Hedrick, Veva Galena.
1115 E. 10th.
Bloomington,
Ind.

A FRENCH GRAMMAR

By
E. F. HACKER
Ohio State University

R. G. ADAMS AND COMPANY
COLUMBUS, OHIO
1924

Copyright, 1924 by
E. F. Hacker

COMPOSED, PRINTED AND BOUND BY
The Collegiate Press
GEORGE BANTA PUBLISHING COMPANY
MENASHA, WISCONSIN

TO THE MEMORY OF

MY MOTHER

PREFACE

It is scarcely necessary to apologize for the appearance of another beginners' book in French: teachers of modern languages generally welcome a new text, we are always ready to vary our routine by using fresh material. In writing this book, the author is in no sense a reformer; he has no pet hobby, and he does not radically depart from the methods of other French Grammars. The book embodies features of the grammatical, phonetic, translation, conversational and psychological methods. It is the result of fifteen years' experience in college teaching, and is designed to meet the needs of college students.

I. Pronunciation. A most careful phonetic introduction seeks to give the student a reasonable understanding of French sounds and the values of the letters. The alphabet of the International Phonetic Association is used throughout the book. After a discussion of French sounds and a statement of some general principles, we find more specific rules for the pronunciation of certain letters in certain combinations. The less important rules are printed in smaller type, so that the student is not lost in the attempt to learn a great number of rules at once. This introduction is followed up in the earlier lessons, in which there are exercises in syllabication and the determination of pronunciation according to the principles laid down. In fifteen lessons there is an interlinear phonetic transcription for the French exercises, which obviates at the very beginning the difficulty of the students' forming incorrect habits of pronunciation. In all the lesson vocabularies and also in the general vocabulary at the back of the book, each French word appears in phonetic transcription.

II. Grammar. The grammatical material has been prepared with special care. This is not a book for small children; therefore an attempt is made to present the French language on a logical basis. The author believes that every intelligent student of college age feels the necessity of understanding his constructions. Principles are stated clearly and concisely. The author abhors the methods of some books, which seek to simplify matters by making statements which are inexact and unscientific, which tell only half the truth when not entirely misleading, and which necessitate corrections and endless additions later. Let this not be construed to mean that the book is complete in every detail: it is not a reference grammar, but it aims to give the beginner the essentials stated in a manner that will hold.

III. Vocabulary and **Exercises.** From the beginning the exercises are based on topics. The early lessons deal with every-day affairs, such as classroom, home, meals, family, friends, visiting, shopping, etc. With Lesson XVI begin preparations for a journey, and the rest of the forty lessons deal with a trip to France. All of this material was prepared during a recent sojourn in France, and was carefully read and corrected by French friends of the author. The first section of the exercise is a French model, with interlinear phonetic transcription through Lesson XVII. Next appears an oral exercise which is a drill on the points taken up in the grammar lesson. The third section is made up of English sentences to be written in French. Some of the earlier lessons have an exercise on pronunciation. Beginning with Lesson VI, there is a conversation exercise in each lesson.

An attempt has been made to conform somewhat to a vocabulary suggested by a colleague of the author.[1] How-

---

[1] George R. Havens: A Minimum Requirement for Elementary French—The College Book Company, Columbus, Ohio.

ever, a considerable number of other words, naturally suggested by the topics discussed, appear in the French exercises, but are generally not used in the English-French composition. Some words that do not occur at all in the exercises will be found in the general vocabulary at the back of the book, simply because they appear as illustrations somewhere in the text. For instance, a footnote gives the seven nouns in *-ou* which add *x* for the plural; to satisfy the inquiring student, *pou* is given in the vocabulary, but it is not used in the exercises! The author has tried to keep the length of the vocabularies as nearly uniform as possible. Some lessons will seem at first glance to have a much longer vocabulary than others; however a more careful examination will show that such vocabularies contain words which the student can guess because of their similarity to English words and which require no great effort to learn.

Lessons are planned to occupy two class periods. The fortunate teacher who can afford to go very slowly and do everything thoroughly, may find in a lesson enough material for three days.

Every sixth lesson is a thorough review of grammar principles and vocabulary.

IV. Verbs. The author believes that, while verbs present one of the main difficulties of the beginning student of French, it is essential that he learn them as early as possible. In this book a discussion of the tenses and their uses is completed in Lesson XXV, which treats of the past definite and the imperfect subjunctive. This makes it possible to begin a reading text in connection with further grammatical study, if the teacher is so inclined.

The formation of tenses from the principal parts is taught from the beginning. The regular conjugations, **avoir, être, aller, faire** and **voir** are taken up tense by tense. In Lesson

XXVI, the complete scheme of derivation[1] is given in tabular form and fully explained. From that point on, irregular verbs are introduced in each lesson, the student being encouraged to learn a minimum of forms and derive all others from the principal parts.

V. Appendix. An appendix gives the complete conjugations of regular verbs and of **avoir** and **être,** with a fairly complete list of irregular verbs, in which only the principal parts and other irregularities occur. There is also some grammatical reference material not deemed of sufficient importance to the beginner to be included in the lessons. Among other things is a study of the infinitive rarely found in French grammars.

The author wishes to thank D. C. Heath & Company and Dr. P. H. Churchman of Clark University for kind permission to use material which appears in another form elsewhere.[2]

For aid in the preparation of the manuscript and in the reading of the proof, the author desires to express his sincere gratitude to Madame Charlotte Carré of Paris, formerly head-mistress of French in Kensington High School, London; to Professor Paul Parant of Paris; and to these colleagues in the Department of Romance Languages in the Ohio State University: Mrs. Bertha Arthur, Miss Marie Davis, Madame Hélène Fouré, Miss Florence Hier.

Columbus, Ohio,
    July, 1924.

E. F. H.

---

[1] With a few variations and amplifications this is the system employed in A French Grammar by Thieme and Effinger (Macmillan).

[2] Churchman and Hacker: A First Phonetic French Course (D. C. Heath & Co.)

TABLE OF CONTENTS

FRENCH SPELLING AND PRONUNCIATION

	Page
A. Introduction..................................	1

    I. Differences between English and French; II. Phonetic Symbols; III. Table of Phonetic Symbols; IV. Vowels; V. Semi-Consonants; VI. Consonants; VII. Orthographic Signs; VIII. Syllabication; IX. Mute **e**; X. Nasalization; XI. Silent Consonants; XII. Elision; XIII. Linking or Liaison; XIV. Quantity.

B. Relation between Spelling and Pronunciation   16

FRENCH GRAMMAR

LESSON

    I. 1. Agreement of Adjective and Noun; 2. Gender; 3. Number; 4. Definite Article; 5. Indefinite Article..   39

    II. 6. Agreement of Verb and Subject; 7. Present Indicative of **avoir;** 8. Present Indicative of **être;** 9. Agreement of Pronoun and Antecedent............   41

    III. 10. Negation; 11. Interrogation; 12. Possessive—Dative—Contractions............................   44

    IV. 13. Principal Parts of French Verbs; 14. Present Indicative of Regular Verbs.........................   49

    V. 15. Possessive Adjectives; 16. Interrogative Adjectives; 17. Demonstrative Adjectives......................   52

    VI. Review   56

    VII. 18. Partitive Defined; 19. Regular Partitive; 20. Partitive Pronoun; 21. Pronominal Adverbs; 22. Distinction between **il y a** and **voilà**....................   59

    VIII. 23. Present Indicative of **aller, faire, voir;** 24. Relative Pronouns **qui** and **que;** 25. Interrogative Pronouns **qui** and **que**......................................   63

    IX. 26. Compound Tenses; 27. Word Order; 28. Agreement of Past Participle; 29. Idiomatic Use of the Present..   67

    X. 30. Irregular Plurals; 31. Irregular Feminines; 32. Position of Adjectives............................   72

XI.	33. Irregular Partitive Construction; 34. Omission of Expression of the Partitive....................	78
XII.	Review	82
XIII.	35. Conjunctive Personal Pronouns; 36. Object Forms; 37. Position; 38. Reflexive Verbs; 39. Order of Pronoun Objects...................................	85
XIV.	40. Être as Auxiliary; 41. Agreement of Past Participle	90
XV.	42. Indefinite Pronoun **on;** 43. General Noun; 44. Definite Article for Possessive......................	95
XVI.	45. Comparison; 46. Position of Adverbs............	99
XVII.	47. Imperfect Indicative; 48. Meanings of the Imperfect Indicative; 49. Idiomatic Use of the Imperfect.......	104
XVIII.	Review	109
XIX.	50. Disjunctive Pronouns; 51. Uses of Disjunctive Pronouns...	111
XX.	52. Future; 53. Conditional; 54. Conditional Sentences; 55. Future after **quand**.............................	115
XXI.	56. Some Uses of Prepositions; 57. Idiomatic Uses of **avoir;** 58. Impersonal Verbs........................	119
XXII.	59. Present Subjunctive; 60. Uses of the Subjunctive; 61. Sequence of Tenses in Subjunctive Clauses......	124
XXIII.	62. Imperatives; 63. Position and Order of Pronoun Objects; 64. Present Subjunctive as Imperative......	128
XXIV.	Review	133
XXV.	65. Past Definite; 66. Imperfect Subjunctive; 67. Uses of the Past Definite and the Imperfect Subjunctive...	135
XXVI.	68. Derivation of Verb-Forms: Table; 69. Explanation of the Derivation from the Principal Parts; 70. Illustration: **aller**..	138
XXVII.	71. Demonstrative Pronouns; 72. Uses of **ce;** 73. Uses of **ceci** and **cela;** 74. Uses of Variable Forms; 75. **partir, sortir, dormir**....................................	143
XXVIII.	76. Peculiarities of First-Conjugation Verbs; 77. **envoyer**...	148
XXIX.	78. Possessive Pronouns; 79. Forms; 80. Uses; 81. Possession Expressed in the Predicate; 82. **pouvoir**......	154
XXX.	Review	158
XXXI.	83. Negatives; 84. **vouloir, falloir**.................	160
XXXII.	85. Relative Pronouns: Forms; 86. Uses of Relative Pronouns; 87. **écrire, connaître**....................	166

XXXIII.	88. Interrogative Pronouns: Forms; 89. Uses of Interrogative Pronouns; 90. **lire, dire**.....................	170
XXXIV.	91. Infinitive Complementary to a Verb; 92. Infinitive Complementary to a Noun or an Adjective; 93. Infinitive as Logical Subject; 94. Infinitive Governed by a Preposition; 95. **savoir**.......................	175
XXXV.	96. Infinitive with Change of Subject; 97. Present Participle; 98. **devoir, recevoir**..........................	181
XXXVI.	Review	186
XXXVII.	99. Compound Tenses; 100. Passive Voice; 101. Reciprocal Value of Reflexive Form; 102. **venir, tenir**....	189
XXXVIII.	103. Cardinal Numerals; 104. Observations on Forms and Pronunciation; 105. Ordinal Numerals; 106. Fractions; 107. Dates and Titles; 108. **ouvrir**..............	194
XXXIX.	109. Indefinite Pronouns and Adjectives; 110. **prendre, boire**	199
XL.	111. Omission of Article; 112. Definite Article Used Distributively; 113. Expressions of Time of Day; 114. **mettre**...	204

APPENDIX

1.	Some Common Irregular Feminines: I. Nouns, II. Adjectives	211
2.	On the Gender of Nouns................................	213
3.	Table of Personal Pronouns.............................	215
4.	Table of Relative and Interrogative Pronouns.............	216
5.	Negation...	218
6.	Subjunctive..	220
7.	Infinitive...	223
8.	Lists of Verbs Showing the Construction of Following Infinitives: I. Without Sign, II. Sign **à**, III. Sign **de**..........	225
9.	Simple Tenses of Regular Verbs, of **avoir**, and of **être**........	228
10.	Irregular Verbs: Forms................................	230
	Alphabetical List of Irregular Verbs (with Index)..........	240

GENERAL VOCABULARY 245

LIST OF ILLUSTRATIONS

Map of France..	*Frontispiece*
Le Château d'Azay le Rideau....................... *Opposite page*	56
La Place de la Concorde, Paris....................................	57
La Chapelle du Château d'Amboise...............................	94
La Place de la Bastille...	95
Le Château de Chaumont...	130
L'Arc de Triomphe de l'Étoile, Paris.............................	131
Le Palais du Louvre, Paris..	150
Le Musée de Cluny, Paris...	151
Une Aile du Palais de Versailles..................................	178
La Cathédrale de Notre-Dame de Paris...........................	179
La Tour Eiffel, Paris..	196
Le Grand Escalier, Château de Blois.............................	197
La Maison Carrée (Reste Romain), Nîmes.......................	206
Le Mont-Saint-Michel...	207

FRENCH SPELLING AND PRONUNCIATION

FRENCH SPELLING AND PRONUNCIATION

A. INTRODUCTION

I. Differences Between English and French

There are several marked differences between English pronunciation and French pronunciation:

1. English vowels are often pronounced indistinctly; the different vowels often sound alike, especially when in unstressed position. French vowels are very carefully and very distinctly pronounced, the only one that can ever be slighted (if pronounced at all) being mute **e**.

2. English vowels tend to be lengthened, often gliding off into another sound.[1] A French vowel is generally short, and pure: i. e. *one* sound.

3. English consonants are generally pronounced with very little action of the organs of speech. French consonants are forcefully enunciated.

4. In English words, some syllables receive marked stress while others are slighted or practically disappear. In French words, each syllable receives its full time; and the emphasis, not nearly so strong as in English, is ordinarily on the last pronounced vowel—not, however, on a mute **e**.

II. Phonetic Symbols

In French as in English, a letter may have more than one sound,[2] and one sound may be represented by more than one letter.[3] To facilitate the study of sounds, there has been devised a phonetic alphabet, known as the alphabet of the International Phonetic Association, in which each symbol has only one sound and a sound is always represented by the same symbol.

---

[1] For example: ā=eh+ēē; ī=ä+ēē; ē=ēē+y; ō=o+ōō; etc.

[2] Cf. **a** in man and in mar; **o** in come and in home; **g** in **g**et and in **g**entle.

[3] Cf. **e**ight, ate; meat, m**ee**t, mete; place, vase; **c**an, **k**ick.

A table of these symbols is here given with key words in English and in French, so that the student may form some idea of the sounds represented by the symbols; but since habits of speech of English speaking people and French people differ so radically, the English equivalents cannot be very satisfactory. A correct French pronunciation can be acquired only through careful drill under the guidance of a competent teacher.

III. Table of Phonetic Symbols

Symbol		English key		French key	
[a]	(front a)	mat	(less flat)	bague	baɡ
[ɑ]	(back a)	far	(mouth open)	pas	pɑ
[ɑ̃]	(nasal a)	calm		banc	bɑ̃
[b]		bat		banc	bɑ̃
[d]		did	(tongue touching teeth)	dent	dɑ̃
[e]	(close e)	made	(one sound; avoid glide)	fée	fe
[ɛ]	(open e)	met	(mouth wide open)	bec	bɛk
[ɛ̃]	(nasal e)	sang	(avoid **ng**-sound)	fin	fɛ̃
[ə]	(mute e)	the man	(slightly rounded)	de	də
[f]		far		fait	fɛ
[g]		game		vague	vaɡ
[h]		hat		(Almost never pronounced)	
[i]	(vowel i)	meet	(avoid glide)	ami	ami
[j]	(liquid l *or* semi-consonant i)	yet		fille papier	fiːj papje
[k]		cat		avec	avɛk
[l]		long	(tongue forward)	la	la
[m]		my		me	mə
[n]		no	(tongue forward)	ne	nə
[ɲ]	(liquid n)	onion	(pronounced as one sound, with tip of tongue pressed against lower teeth)	vigne	viɲ
[o]	(close o)	note	(avoid glide)	mot	mo
[ɔ]	(open o)	bun		homme	ɔm
[õ]	(nasal o)		*between* long *and* lone (avoid **n** or **ng**-sound)	mon	mõ
[ø]	(close eu)		(No English equivalent) (See **Triangle** below)	feu	fø
[œ]	(open eu)		(No English equivalent) (See **Triangle** below)	neuf	nœf

[œ̃] (nasal eu)	su**ng**	(avoid **ng**-sound)	un	œ̃
[p]	**p**art		papier	papje
[r]		(Tongue-tip trill or uvular. See below.)	sœur	sœːr
[s]	**s**ing	(hissing)	son	sɔ̃
[ʃ]	**sh**oe		cheval	ʃəval
[t]	**t**o	(tongue touching teeth)	tante	tãːt
[u]	t**oo**	(lips rounded; avoid glide)	toute	tut
[w]	**w**ant		oui	wi
[v]	**v**ote		vont	vɔ̃
[y] (vowel u)	(No English equivalent. An [i] sound made through rounded lips as for [u]. See **Triangle** below.)		une	yn
[ɥ] (semi-consonant u)	(A shortening of [y] when followed by a pronounced vowel.)		nuit	nɥi
[z]	bu**zz**	(strongly voiced)	base	baːz
[ʒ]	plea**s**ure	(strongly voiced)	je	ʒə
[ː] (sign of length)	(Placed after a vowel to indicate that it is lengthened, French vowels ordinarily being very short.)		base	baːz

IV. Vowels

1. Front Vowels. The vowels [i], [e], [ɛ], [a], are known as "front" vowels, because in making these sounds, the tongue is brought forward against the lower teeth.

For [i], the corners of the mouth are drawn back, the lips form a narrow slit, the tongue is pressed firmly against the lower teeth, and the tip is raised to the edges of the lower teeth. Avoid the English tendency to glide off into [j]; and by all means, avoid a short English **i** as in **sit**.

For [e], the corners of the mouth are slightly less retracted than for [i], the lips are slightly opened. The tip of the tongue is not quite so high as for [i]. The sound is much like the first part of **ā** in **day**. Avoid drawing out the sound and gliding into [i].

For [ɛ], the lips are more retracted than for the English **ĕ** in **met**, and the mouth is more widely opened. The tip of the tongue is much lower than for [e].

For [a], the tongue is very low although the tip still touches the lower teeth; the mouth is wide open but not round, the corners being slightly retracted. The sound is very much like ă in **patty** (pronounced very short) or like the Englishman's **a** in **hat.**

The position in the triangle will show that [i] and [e] are close together, and that there is little difference between [ɛ] and [a]:

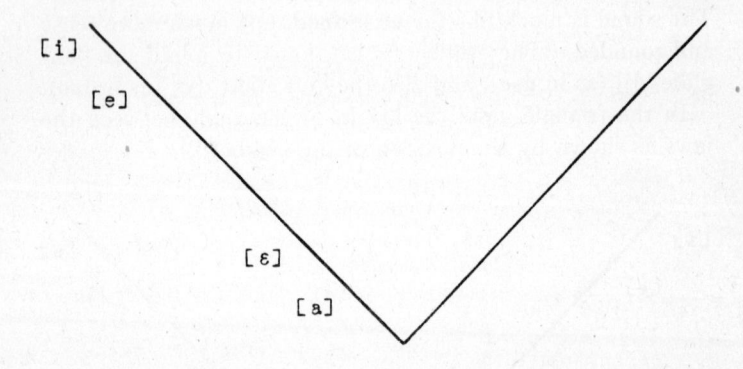

```
[i]
   [e]


          [ɛ]
            [a]
```

2. Back Vowels. The vowels [ɑ], [ɔ], [o], [u] are known as the "back" vowels, because in making these sounds, the tongue is retracted; and as we progress from [ɑ] to [u], the back of the tongue is more and more raised toward the soft palate.

For [ɑ], the height of the angle between the jaws is slightly greater than for [a]; the corners of the mouth are not retracted, the lips are only very slightly rounded (practically neutral); the tongue no longer touches the teeth, but lies quite flat. The sound is much like **a** in **father,** pronounced without rounding.

For [ɔ], the angle between the jaws is about the same as for [ɛ], but the lips are rounded; the tongue is slightly retracted and the back is slightly raised. The sound is much like **u** in **bun,** but open and rounded.

For [o], the angle between the jaws is about the same as for [e], but the lips are protruded and definitely rounded, and the opening is smaller than for [ɔ]. The back of the tongue is somewhat higher than for [ɔ]. The sound is much like **o** in **so,** but without the [u] glide.

For [u], the angle between the jaws is about the same as for [i]. The lips are pushed forward as for whistling and form a very small circle, very definitely rounded. The tongue is drawn backward and forcibly raised toward the soft palate. The sound is much like the **oo** in **food,** but much more tense and rounded. The student is cautioned to avoid the "on-glide" [j] (as in **use**), and also the "off-glide" [w] (as in **too**).

In the triangle, note the height of the angle between the jaws as shown by the position of the symbol:

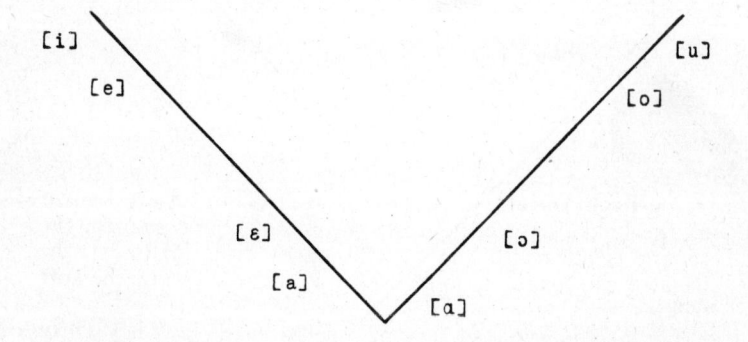

```
[i]                                    [u]
   [e]                              [o]

      [ɛ]                     [ɔ]
         [a]              [ɑ]
```

3. **Mixed Vowels.** The vowels [y], [ø], [ə], [œ], are known as "mixed" vowels, because these sounds are produced by combining features of the "fundamental" vowels above. These sounds are all foreign to the English; so they require a special effort.

For [y], the tongue is in almost the same position as for [i] (very slightly lower); the lips are in the position for [u]. Care must be taken not to pronounce [u]: the sound of [y] resembles [i] much more than [u]. Practice before a mirror is suggested.

For [ø], the tongue is slightly lower than for [e]. With the tongue held firmly in that position, the lips are rounded as for [o] (more open than for [y]).[1]

For [œ], the tongue is slightly lower than for [ɛ] (almost the position for [a]), and the lips are open and rounded as for [ɔ].

[ə] is midway between [ø] and [œ]. It is the one sound in French which is slighted. In the stressed position it becomes [ø]: **Voyez-le** [vwaje lø]. [ə] may be produced by rounding the indistinct sound of **e** in the English word **the** (unstressed): **the man**.

Note the triangle:

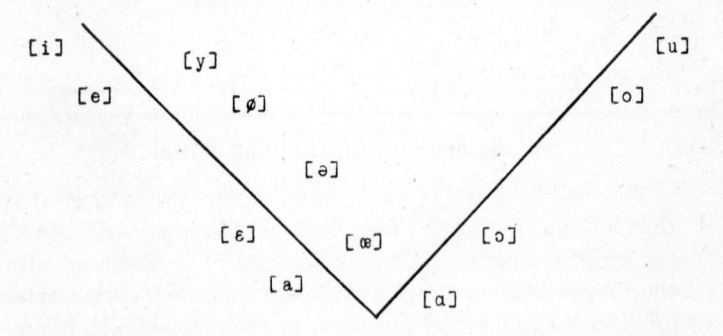

```
[i]                                    [u]
   [e]    [y]                     [o]
           [ø]
             [ə]
         [ɛ]   [œ]   [ɔ]
             [a]   [ɑ]
```

4. Nasal Vowels. The above twelve vowels are known as the oral vowels: in producing them, the sound passes through the mouth. The nasal vowels, [ɛ̃], [ɑ̃], [ɔ̃], [œ̃], are produced by dropping the uvula, thus opening the nasal passage, and permitting a part of the sound to pass through the nose. Care must be taken to avoid the sound of **m, n,** or **ng** after a French nasal vowel.

---

[1] The tendency to produce an **r** after this sound, often noted among English speaking people (even some teachers of French), is distinctly bad, and should be carefully avoided.

[ɛ̃] is produced by nasalizing an oral vowel between [ɛ] and [a]; [ɑ̃] is a nasalization of [ɑ]; [ɔ̃] is a nasalization of an **o** much closer to [o] than to [ɔ]; [œ̃] is a nasalization of [œ].[1]

We may now complete our vowel triangle:

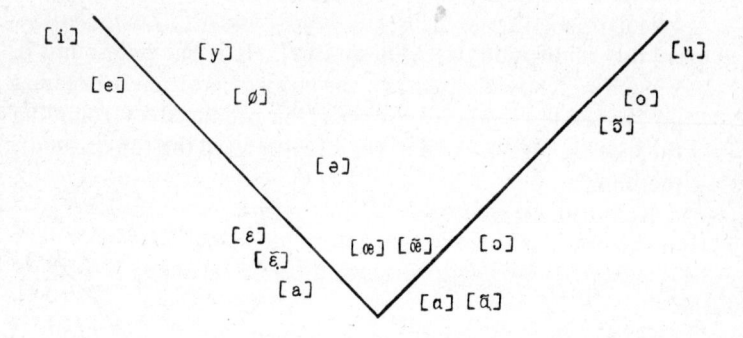

```
[i]                                    [u]
   [e]      [y]                     [o]
         [ø]                     [ɔ̃]

            [ə]

   [ɛ]
   [ɛ̃]   [œ] [œ̃]    [ɔ]
     [a]
            [ɑ] [ɑ̃]
```

V. Semi-Consonants (Semi-Vowels)

The vowels [i], [u], [y], may be so rapidly pronounced that they lose much of their vowel value and become semi-vowels (or semi-consonants). Thus, [i] becomes [j], pronounced with the tongue higher than for [i]; [u] becomes [w]; [y] becomes [ɥ], a sound which does not occur in English, but which may be produced by shortening [y] before a pronounced vowel. The change from vowel to semi-consonant may readily be observed by pronouncing [ia], [ua], and [yi] more and more rapidly until they become [ja], [wa], and [ɥi].

In general, **i, u,** or **ou,** becomes semi-consonant when followed by a pronounced vowel and not preceded by two consonants the second of which is **l** or **r**. This rule practically always holds for **i**, the only exceptions occurring in compounds: **nier** [nje], **voulions** [vuljɔ̃]; but **ni** [ni], **nie** (silent

---

[1] Note that the tilde (˜) is used in phonetics to indicate nasalization.

vowel) [ni], **lire** (consonant) [liːr], **plier** (preceded by two consonants the second of which is **l**) [plie], **criant** (preceded by two consonants the second of which is **r**) [kriɑ̃]. Applied to **u**, the rule has many exceptions: **nuage** [nɥaːʒ], **lui** [lɥi]; but **duo** [dyo], **bruit** [brɥi], **fruit** [frɥi], **pluie** [plɥi], etc. Applied to **ou**, the rule generally holds: **oui** [wi], **Louis** [lwi], **louer** [lwe]; but **loue** [lu], **clouer** [klue], etc.

VI. Consonants

All French consonants are more forcefully enunciated than English consonants, and the organs of speech are more tense. Except for these differences, there will be no difficulty in the pronunciation of the following: [b], [f], [g], [k], [m], [p], [s] (hissing), [ʃ] (strongly fricative),[1] [v], [z] (strongly voiced), [ʒ].[2]

The sounds [d], [l], [n], [t], are made with the tongue thrust forward against the upper teeth.

[ɲ] *slightly* resembles **ny** in **union,** but it is one sound—not two. Notice that although English **n** is not the same as French [n], the tip of the tongue is raised for both of them. To pronounce [ɲ], the tongue must be thrust against the lower teeth and the *middle* of the tongue raised to the hard palate.

[r] has no English equivalent. It may be made by trilling the tip of the tongue against the upper gums. Another [r] (strictly, the symbol should be [R]), heard especially in Paris and other large cities, is the "uvular" **r**. This is made by raising the back of the tongue and causing the uvula to vibrate against the tongue. The action of the vocal organs in producing this sound is very much like that of gargling. Either sound is acceptable.

[1] [ʃ] is generally spelled **ch.** Care must be taken not to put a [t] before the **sh**-sound as in the English word **chant.**

[2] In pronouncing [ʒ] (like **z** in **azure**), care must be taken to voice the sound strongly and to avoid prefixing a [d] as in **jolly.**

Consonants are "voiced" or "voiceless." Consonants which have voice, produced by a vibration of the vocal chords, are said to be "voiced." They are [b], [d], [g], [v], [z], [ʒ], [m], [n], [ɲ], [l], [r], and the three semi-consonants [j], [ɥ], [w]. The first six may be "unvoiced" or "devocalized," producing the "voiceless" consonants: [p], [t], [k], [f], [s], [ʃ]. These are formed by a stopping or compressing of the expiratory current, unaccompanied by vibration of the vocal chords. The difference can be noticed in placing the fingers on the throat while pronouncing the sounds.

Because of the difficulty in pronunciation, a voiced and a voiceless consonant are rarely found in juxtaposition. If a voiceless consonant be followed by a voiced consonant, the voiceless consonant is generally vocalized: **tasse** [tɑːs], but **tasse de thé** [tɑz də te]. Here the voiceless [s] changes to the voiced [z] before the voiced [d]. If a voiced consonant that has a corresponding voiceless consonant be followed by a voiceless consonant, the voiced consonant is generally devocalized: **médecin** [mɛtsɛ̃], **absent** [apsɑ̃]; if there be no corresponding voiceless consonant, both are sometimes voiced: **Alsace** [alzas]. Sometimes the influence of a first consonant changes a second even when there is a corresponding consonant of the other group: **un cheval** [œ̃ ʃfal]. This phenomenon is known as "assimilation." Cf. English **cupboard, blackguard, John's book** (**s** = [z] because of **n**), **Edith's book** (**s** = [s] because of **th**), etc.

Devocalization may be indicated in phonetics by placing a small circle over or under a symbol: [ʒ̊], [z̥]; vocalization may be indicated by the sign [ˬ]: [s̬].

VII. Orthographic Signs

1. Three "accents" are used with French vowels: acute (**é**), grave (**è**), and circumflex (**ê**). They have nothing to do with stress; they are a part of the spelling. They may or

may not affect the pronunciation. The acute accent, which is used only with **e**, always affects the sound of **e**: **donne** [dɔn], **donné** [dɔne]. The other two accents when used with **e** always affect the pronunciation: **tête** [tɛːt], **père** [pɛːr]; but when used with other vowels they sometimes merely distinguish two words similarly spelled: **la** [la] *the, her, it,* **là** [la] *there;* **ou** [u] *or,* **où** [u] *where;* **sur** [syːr] *upon,* **sûr** [syːr] *sure.* The circumflex often indicates the derivation of a word, in many cases showing the omission of **s**: **tête** (from Latin **testa**), **pâte** (from Latin **pasta**), **rôtir** (from Germanic **rostjan**).

2. The cedilla is written under **c** (ç) when it is desired to give the sound [s] to a **c** which would otherwise be pronounced [k]: **conte** [kɔ̃ːt], **garçon** [garsɔ̃].

3. The diæresis written over one of two contiguous vowels, breaks up the group: **hais** [ɛ], **haïs** [ai]; **roi** [rwa], **héroïque** [erɔik]. Note also **vague** (va-gue) [vag] and **aiguë** (ai-gu-ë) [ɛgy].

4. The letters **u** and **e** are sometimes inserted to change the value of a preceding consonant; when so used, they are no more than orthographic signs: **manger** [mɑ̃ʒe], **distinguer** [distɛ̃ge]; **gai** [ge], **mangeai** [mɑ̃ʒe]. In verbs like **distinguer**, in which **u** is inserted to make **g** hard before **e**, **u** is retained throughout the conjugation but has no value of its own: **distinguons** [distɛ̃gɔ̃].

VIII. Syllabication

Correct syllabication is essential to good French pronunciation: French people are careful to pronounce a consonant in the syllable to which it belongs, and the sound of a letter (especially a vowel) is very often determined by syllabication.

Rule 1. A single consonant (except **x**) between vowels goes with the following vowel. This rule includes the consonantal digraphs (**ch, ph, th, gn**), each of which represents one sound: **é-lè-ve, a-che-ter, é-lé-phant, ma-thé-ma-ti-ques, ga-gner, ex-act.**

Rule 2. Two consonants the first of which is not **l, m, n, r,** or **s,** and the second of which is **l** or **r,** go with a following vowel: **ta-bleau, li-vre, fe-nê-tre, dé-cla-rer;** but **par-ler, Hen-ri, dis-lo-quer.**

Rule 3. Other groups of consonants, including double consonants,[1] are divided: **ar-gent, por-te, en-fant, res-ter, ac-tif, dif-fé-ren-ce, don-ner, ap-pel-le.**

When three or more consonants follow each other, the last two will go together if that is possible under the second rule; otherwise only one will go with a following vowel, leaving the rest in the preceding syllable; however, the consonantal digraphs are not separated: **en-trer, let-tre, es-pla-na-de, ar-bre, com-pren-dre, dis-tinc-te-ment, ins-tru-ment, four-chet-te, é-par-gne.**

Rule 4. Independent vowels are divided.[2, 3] Certain vowels, when coming together, form combinations, the values of which vary. Such groups include **ai, au, eau, ei, eu, œu, œ, oi, ou** (see also **Semi-Consonants, V**). Vowels which do

[1] Double consonants are generally pronounced as single consonants, except **cc** and **gg,** which may have two different sounds according to the rules for the pronunciation of **c** and **g,** depending on the letter following (see pp. 19 and 24). Thus: **accorder** [akɔrde], but **accepter** [aksɛpte]; **aggraver** [agrave], but **suggérer** [sygʒere]. Some authorities double the same sound in some words, especially bookish words (**illégal** [illegal], **imminent** [imminã]), but it is doubtful whether the mass of French people so pronounce.

[2] A semi-consonant never occasions a separate syllable: **vou-lions.** Between vowels it goes with the following: **pa-ïen.**

[3] When **u** and **e** are used as orthographic signs, they have no effect upon syllabication: **dis-tin-guer, man-geons.** The same is true of **u** following **q**: **ac-qué-rir.**

not form combinations are said to be independent, and are divided: **thé-â-tre, a-é-ro-pla-ne, a-or-te, la-ï-que.**[1, 2]

IX. Mute e[3]

An **e** is mute when final in a syllable and unaccented: **ne** (mute); **né** (acute, close); **a-che-tons** (mute); **a-chè-te** (grave, open, in second syllable; mute in third); **je-ter** (mute in first syllable, close in second); **jet-te** (open in first syllable, mute in second).

Note that **s** and **nt** when added for inflection are regularly silent and do not affect a preceding **e**: **je donne** [dɔn], **tu donnes** [dɔn], **ils donnent** [dɔn]; **table** [tabl], **tables** [tabl].

Mute **e** is usually silent in prose (**a-che-ter** [aʃte], **ap-pe-ler** [aple]); but must ordinarily be pronounced in monosyllables (**le** [lə], **me** [mə]), and elsewhere when it is in the initial syllable (**fe-nê-tre** [fənɛːtr]), when the omission of it would cause three or more consonant sounds to come together (**mar-che-rons** [marʃərɔ̃]), and when the omission of it would cause an impossible combination of consonants (**seize cents** [sɛzə sɑ̃]). In connected prose these rules apply to the group of words as if the group made up one word: **la fe-nê-tre** [laf-nɛɪtr]; **je ne le fe-rai pas** [ʒən-lə-fre-pɑ]; **vo-tre** [vɔtr], but **vo-tre pè-re** [vɔ-trə-pɛɪr]. When a mute **e** is dropped, the consonant or consonants of the syllable in which it occurs must be attached to a preceding or a following vowel.

---

[1] Notice that while compounds are divided according to the parts that make the compounds, the pronunciation often follows the rules for orthographic syllabication. Thus, while **inégal** is syllabicated **in-é-gal** (which should give [ɛ(n)egal]), it is pronounced as if it were syllabicated **i-né-gal**: [i-ne-gal].

[2] Orthographic syllabication and phonetic syllabication do not always correspond, especially when a mute **e** is dropped (see next section): **ma-de-moi-sel-le** [mad-mwa-zɛl], **a-che-ter** [aʃ-te], **fai-tes** [fɛt], **cé-de-rai** [se-dre], **in-ex-act** [i-nɛg-zakt].

[3] Note that "mute," as applied to **e**, does not necessarily mean "silent."

In verse, however, a mute **e** (except when immediately followed by a vowel or at the end of a line) counts as a syllable, and is generally pronounced.

A mute **e** in the stressed position becomes [ø] (or [œ]): **Voyez-le** [vwaje lø].

X. Nasalization

A vowel is nasal when followed *in the same syllable* by **m** or **n**, unless the **m** or **n** is doubled: **en-trons** [ɑ̃trɔ̃], **grand** [grɑ̃], **prin-ce** [prɛ̃ːs], **un** [œ̃]; but **a-mi** [ami], **u-ne** [yn], **hom-me** [ɔm], **don-ne** [dɔn]. However, when a word begins with **emm-** or **enn-**, the **e** is generally nasal: **emmener** [ɑ̃mne], **ennui** [ɑ̃nɥi]; but **ennemi** [ɛnmi]. A vowel followed by **mn** is not nasal (**gymnaste** [ʒimnast]); in such a case the **mn** is sometimes treated as if it were **nn** (**automne** [otɔn]). Initial **en-**, followed by a vowel, is treated as initial **enn-**: **enamourer** [ɑ̃namure].

The **m** or **n** which nasalizes a vowel is usually silent.

XI. Silent Consonants

1. Four consonants, **c, f, l,** and **r,** are usually pronounced when final: **sec** [sɛk], **chef** [ʃɛf], **mal** [mal], **car** [kaːr]. However, **r** is generally silent in **-er** at the end of a word of more than one syllable (always at the end of a first conjugation infinitive): **boulanger** [bulɑ̃ʒe], **donner** [dɔne]; but **hiver** [ivɛːr]. Except in **donc** [dɔ̃(ːk)], final **c** is silent after a nasal: **banc** [bɑ̃].

2. Other consonants are usually silent when final: **rang** [rɑ̃], **trop** [tro], **mes** [me], **et** [e]. However, every consonant (except **h**) is sometimes pronounced when final, and even **c, f, l,** and **r** are sometimes silent. Consonants within a word may likewise be silent; rules are of little value. See also **Nasalization,** above.

3. An **h** may be "mute," in which case it permits linking (see XIII) and elision (see XII); or it may be "aspirate," in which case it prevents linking and elision: **l'homme** [l ɔm], **les hommes** [lez‿ɔm]; but **le héros** [lə ero], **les héros** [le ero]. A mute **h** is always silent. An aspirate **h** is unpronounced by most French people; the sounding of the **h** is always affected.

XII. Elision

The vowels **a**, **e**, and **i** disappear and are replaced by the apostrophe (') in the following cases:

1. **a** in **la** (article or pronoun) before an initial vowel or mute **h**: **l'école, l'heure, je l'ai.**

2. **e** in **de, je, le, me, ne, se, te, que,** and some compounds of **que,** before an initial vowel or mute **h**; likewise in **ce** *when it is a pronoun*: **d'une école, j'ai, je l'ai, l'homme, il m'a vu, il n'est pas, il s'en va, tu t'en vas, qu'il vienne, quoiqu'il vienne, c'est moi.**

However, there is no elision when **ce** or **je** follows the verb of which it is the subject or when **la** or **le** follows an affirmative imperative of which it is the object: **Est-ce un livre? Ai-je un livre? Donnez-le aux enfants. Donnez-la aux enfants.** Note, however, **Envoyez-l'y.**

3. **i** in **si** only before **il** or **ils**: **s'il va, s'ils vont.**

XIII. Linking or Liaison

When the first of two words closely connected in construction ends in a silent consonant, and the second word begins with a vowel or mute **h**, the final consonant of the first may be carried over and pronounced as the initial letter of the second. **d** links as [t]: **un grand homme** [œ̃ grɑ̃t‿ɔm]; **g** links as [k]: **sang impur** [sɑ̃k‿ɛ̃pyːr]; **s** and **x** link as [z]: **les enfants** [lez‿ɑ̃fɑ̃], **aux enfants** [oz‿ɑ̃fɑ̃].

When an **n** that nasalizes is carried over, the preceding vowel is sometimes partly or wholly denasalized: **mon ami** [mɔ̃‿ami] or [mɔn‿ami], **en plein air** [ã plɛn‿ɛɪr]. An **m** is never linked.

XIV. Quantity

As has been said above, French vowels are generally quite short. We shall not consider "half long" vowels, but only those that have "full length." In the rules given below, "stressed syllable" means the syllable in which the last pronounced vowel occurs, disregarding a mute **e**.

1. Any vowel in the stressed syllable is long before the sounds [j], [v], [z], [ʒ], or a phonetically final [r]: **fille** [fiːj], **livre** [liːvr], **douze** [duːz], **page** [paːʒ], **fort** [fɔːr]; but **forte** [fɔrt].

2. The nasal vowels ([ɑ̃], [ɛ̃], [ɔ̃], [œ̃]), [ɑ], [o], [ø], and sometimes **ê** and **î**, are long when in the stressed syllable and followed by any consonant sound: **tante** [tɑ̃ːt], **prince** [prɛ̃ːs], **oncle** [ɔ̃ːkl], **humble** [œ̃ːbl], **classe** [klɑːs], **faute** [foːt], **meute** [møːt], **tête** [tɛːt], **île** [iːl].

Note 1. The rules here given do not cover all cases of length. There are a few exceptions to the rules.

Note 2. Notice that length occurs only in a stressed syllable that is closed, i. e. which is followed in the same word by a consonant sound.

Note 3. In connected French, when a word which ordinarily has a long vowel is not at the end of a group of words, the length disappears partly or entirely: **Où est votre fille?** [u ɛ vɔtrə fiːj?] **Ma fille est partie.** [ma fij ɛ parti].

B. RELATION BETWEEN SPELLING AND PRONUNCIATION

The student to whom English is a foreign language is quite at a loss to formulate rules for pronunciation. There seems to be no reason, for instance, for the different values of **ough** in **through, though, tough, cough, bough.** While French spelling is not phonetic, it is much less haphazard than English spelling; an effort has been made to make spelling conform to French ideas of how certain combinations of letters should be pronounced. The student's preconceived ideas may not be correct; hence the seeming strangeness of the foreign tongue. A mastery of the principles stated in the following pages will lead to the conviction that French pronunciation is, after all, fairly regular. However, it should be stated at the beginning that a considerable number of French words, although a very small proportion of the words in the language, are irregular in pronunciation; among them are some of the most common in the language.

Note—The material of the following pages is arranged in five columns: 1. the letters, 2. the phonetic symbols, 3. the rules (explanations as to when the letters have the sounds indicated), 4. examples in standard French spelling, 5. examples in phonetic transcription. The size of the type is meant to indicate to the beginning student the relative importance of the rules.

		1. a		
a	1 [a]	Usually:[1]	la table avec	la tabl avɛk
		[1] Rarely silent:	août Saône	u *or* au soːn

1. a (continued)

2	[ɑ]	**â** (circumflex): [2]	âge théâtre	ɑːʒ teɑːtr
3	[ɑ]	Before endings **-tion** and **-sion**: But:	nation occasion national	nɑsjɔ̃ ɔkɑzjɔ̃ nasjɔnal
4	[ɑ]	Often before phonetically final [s] or [z]: [3] But:	hélas base place	elɑːs bɑːz plas
5	[ɑ]	Often before final silent **s**: Except in verbs: [4]	pas vas auras donnas	pɑ va ɔra dɔna
6	[ɑ̃]	Nasal (see X, p. 13):	dans quand camp	dɑ̃ kɑ̃ kɑ̃
		[2] Except in endings of first conjugation verbs:	allât donnâmes parlâtes	ala dɔnam parlat
		[3] Note also: But:	écraser paille passer damner damnation	ekrɑze pɑːj pɑse dɑne dɑnɑsjɔ̃
		[4] Note also:	bras	brɑ

1. a (continued)

ai	7 [ɛ]	Usually[5]:	faire vrai aurait donnais	fɛːr vrɛ ɔrɛ dɔnɛ
	8 [e]	Final in verbs:[6]	aurai donnai	ɔre dɔne
	9 [ɛ̃]	Nasal:	faim main	fɛ̃ mɛ̃
au	10 [o]	Usually:	chaud	ʃo
	11 [ɔ]	Before **r**:[7]	aurai	ɔre
eau	12 [o]	Usually:[8]	beau	bo
		[5] In the present participle of **faire** and in all forms derived from it, **ai** = [ə]:	faisant faisons faisait	fəzɑ̃ fəzɔ̃ fəzɛ
		[6] Also:	je vais je (tu) sais il sait gai geai quai mais maison	ve *or* vɛ se *or* sɛ se *or* sɛ ge ʒe ke mɛ *or* me mɛzɔ̃ *or* mezɔ̃
		[7] Also in a few other words:	Paul aujourd'hui	pɔl ɔʒurdɥi *or* oʒurdɥi
		[8] Rarely [ɔ]:	bureaucratie	byrɔkrasi

2. b

b	1 [b]	Usually:[1]	base	bɑːz
	2 [p]	Before **s** or **t**: .	absent obtenir	apsɑ̄ ɔptəniːr
		[1] When final, **b** is usually silent: But:	plomb cab	plɔ̄ kab

3. c

c	1 [k]	Usually:[1]	carte cousin culte crayon avec	kart kuzɛ̃ kylt krɛjɔ̃ avɛk
	2 [s]	Before **e, i, y**:[2]	ce ici cylindre	sə isi silɛ̃ːdr
		[1] When final, **c** is generally pronounced except after a nasal: But:	sec banc estomac tabac	sɛk bɑ̄ ɛstɔma taba
		[2] When **c** is doubled, the rules are applied to each **c**; if, according to rule, the two sounds are alike, only one is pronounced; if they differ, both are pronounced: The procedure is the same in the case of **sc**:	occupé accident scène escapade	ɔkype aksidɑ̄ sɛːn ɛskapad

3. c (continued)

ç	3 [s]	Always:	garçon	garsɔ̃
ch	4	See **h**.		

4. d

d	1 [d]	Usually:[1]	donner	dɔne
	2 [t]	Linked:	grand homme	grɑ̃t‿ɔm
		[1] When final, **d** is usually silent:	pied	pje
		But:	sud	syd

5. e

e	1 [ɛ]	è (grave):	père	pɛːr
	2 [ɛ]	ê (circumflex):	fenêtre	fənɛːtr
	3 [ɛ]	Followed in the same syllable by a pronounced consonant:[1]	elle fermer mienne	ɛl fɛrme mjɛn
		[1] In words in which a monosyllabic prefix ending in a mute **e** is joined to a word beginning with an **s**, the **s** is doubled to retain the sound [s], but the **e** remains mute although not final in the syllable: See also **eff-**, etc. under **e** = [e].	ressembler dessous dessus	rəsɑ̃ble dəsu dəsy

FRENCH PRONUNCIATION 21

\multicolumn{4}{c}{**5. e** (continued)}
4 [ɛ]	Before final silent **t**,[2] **ts, ct, cts**:	met(s) effet(s) aspect(s)	mɛ efɛ aspɛ
5 [ɛ]	Before the sound [j]:	meilleur sommeil	mɛjœːr sɔmɛːj
6 [e]	é (acute):[3]	école	ekɔl
7 [e]	Before a final silent consonant other than **t, ts, ct, cts**:	aller mes[4] clef	ale me kle
8 [e]	Usually in the initial groups **eff-, ess-, desc-, dess-**:[5]	effet essayer description dessert	efɛ esɛje deskripsjɔ̃ desɛːr
	[2] Note:	et (*and*) es (*art*) est (*is*) est (*east*)	e ɛ ɛ ɛst
	[3] When a first person singular verb ending in a mute **e** is inverted, **e** is written **é** but pronounced open:	donné-je puissé-je	dɔnɛːʒ pɥisɛːʒ
	[4] In formal declamation, some teachers of diction prefer [ɛ] in **ces, des, les, mes, ses, tes.**		
	[5] In these combinations, when initial, the usually accepted sound of **e** is [e]; but some authorities give [ɛ].		

5. e (continued)

9 [ə]	Mute (pronounced).[6] See IX, p. 12:	de venir comprenez	də vəniːr kɔ̃prəne
10 [a]	First **e** in the adverbial ending **-emment**:[7]	évidemment	evidamɑ̃
11 [ɑ̃]	Nasal:[8]	dent sembler	dɑ̃ sɑ̃ble
12 [ɛ̃]	In **-ien** final:	rien combien	rjɛ̃ kɔ̃bjɛ̃
13 [ɛ]	In **-ien-** in forms of **venir** and **tenir** and their compounds, except when **n** is doubled:	vient tiendrai revient reviennent	vjɛ̃ tjɛ̃dre rəvjɛ̃ rəvjɛn
	[6] An **e** may be used to soften a **g** (rarely a **c**); and when so used, it has no value of its own:	mangeons mangeait douceâtre	mɑ̃ʒɔ̃ mɑ̃ʒɛ dusɑːtr
	[7] Note also:	femme solennel hennir	fam sɔlanɛl aniːr *or* ɛniːr
	[8] When **e** initial is followed by a single **n** and a vowel, it may always be treated like **enn-** initial, giving a nasal:	enamourer enorgueillir	ɑ̃namure ɑ̃nɔrgœjiːr

5. e (continued)

	14	[ɛ̃]	In **-éen** final:[9]	européen	œrɔpeɛ̃
eau	15		See **a.**		
ei	16	[ɛ]	Usually:	seize	sɛɪz
	17	[ɛ̃]	Nasal:	plein	plɛ̃
eu	18	[ø]	Phonetically final, or before [t] or [z]:	feu veut neutre heureuse	fø vø nø:tr œrø:z
	19	[œ]	Except as above, unless nasal:[10, 11]	heure	œ:r
	20	[œ̃]	Nasal:	jeun	ʒœ̃
œu	21	[ø]	Like **eu** (see above):	bœufs	bø
			[9] Note also:	examen benzine Benjamin	ɛgzamɛ̃ bɛ̃zin bɛ̃ʒamɛ̃
			[10] In forms of **avoir**, **eu** = [y]:	eut eurent	y yːr
			[11] **U** may be inserted after **c** or **g** to give the consonant the hard sound, and in some cases this **u** causes a **u** after a following **e** to disappear. In such cases the sound of **eu** remains, however:	cueillir orgueil	kœjiːr ɔrgœːj

5. e (continued)

	22	[œ]	Like **eu** (see above):	bœuf	bœf
œ	23	[œ]	In a few words:	œil œillade	œ:j œjad
	24	[e]	In a few bookish words:	œsophage œdipe	ezɔfa:ʒ edip

6. f

f	1	[f]	Usually:[1]	fils	fis
	2	[v]	Linked:	neuf heures	nœv‿œ:r
			[1] When final, **f** is usually pronounced: But:	chef clef	ʃɛf kle

7. g

g	1	[g]	Usually:[1]	grand gant guide	grɑ̃ gɑ̃ gid
	2	[ʒ]	Before **e, i, y**:[2]	manger gigot gymnaste	mɑ̃ʒe ʒigo ʒimnast
			[1] When final, **g** is generally silent: But:	rang grog	rɑ̃ grɔg
			[2] For **gg**, cf. **cc**:	aggraver suggérer	agrave sygʒere

7. g (continued)

	3 [k]	Linked:	sang impur	sɑ̃k‿ɛ̃pyːr
gn	4 [ɲ]	Usually:	compagnon	kɔ̃paɲɔ̃
	5 [gn]	In a few bookish words:	ignition	ignisjɔ̃

8. h

h	1 silent	Always:[1]	homme	ɔm
			cahier	kaje
			ah	ɑ
ch	2 [ʃ]	Usually:	cheval	ʃəval
	3 [k]	In a few words of Greek origin:	orchestre	ɔrkɛstr
sch	4 [ʃ]	Occurs in a few bookish words:	schisme	ʃism
	5 [sk]	Rare — occurs in a few bookish words:	sc(h)olaire	skɔlɛːr
sh	6 [ʃ]	Occurs in a few bookish words:	shako	ʃako
ph	7 [f]	Always:	philosophe	filɔzɔf
th	8	See **t**.		

[1] See XI, 3, p. 14.

9. i

i	1 [i]	Usually:	il livre	il liːvr
	2 [j]	Semi-consonant (see V, p. 7): But:	bien papier prier oubliant	bjɛ̃ papje prie ubliã
	3 [j]	In **-ill-** in the body of a word:[1]	mouillé	muje
	4 [j]	In **-il** final preceded by a vowel:	travail	travaːj
	5 [ɛ̃]	Nasal:	matin impossible	matɛ̃ ɛ̃pɔsibl
ai	6	See **a**.		
ei	7	See **e**.		
oi	8 [wa]	Usually:	moi	mwa
	9 [wɑ]	After **r**, or before a final silent consonant:[2]	roi mois	rwɑ mwɑ
	10 [wɛ̃]	Nasal:	besoin	bəzwɛ̃
		[1] The rule does not always hold: Note:	mille ville village gentilhomme	mil vil vilaːʒ ʒãtijɔm
		[2] The rule does not hold in verbs: Note:	je vois je bois fois foi foie voix voie (noun)	vwa bwa fwɑ fwɑ fwɑ vwa vwɑ

10. j

| j | [ʒ] | Always: | jardin | ʒardɛ̃ |

11. k

| k | [k] | Occurs only in foreign words: | kilo | kilo |

12. l

l	1 [l]	Usually:[1]	plus	ply
	2 [j]	In **-ill-** in the body of a word:[2]	brillant fille meilleur	brijɑ̃ fiːj mɛjœːr
	3 [j]	In **-il** final preceded by a vowel:	travail	travaːj
		[1] When final, **l** is generally pronounced: But:	bel fil gentil fusil	bɛl fil ʒɑ̃ti fyzi
		[2] The rule does not always hold (see **i**, note 1):	million billion tranquille	miljɔ̃ biljɔ̃ trɑ̃kil

13. m

m	1 [m]	Usually:[1, 2]	matin	matɛ̃
mn	2 [mn]	In some words:	omnibus	ɔmnibys
	3 [n]	In a few words:	automne damner	otɔn dɑne
		[1] When final, **m** is usually silent: Except in a few foreign words:	nom album rhum islam maximum	nɔ̃ albɔm rɔm islam maksimɔm
		[2] See X, p. 13.		

14. n

n	1 [n]	Usually:[1, 2]	donne nombre	dɔn nɔ̃ːbr
gn	2	See **g**.		
mn	3	See **m**.		
		[1] When final, **n** is usually silent: Except in a few foreign words: See X, p 13	non spécimen	nɔ̃ spesimɛn

15. o

o	1 [ɔ]	Usually:[1]	école	ekɔl
	2 [o]	ô (circumflex):[2]	le nôtre	noːtr
	3 [o]	Phonetically final:	zéro gros	zero gro
	4 [o]	Before [z]:[3]	oser	oze
	5 [o]	Before the ending **-tion**:	notion	nosjɔ̃
	6 [ɔ̃]	Nasal:	monde tromper	mɔ̃ːd trɔ̃pe
œ	7	See **e**.		
œu	8	See **e**.		
oi	9	See **i**.		
ou	10 [u]	Usually:	vous	vu
	11 [w]	Semi-consonant (see V, p. 7): But:	oui louer clouer	wi lwe klue
		[1] Silent in a few words:	faon paon taon Laon	fɑ̃ pɑ̃ tɑ̃ lɑ̃
		[2] A few exceptions:	hôpital hôtel rôtir	ɔpital ɔtɛl rɔtiːr
		[3] Very few exceptions:	philosophe	filɔzɔf

16. p

p	1 [p]	Usually:[1]	pas	pɑ
ph	2	See **h**.		

[1] When final, **p** is usually silent:

	drap	dra
	trop	tro
	camp	kɑ̃
But:	cep	sɛp
	hanap	anap

17. q

q	[k]	Usually:[1]	quand	kɑ̃

[1] Rarely used without **u**. When final (very rare), **q** is pronounced:

	cinq	sɛ̃ːk
	coq	kɔk
But:	cinq livres	sɛ̃ liːvr

18. r

r	[r]	Usually:[1, 2]	arbre	arbr

[1] See XI, 1, p. 13.

[2] In words ending in **r**+a consonant, **r** is generally pronounced:

fort	fɔːr
vers	vɛːr

19. s

s	1 [s]	Usually:[1, 2]	sac classe fils	sak klɑɪs fis
	2 [z]	Single between vowels:[3, 4, 5]	maison	mɛzɔ̃
	3 [z]	Linked:	les hommes	lez‿ɔm
sch	4	See **h**.		
sh	5	See **h**.		
		[1] When final, **s** is usually silent: But final **s** is pronounced in **fils** (*son*), **hélas, mars, mœurs, ours, os, omnibus, jadis, bis** (*twice*), **blocus, tous,** (pronoun), **lis** (*lily*), etc.	bas gros	bɑ gro
		[2] **S** added to make the plural rarely affects the pronunciation: **table, tables** [tabl]. But: **œuf** [œf], **œufs** [ø]; **bœuf** [bœf], **bœufs** [bø].		
		[3] Note the following compounds:	antisocial entresol vraisemblable	ātisɔsjal ātrəsɔl vrɛsāblabl
		[4] In **trans-**+a vowel, **s** is usually pronounced [z]: But:	transatlantique transitif transept	trāzatlātik trāzitif trāsɛ
		[5] See Assimilation, under Consonants (VI, p. 9). Notice:	Alsace asbeste balsamique presbytère transverse	alzas azbɛst balzamik prɛzbitɛːr trā'zvɛrs

20. t

t	1	[t]	Usually:[1]	petite	pətit
	2	[s]	Often when followed by i+a vowel,[2] unless preceded by **s** or **x**, or in verb endings:	nation prophétie question mixtion (nous) montions	nasjɔ̃ prɔfesi kɛstjɔ̃ mikstjɔ̃ mɔ̃tjɔ̃
th	3	[t]	Always:	théâtre	teɑːtr
			[1] When final, **t** is usually silent: But:	mot part dot est (*east*) ouest	mo paːr dɔt ɛst wɛst
			[2] Note:	amitié moitié pitié huitième métier	amitje mwatje pitje ɥitjɛm metje

21. u

u	1	[y]	Usually:[1, 2]	rue du	ry dy
	2	[ɥ]	Semi-consonant (see V, p. 7):[3]	lui suis	lɥi sɥi
			[1] See Note 11 under **e**. [2] See Orthographic Signs, VII, 4, p. 10. [3] The rule does not always hold:	 duo bruit	 dyo brɥi

FRENCH PRONUNCIATION

21. u (continued)

	3 [œ̃]	Nasal:	un humble	œ̃ œ̃ːbl
	4 silent	Usually in **qu**, also when inserted to make **c** or **g** hard:	quand cueillir guide	kɑ̃ kœjiːr gid
	5 [w]	Before **a** in a number of bookish words:	aquatique lingual	akwatik lɛ̃gwal
au	6	See **a**.		
eau	7	See **a**.		
eu	8	See **e**.		
œu	9	See **e**.		
ou	10	See **o**.		

22. v

v	[v]	Always:	vivre vrai	viːvr vrɛ

23. w

w	1 [w]	Occurs in some foreign words:[1]	tramway watt	tramwe wat
	2 [v]	Occurs in some foreign words:[1]	wagon	vagɔ̃

[1] Frenchmen differ in their pronunciation of **w**: some usually (or always) pronounce it [v], some usually (or always) pronounce it [w].

24. x

x	1 [ks]	Usually:[1]	exprès sexe	ɛksprɛ sɛks
	2 [gz]	In **ex-** or **hex-** initial followed by a vowel; also **x** initial in a few Greek proper nouns:	exact exercice hexagone Xantippe	ɛgzakt ɛgzɛrsis ɛgzagɔn gzãtip
	3 [s]	In a few words:	Bruxelles soixante six dix	brysɛl swasã:t sis dis
		But:	six livres six hommes dix livres dix hommes	si li:vr siz‿ɔm di li:vr diz‿ɔm
	4 [z]	In a few words:	deuxième sixième dixième dix-huit dix-neuf	dØzjɛm sizjɛm dizjɛm dizɥit diznœf
	5 [z]	Linked:	aux hommes	oz‿ɔm
		[1] When final, **x** is usually silent:	heureux paix voix	œrØ pɛ vwa
		Final **x** is pronounced [s] in **six** and **dix**. Final **x** is pronounced [ks] in **borax, index, larynx, lynx, préfix, sphinx,** etc.		

25. y

y	1	[j]	Y or **hy** initial before a vowel:	yeux hyacinthe	jø jasɛ̃ːt
	2	[i]	Except as above, unless nasal or combined with another vowel:[1] But:	Yves hymne lyre Chantilly tramway	iːv imn liːr ʃɑ̃tiji tramwe
	3	[ɛ̃]	Nasal:	lynx symbole	lɛ̃ːks sɛ̃bɔl

			[1] N.B. Between vowels and in **pays** and its derivatives, y = i+i. Each **i** is treated according to the rules for **i**:	crayon (crai-ion)
				moyen (moi-ien)
				ployiez
				    (ploi-i-iez)
				pays (pai-is)
				
				paysan
				    (pai-i-san)
				paysage
				    (pai-i-sa-ge)
					krɛjɔ̃
					mwajɛ̃
					
					plwaije
					pɛi
					pei
					pɛji (peji)
					
					pɛizɑ̃, etc.
					
					pɛizaːʒ, etc.

26. z

z	[z]	Usually:[1] [1] When final, **z** is usually silent: But:	douze nez gaz	duːz ne gɑːz

FRENCH GRAMMAR

LESSON I

1. Agreement. An adjective agrees in gender and number with the noun it modifies.

2. Gender. French nouns are either masculine or feminine: **homme** (masc.), *man*; **femme** (fem.), *woman*; **livre** (masc.), *book*; **encre** (fem.), *ink*. A few nouns are of both genders: **enfant,** *child*; **élève,** *pupil*; **après-midi,** *afternoon*.

An adjective regularly forms its feminine by the addition of **e** to the masculine: **grand homme,** *tall man*; **grande femme,** *tall woman*. When the masculine form ends in **e**, the feminine is the same as the masculine: **jeune homme,** *young man*; **jeune femme,** *young woman*.

3. Number. Nouns and adjectives commonly form their plurals by the addition of **s**: **grand homme, grands hommes; grande femme, grandes femmes.**

4. Definite Article. The definite article has four forms: (1) **le,** used before a masculine singular noun beginning with a consonant: **le livre;** (2) **la,** used before a feminine singular noun beginning with a consonant: **la femme;** (3) **l',** used before a singular noun beginning with a vowel or mute **h**: **l'enfant, l'encre, l'homme;** (4) **les,** used before a plural noun: **les enfants, les livres.**

5. Indefinite Article. The indefinite article has two forms: (1) **un,** used with a masculine singular noun: **un homme, un livre;** (2) **une,** used with a feminine singular noun: **une femme, une enfant.**

The definite and the indefinite articles must be repeated before each noun modified: *the women and children*, **les femmes et les enfants.**

EXERCISE I

avec [avɛk] *with*
deux [dø] *two*
élève [elɛːv] m. *or* f. *pupil*
encre [ãːkr] f. *ink*
enfant [ãfã] m. *or* f. *child*
et [e] *and*
femme [fam] f. *woman, wife*
grand, -e [grã, grãːd] *tall, great, grand*
homme [ɔm] m. *man*

le [lə], la [la], l', les [le] *th.*
livre [liːvr] m. *book*
montrez-moi [mɔ̃tre mwa] *show me*
petit, -e [pəti, pətit] *small, little*
sur [syːr] *on, upon, over*
table [tabl] f. *table*
un, -e [œ̃, yn] *a, an,*
voici [vwasi] *here is, here are*
voilà [vwala] *there is, there are*

A. 1. Un homme et une femme. 2. Un grand homme et
   œ̃n‿ɔm   e yn fam.   œ̃   grãt‿ɔm   e
une grande femme. 3. Deux hommes et deux femmes. 4. Deux
yn grãːd fam.   døz‿ɔm   e dø fam.   dø
grands hommes. 5. L'homme et la femme. 6. Le grand homme
grãz‿ɔm.   lɔm   e la fam.   lə   grãt‿ɔm
et la grande femme. 7. Les deux grands hommes. 8. Montrez-
e la grãːd fam.   le dø   grãz‿ɔm.   mɔ̃tre
moi les grands livres. 9. Voilà les grands livres sur la table.
mwa le grã   liːvr.   vwala le grã   liːvr syr la tabl.
10. Un petit livre. 11. Deux petits livres. 12. Une petite enfant.
œ̃ pti liːvr.   dø pti liːvr.   yn pətit ãfã.
13. Les petits enfants. 14. La petite enfant. 15. Montrez-moi
   le ptiz‿ãfã.   la ptit ãfã.   mɔ̃tre mwa
l'encre. 16. Voici l'encre avec le grand livre sur la petite table.
lãːkr.   vwasi lãːkr avɛk lə grã   liːvr syr la ptit tabl.
17. Montrez-moi l'élève. 18. Voilà le petit élève avec l'homme.
   mɔ̃tre mwa lelɛːv.   vwala lə ptit‿elɛːv avɛk lɔm.

B. (*Oral*) 1. A man. 2. A woman. 3. The man. 4. The tall man. 5. The tall woman. 6. Two men. 7. Two women. 8. The two little children. 9. A pupil (*m*.). 10. A child (*f*.). 11. The pupil (*m*.). 12. The pupil (*f*.). 13. The little child (*m*.). 14. The little child (*f*.). 15. Two little books.

C. *Write:* 1. Show me the man and the woman. 2. There are the man and the woman. 3. There is the man with the small child. 4. Two large books on one small table. 5. Two small children with a tall man. 6. The pupils, the two women, and the tall men. 7. Here is a book on the table. 8. Here are the two books with the ink. 9. Show me the tables. 10. There are the small tables.

D. (*Pronunciation*) 1. Divide the words of the vocabulary into syllables, applying the rules (VIII, p. 11). 2. Point out the words in which there are nasal vowels (X, p. 13). 3. Why isn't the **o** in **homme** nasal? 4. Point out the words in which **e** is mute (IX, p. 12). 5. In which ones is the mute **e** pronounced? Why? 6. Note that the mute **e** in the first syllable of **petit** is silent in A 10, 11, 13, 14, 16, and 18; but pronounced in A 12. Can you tell why? 7. Note which of the final consonants are pronounced (XI, 1, p. 13). 8. Note the difference in pronunciation between **un** and **une, grand** and **grande.** Why? 9. Explain the two pronunciations for (a) **deux** (A3); (b) **petits** (A 11 and 13); (c) **grand** (A 2 and 16); (d) **grands** (A 7 and 8). See XIII, p. 14. 10. Note the irregular pronunciation of **et** and of **femme.**

LESSON II

6. Agreement. A verb agrees in person and number with its subject.

7. Present Indicative of **avoir,** *to have.*

j'ai [ʒ e] *I have*
tu as [ty a] *thou hast* [1]
il a [il a] *he has*
elle a [ɛl a] *she has*

nous avons [nuz‿avɔ̃] *we have*
vous avez [vuz‿ave] *you have*
ils ont [ilz‿ɔ̃] *they* (masc.) *have*
elles ont [ɛlz‿ɔ̃] *they* (fem.) *have*

[1] The pronoun in the second person singular is used in addressing a familiar friend, a member of one's family, a small child, or a lower animal. In other cases, "**vous**" is used. "**Vous**" is always used in addressing more than one person. The student is cautioned to avoid the use of "**tu**", unless the context demands it.

8. Present Indicative of être, *to be*.

je suis [ʒə sɥi] *I am*	**nous sommes** [nu sɔm] *we are*
tu es [ty ɛ] *thou art*	**vous êtes** [vuz‿ɛt] *you are*
il est [il ɛ] *he is*	**ils sont** [il sɔ̃] *they* (masc.) *are*
elle est [ɛl ɛ] *she is*	**elles sont** [ɛl sɔ̃] *they* (fem.) *are*

9. Agreement.
A pronoun agrees in gender and number with its antecedent:

Où est l'homme? **Il** est à l'église. *Where is the man? He is at church.*
Où est la femme? **Elle** est avec l'homme. *Where is the woman? She is with the man.*

Since French nouns are either masculine or feminine, a pronoun referring to a noun is either masculine or feminine:

Où est le livre? **Il** est sur la table. *Where is the book? It is on the table.*
Où est la plume? **Elle** est aussi sur la table. *Where is the pen? It is also on the table.*

A compound, one member of which is masculine, requires any agreement (such as a pronoun with its antecedent, an adjective with the noun modified, etc.) to be masculine plural:

Où sont le livre et le papier? **Ils** (*two masculines*) sont sur la table. *Where are the book and the paper? They are on the table.*
Où sont la plume et l'encre? **Elles** (*two feminines*) sont sur la table. *Where are the pen and the ink? They are on the table.*
Où sont la plume, l'encre et le papier? **Ils** (*two feminines and a masculine*) sont sur la table. *Where are the pen, the ink and the paper? They are on the table.*

EXERCISE II

à [a] *at, to, in*
aussi [osi] *also*
autre [oːtr] *other*
bureau [byro] m. (*large*) *desk*
cahier [kaje] m. *notebook*
classe [klɑːs] f. *class, classroom*
craie [krɛ] f. *chalk*
crayon [krɛjɔ̃] m. *pencil*
dans [dɑ̃] *in, into*
de [də] *of, from*
école [ekɔl] f. *school*
leçon [ləsɔ̃] f. *lesson*
main [mɛ̃] f. *hand*
maître [mɛːtr] m. *master, teacher*

LESSON II 43

morceau [mɔrso] m. *piece*
noir, -e [nwaːr] *black*
où [u] *where*
papier [papje] m. *paper*
plume [plym] f. *pen*
pupitre [pypitr] m. *(pupil's) desk*
quatre [katr] *four*
salle [sal] f. *room, hall*
tableau [tablo] m. *picture, blackboard*
trois [trwɑ] *three*

  à la main *in my (his, her, your, etc.) hand*
  à l'école *in school, at school, to school*
  la (salle de) classe *the classroom*

A. 1. Où est l'élève? 2. Il est à l'école. 3. Les élèves et
    u ɛ lelɛːv?   il ɛt‿a lekɔl.   lez‿elɛːv e
le maître sont dans la salle de classe. 4. Les élèves sont
l(ə) mɛːtr(ə) sɔ̃ dɑ̃ la sal də klɑːs.   lez‿elɛːv sɔ̃
petits. 5. Le maître est grand. 6. Il a un morceau de craie à la
pti.   lə mɛtr ɛ grɑ̃.   il a œ̃ mɔrso d krɛ a la
main. 7. La leçon est sur le tableau noir. 8. L'élève a un
mɛ̃.   la lsɔ̃   ɛ   syr lə tablo nwaːr.   lelɛːv a œ̃
pupitre. 9. Le maître a un bureau. 10. Les enfants ont trois
pypitr.   lə mɛːtr a œ̃ byro.   lez‿ɑ̃fɑ̃ ɔ̃ trwɑ
livres et deux cahiers. 11. Un élève a un crayon; l'autre a
liːvr e dø kaje.   œ̃‿elɛv a œ̃ krɛjɔ̃;   loːtr a
une plume. 12. Le papier et les plumes sont avec les livres sur
yn plym.   lə papje e le plym sɔ̃t‿avɛk le liːvr syr
les pupitres. 13. Vous êtes à l'école. 14. Je suis à l'école
le pypitr.   vuz‿ɛts‿a lekɔl.   ʒə sɥiz‿a lekɔl
aussi avec les autres élèves. 15. Vous avez un petit livre
osi avɛk lez‿otrəz‿elɛːv.   vuz‿avez‿œ̃ pti liːvr
et un cahier. 16. Nous avons quatre grands livres aussi. 17.
e œ̃ kaje.   nuz‿avɔ̃ katrə grɑ̃ liːvr osi.
L'encre est sur le bureau; elle est noire. 18. Les livres sont
lɑ̃ːkr ɛ syr lə byro;   ɛl ɛ nwaːr.   le livrə sɔ̃
sur la table; ils sont grands. 19. J'ai un livre à la main. 20.
syr la tabl; il sɔ̃ grɑ̃.   ʒe œ̃ liˑvr a la mɛ̃.
Vous avez un livre à la main aussi.
vuz‿avez‿œ̃ liˑvr a la mɛ̃ osi.

B. (*Oral*) 1. One pen. 2. One pencil. 3. Four books.
4. Three other books. 5. Another school. 6. Another

teacher. 7. At school. 8. In my hand. 9. In his hand. 10. In the classroom. 11. In school. 12. One piece of chalk. 13. They have; they are. 14. We have; we are. 15. I am; I have. 16. You are; you have. 17. He is; she has.

C. *Write:* 1. Where are the children? 2. They are at school. 3. Show me the classroom. 4. Here is the classroom. 5. You have two books. 6. We have three pens. 7. They are on the table with the pencils. 8. We are the pupils. 9. You are the teacher. 10. You have a piece of chalk in your hand. 11. The other children are at school. 12. They are in the classroom. 13. Where are the pen and the ink? 14. They are on the (large) desk. 15. I have a pen and a pencil; they are at school. 16. The teacher is a tall man. 17. Show me the teacher. 18. There is the teacher with a piece of chalk in his hand.

D. 1. Pronounce the sounds represented by these combinations of vowels: **ai, au, eau, ou, oi.** 2. Note the sound of **ai** when it is nasal, as in **main.** 3. Note that the value of **oi** in **trois** differs from that in **moi, voici, voilà.** The latter is the more common. See **oi,** p. 26. 4. Why isn't the **u** in **plume** nasal? 5. Note that in **quatre** there is only one sound for **qu.** 6. Compare the sound of **c** in **morceau** and **voici** with that in **cahier, école, avec,** and **encre;** and tell when **c** has the sound [s]. 7. Compare **école** and **leçon,** and state the effect of the cedilla. 8. Note the omission of the mute **e** in **leçon** in A 7, and its insertion in **autres, quatre, livres** in A 14, 16, 18 respectively. Can you explain the reason?

LESSON III

10. Negation. Negation is ordinarily expressed by placing **ne** before the verb and **pas** after the verb:

Je suis. *I am.* Je **ne** suis **pas.** *I am not.*
Il a. *He has.* Il **n'**a **pas.** *He has not.*

11. Interrogation. 1. When the subject is a personal pronoun (or **ce** or **on**—see §§ 42 and 51, 2), interrogation may be expressed by inverting the order of the verb and subject, as in English:

Il est. *He is.* Est-il? *Is he?*
Nous avons. *We have.* Avons-nous? *Have we?*

The verb and its following pronoun subject (**je, tu, il, elle, nous, vous, ils, elles, ce, on**) are joined by the hyphen. When a verb in the third person singular ends in a vowel-letter and a following pronoun subject (**il, elle, on**) begins with a vowel, **-t-** is inserted between them:

Il a. *He has.* A-t-il? *Has he?*

2. When the subject is not a personal pronoun (or **ce** or **on**) inversion rarely takes place. We may place the subject first and repeat it after the verb by a personal pronoun to obtain inverted order:

Jean a-t-il un livre? *Has John a book?*
Les hommes sont-ils dans la maison? *Are the men in the house?*

Or, we may use a fixed expression **est-ce que** [ɛskə], which we place before the sentence in the normal order, and which indicates that the sentence is interrogative. The inversion then occurs in **est-ce**:

Jean a un livre. Est-ce que Jean a un livre? *Has John a book?*
Les hommes sont dans la maison. Est-ce que les hommes sont dans la maison? *Are the men in the house?*

3. This expression, **est-ce que**, is commonly used even when the subject is a personal pronoun (or **ce** or **on**). It is well to use it when in doubt, especially in the first person singular, as some verbs do not permit inversion of this form:

Est-ce qu'il a un livre? *Has he a book?*

4. One of the comparatively few cases of inversion when the subject is not a personal pronoun (or **ce** or **on**) occurs

when a sentence having a verb in a simple tense is introduced by the interrogative **où** (*where*):

Où est Jean? Where is John? *Où sont les hommes? Where are the men?*

12. Possessive—Dative—Contractions. The possessive case of a noun is expressed with the preposition **de** (*of*):

John's book = the book of John: Le livre **de** Jean.
the man's book = the book of the man: le livre **de** l'homme.

The dative case (indirect object) of a noun is expressed with the preposition **à** (*to*):

Show John the book = Show the book to John: Montrez le livre **à** Jean.
Show the man the book = Show the book to the man: Montrez le livre **à** l'homme.

The prepositions **de** and **à**, when followed by the definite article **le** or **les,** form the following contractions: **de+le maître = du maître; de+les maîtres = des maîtres; à+le maître = au maître; à+les maîtres = aux maîtres.** Note the following:

du maître *of the master*	**au** maître *to the master*
de la femme *of the woman*	**à la** femme *to the woman*
de l'enfant *of the child*	**à l'**enfant *to the child*
des maîtres *of the masters*	**aux** maîtres *to the masters*
des enfants *of the children*	**aux** enfants *to the children*
des femmes *of the women*	**aux** femmes *to the women*

EXERCISE III

à [a] *with* (in descriptions), *on*
bain [bɛ̃] m. *bath*
bibliothèque [bibliɔtɛk] f. *library*
campagne [kɑ̃paɲ] f. (*open*) *country*
ce [sə] *this, that, it,* etc. See §72
chaise [ʃɛːz] f. *chair*
chambre [ʃɑ̃ːbr] f. (*private*) *room*
cinq [sɛ̃ːk] [sɛ̃] *five*
cuisine [kɥizin] f. *kitchen*

derrière [dɛrjɛːr] *behind*
devant [dəvɑ̃] *before, in front of*
étage [etaːʒ] m. *story* (*of a house*)
fenêtre [fənɛːtr] f. *window*
Jean [ʒɑ̃] *John*
lit [li] m. *bed*
maison [mɛzɔ̃] f. *house*
manger [mɑ̃ʒe] *to eat*
Marie [mari] *Mary*

LESSON III

ne - pas [nə - pa] *not*
pièce [pjɛs] f. *(any) room*
porte [pɔrt] f. *door, gate*
premier [prəmje] *first*
rayon [rɛjɔ̃] m. *shelf*
salon [salɔ̃] m. *drawing-room*
se trouvent [sə truːv] *are*

à la campagne *in the country*
au premier (étage) [1] *on the second (or third) floor*
au rez-de-chaussée [re d̥ ʃose] *on the ground floor*
en bas [bɑ] *downstairs*
en*haut [2] [o] *upstairs*
la chambre à coucher *the bedroom*
la salle à manger *dining-room*
la salle de bain(s) *bath-room*

A. 1. Nous avons une maison à la campagne. 2. La maison
nuz‿avɔ̃z‿yn   mɛzɔ̃ a la kɑ̃paɲ.   la mɛzɔ̃
a quatre pièces au rez-de-chaussée et cinq au premier étage.
a katrə pjɛs o re d̥ ʃose   e sɛ̃ːk o prəmjer‿etaːʒ.
3. Le salon, la bibliothèque, la salle à manger, et la cuisine
   lə salɔ̃, la bibliɔtɛk,   la sal a mɑ̃ʒe, e la kɥizin
sont au rez-de-chaussée. 4. Au premier se trouvent quatre
sɔ̃t‿o re d̥ ʃose.   o prəmje sə truv   katrə
chambres à coucher et une salle de bains. 5. J'ai une chambre
ʃɑ̃ːbr   a kuʃe   e yn sal də bɛ̃.   ʒe yn ʃɑ̃ːbr
à un lit au premier; le lit est devant la fenêtre. 6. Où est la
a œ̃ li o prəmje; lə li ɛ dvɑ̃   la fnɛːtr.   u ɛ la
chambre de l'enfant? 7. L'enfant n'a-t-il pas une chambre
ʃɑ̃ːbrə d̥ lɑ̃fɑ̃?   lɑ̃fɑ̃   na til paz‿yn ʃɑ̃ːbr
au rez-de-chaussée? 8. Les enfants ont une chambre à deux
o re d̥ ʃose?   lez‿ɑ̃fɑ̃   ɔ̃t‿yn ʃɑ̃ːbr   a dø
lits. 9. La chambre des enfants n'est pas au rez-de-chaussée;
li.   la ʃɑ̃ːbrə dez‿ɑ̃fɑ̃   nɛ   paz‿o re d̥ ʃose;

---

[1] **Un étage** is a story above the ground floor. **Le premier étage** is, therefore, the second floor; when there is an **entresol** (*mezzanine floor*), **le premier étage** is the third floor.

[2] The asterisk before a few words beginning with an "aspirate" **h**, and also before **onze** and **oui**, indicates that there can be no preceding linking or elision.

elle est au premier. 10. Le salon a quatre fenêtres et deux
ɛl ɛt‿o prəmje.   lə salɔ̃ a katrə fnɛːtr e dø
portes. 11. Les portes du salon sont grandes. 12. Les fenêtres
pɔrt.   le pɔrt dy salɔ̃ sɔ̃ grɑ̃ːd.   le fnɛˑtrə
de la cuisine sont petites. 13. Les livres de Jean et de Marie
d la kɥizin sɔ̃ ptit.   le livrə d ʒɑ̃ e d mari
sont sur le bureau dans la bibliothèque. 14. Les livres du maître
sɔ̃ syr lə byro dɑ̃ la bibliɔtɛk.   le livrə dy mɛtrə
de la maison ne sont-ils pas sur les rayons de la bibliothèque?
d la mɛzɔ̃ nə sɔ̃t‿il pɑ syr le rɛjɔ̃   d la bibliɔtɛk?
15. Devant une des fenêtres se trouvent deux chaises.
     dəvɑ̃t‿yn de fnɛːtr sə truv   dø ʃɛːz.
16. Est-ce que le tableau est derrière la porte du salon?
     ɛ s kə l tablo   ɛ dɛrjɛr la pɔrt dy salɔ̃?
17. Nous sommes en haut. 18. N'êtes-vous pas en bas?
     nu   sɔmz‿ɑ̃ o.   nɛt vu pɑz‿ɑ̃ bɑ?

B. *Continue:* 1. je suis, tu es, *etc.* 2. je ne suis pas [ʒə n
sɥi pɑ], tu n'es pas [ty nɛ pɑ], *etc.* 3. suis-je? [sɥiːʒ], *etc.*
4. ne suis-je pas? *etc.* 5. j'ai, tu as, *etc.* 6. je n'ai pas, *etc*
7. ai-je? [ɛːʒ], *etc.* 8. n'ai-je pas? *etc.* 9. est-ce que j'ai?
[ɛ s kə ʒe], *etc.* 10. n'est-ce pas que j'ai? [nɛ s pɑ kə ʒe], *etc.*

C. 1. Where is the library? 2. Is it on the second floor?
3. Is the bath-room on the ground floor? 4. Haven't you
three bedrooms? 5. Are the children downstairs? 6. Are
the men and women in the drawing-room? 7. I am not in
the country. 8. The man's pen and pencil are not on the
table in the dining-room. 9. I have a small book in my hand.
10. Aren't the little children at school? 11. Is the chair in
front of the window? 12. Has the man a room with two
beds? 13. Show me John's and Mary's books. 14. There
are five of the children's books. 15. Are the kitchen windows
(windows of the kitchen) large? 16. Has the house five
rooms?

D. 1. What is the sound of s in **chaise, cuisine, maison?** Why? 2. Note carefully these sounds: **th** in **bibliothèque, gn** in **campagne, ch** in **chaise.** 3. Pronounce carefully the vowel of the first syllable in **devant, fenêtre, premier.** 4. Note that **è** in **derrière** and **ê** in **fenêtre** are pronounced [ɛ]. 5. What is the first syllable in **derrière?** Can you account for the [ɛ]-sound? Does the same rule apply in **avec?** 6. Note that **é** in **étage** and the **e** in **manger** are both pronounced [e].

LESSON IV

13. Principal Parts of French Verbs. 1. French verb-forms are derived from five principal parts: (1) the present infinitive, (2) the present participle, (3) the past participle, (4) the first person singular of the present indicative, and (5) the first person singular of the past definite.

2. Regular verbs are divided into three conjugations according to the ending of the infinitive: donn**er** [dɔne] *to give*, fin**ir** [finiːr] *to finish*, vend**re** [vɑ̃ːdr] *to sell*.

The present participle always ends in **-ant**; the stem in the first and third conjugations is that of the infinitive, but in the second conjugation **-iss-** is inserted: donnant [dɔnɑ̃], finissant [finisɑ̃], vendant [vɑ̃dɑ̃].

The first person singular of the present indicative varies in the three conjugations: je donn**e**, je fin**is**, je vend**s**.

14. Present Indicative. The singular of the present indicative is derived from the fourth principal part:

je donn**e** [dɔn]	je fin**is** [fini]	je vend**s** [vɑ̃]
tu donn**es** [dɔn]	tu fin**is** [fini]	tu vend**s** [vɑ̃]
il donn**e** [dɔn]	il fin**it** [fini]	il vend[1] [vɑ̃]

[1] When the ending of the fourth principal part is **s**, the third person singular of the present indicative ends in **t** unless the stem of the verb ends in **c, d,** or **t,** in which case nothing is added: **je romps, tu romps, il rompt.** But **je vaincs, il vainc; je bats, il bat.**

The plural of the present indicative is derived from the second principal part by adding to the stem of the present participle the endings **-ons, -ez, -ent**:

nous donn**ons** [dɔnɔ̃]	nous finiss**ons** [finisɔ̃]	nous vend**ons** [vãdɔ̃]
vous donn**ez** [dɔne]	vous finiss**ez** [finise]	vous vend**ez** [vãde]
ils donn**ent** [dɔn]	ils finiss**ent** [finis]	ils vend**ent** [vãːd]

There is only one present indicative tense of a French verb; consequently **je donne** means *I give, I do give, I am giving*; **il donne** means *he gives, he does give, he is giving*; *etc.*

Negation is commonly expressed as explained in Lesson III: **je ne donne pas, tu ne donnes pas,** *etc. I do not give (am not giving), etc.*

In the inverted order a mute **e** of a first person singular is written **é** and pronounced [ɛ]: **je donne** [ʒə dɔn], **donné-je?** [dɔnɛːʒ]. It is well to avoid this form, thus: **Est-ce que je donne?** [ɛ s kə ʒ dɔn] *Do I give?*

Note the "euphonic" **t,** the third singular ending in a vowel letter: **il donne** [il dɔn], **donne-t-il?** [dɔn t‿il] *does he give?*

EXERCISE IV

anglais [ãglɛ] *English;* m. *English language*
choisir [ʃwaziːr] *to choose*
donner [dɔne] *to give*
entendre [ãtãːdr] *to hear*
entrer[1] [ãtre] *to enter*
fille [fiːj] f. *daughter,*
   jeune — *girl, young woman*
   petite — *little girl*
fils [fis] m. *son*
finir [finiːr] *to finish*

français [frãsɛ] *French;* m. *French language*
frère [frɛːr] m. *brother*
jeune [ʒœn] *young*
magasin [magazɛ̃] m. *store, shop*
mais [mɛ] *but*
mère [mɛːr] f. *mother*
parler [parle] *to speak, talk*
père [pɛːr] m. *father*
sœur [sœːr] f. *sister*
vendre [vãːdr] *to sell*

    un livre de français *a French book (book on French)*
    une leçon de français *a French lesson (lesson on French)*

---

[1] This verb is intransitive. When the English verb has a direct object, there is a preposition in French: He enters (into) the house.

LESSON IV

A. 1. Le père et la mère de Jean et de Marie ont deux enfants,
lə pɛr e la mɛr də ʒɑ̃ e d mari ɔ̃ døz‿ɑ̃fɑ̃,
un fils et une fille. 2. Marie, la sœur de Jean, parle avec un
œ̃ fis e yn fi:j. mari, la sœr də ʒɑ̃, parl avɛk œ̃
jeune homme. 3. Ils parlent français. 4. Entendez-vous
ʒœn ɔm. il parl frɑ̃sɛ. ɑ̃tɑ̃de vu
les enfants dans le salon? 5. J'entends Jean, mais je n'entends
lez‿ɑ̃fɑ̃ dɑ̃ l salɔ̃? ʒɑ̃tɑ̃ ʒɑ̃, mɛ ʒ nɑ̃tɑ̃
pas Marie. 6. La mère des enfants parle-t-elle français?
pɑ mari. la mɛr dez‿ɑ̃fɑ̃ parl tɛl frɑ̃sɛ?
7. Elle parle français et anglais. 8. Une jeune fille entre dans
ɛl parl frɑ̃sɛ e ɑ̃glɛ. yn ʒœn fij ɑ̃trə dɑ̃
la maison. 9. Elle donne à la petite fille un cahier et un crayon.
la mɛzɔ̃. ɛl dɔn a la ptit fi:j œ̃ kaje e œ̃ krɛjɔ̃.
10. Jean et Marie, finissez-vous la leçon? 11. Nous finissons
ʒɑ̃ e mari, finise vu la lsɔ̃? nu finisɔ̃
la leçon de français. 12. Le père de la jeune fille vend la maison.
la lsɔ̃ də frɑ̃sɛ. lə pɛr d la ʒœn fi:j vɑ̃ la mɛzɔ̃.
13. Ils entrent dans un magasin. 14. Ils choisissent deux
ilz‿ɑ̃trə dɑ̃z‿œ̃ magazɛ̃. il ʃwazis dø
plumes et un crayon. 15. Nous ne vendons pas les plumes.
plym e œ̃ krɛjɔ̃. nu n vɑ̃dɔ̃ pɑ le plym.
16. Nous donnons les crayons aux enfants.
nu dɔnɔ̃ le krɛjɔ̃ oz‿ɑ̃fɑ̃.

B. 1. He speaks. 2. She chooses. 3. He hears. 4. Does he give? 5. Does she finish? 6. Does he sell? 7. Choosing. 8. We are choosing. 9. You are not choosing. 10. Are they not choosing? 11. Do we enter? 12. Do you not enter? 13. They do not enter. 14. The girl speaks. 15. The man's daughter enters. 16. The women's sons enter.

C. 1. There is the pupil's father. 2. The children's mother is the young woman's sister. 3. Has she John's books? 4. Does she not give John the paper, pen and ink? 5. I enter a store. 6. We choose a picture. 7. The man sells the pencil to Mary's brother. 8. The girl gives five books to John's sister. 9. Does she not give a book to Mary also? 10. The teacher gives the pupils a French lesson. 11. They enter the classroom. 12. Show me the teacher's desk. 13. Two of the notebooks are in the dining-room behind the door. 14. Are you finishing the French lesson? 15. Does the teacher speak French to the pupils?

D. 1. Note that the ending **-ent** of a verb in the third person plural is silent. 2. Note the irregular pronunciation of **fils**. 3. Note the pronunciation of **fille** (See **l**, p. 27). 4. Note that the **t** of **et** (*and*) is never linked. See A 7. 5. Divide the words of the vocabulary into syllables, and tell how each letter is pronounced and why.

LESSON V

15. Possessive Adjectives. 1. Forms:

Singular		Plural		
Masculine	Feminine			
mon [mɔ̃]	**ma** [ma]	**mes** [me]	*my*	
ton [tɔ̃]	**ta** [ta]	**tes** [te]	*thy*	
son [sɔ̃]	**sa** [sa]	**ses** [se]	*his, her, its*	
notre [nɔtr]		**nos** [no]	*our*	
votre [vɔtr]		**vos** [vo]	*your*	
leur [lœːr]		**leurs** [lœːr]	*their*	

2. The form of the possessive is determined by the gender and number of the noun modified: **mon livre** (*masc.*), **ma plume** (*fem.*), **mes livres** (*plu.*).

3. The forms **ton, ta, tes,** will be used only when **tu** is the pronoun of address. See § 7, note.

4. Be careful to note that **son, sa, ses,** mean *his* or *her* or *its*, generally indicated by the context:

Où sont Jean et son père? *Where are John and **his** father?*
Où sont Marie et son père? *Where are Mary and **her** father?*
Où sont Jean et sa mère? *Where are John and **his** mother?*
Où sont Marie et sa mère? *Where are Mary and **her** mother?*

In the first sentence **son** is used, not because it means *his* (in the second sentence it means *her*), but because the noun modified is masculine singular; in the fourth sentence **sa** is used, not because it means *her* (in the third sentence it means *his*), but because it modifies a feminine singular noun.

5. The forms **mon, ton, son,** are used instead of **ma, ta, sa,** immediately before a feminine singular noun or adjective beginning with a vowel or mute **h**: **ma plume,** but **mon autre plume; mon encre,** but **ma bonne encre.**

16. Interrogative Adjectives. The interrogative adjectives are **quel** [kɛl] (*masc. sing.*), **quelle** [kɛl] (*fem. sing.*), **quels** [kɛl] (*masc. plu.*), **quelles** [kɛl] (*fem. plu.*): **quel homme?** *which man?*; **quelles femmes?** *which women?*

These forms are used also in interjections. Note the absence of an indefinite article in the singular: **Quel homme!** *What a man!* **Quelle enfant!** *What a girl!* **Quelles femmes!** *What women!*

17. Demonstrative Adjectives. Forms:

Masculine singular before a consonant, **ce** [sə]: **ce livre**
Masculine singular before a vowel or mute **h, cet** [sɛt]: **cet homme**
Feminine singular, **cette** [sɛt]: **cette encre**
Plural (masculine or feminine), **ces** [se]: **ces livres, ces femmes**

The singular forms mean *this* or *that*; the plural form means *these* or *those*. To distinguish between what is near and what is at a distance, **-ci** or **-là** may be added to the noun:

ce livre, *this book* or *that book;* **ce livre-ci,** *this book;* **ce livre-là,** *that book;*
ces livres, *these* or *those books;* **ces livres-ci,** *these books;* **ces livres-là,** *those books.*

The possessive adjectives, the interrogative adjectives, and the demonstrative adjectives must be repeated before every noun modified by them:

my father and mother, **mon père et ma mère**
which men and women? **quels hommes et quelles femmes?**
these boys and girls, **ces garçons et ces jeunes filles.**

EXERCISE V

accompagner [akɔ̃paɲe] *to accompany*
arriver [arive] *to arrive, happen*
chez[1] [ʃe] *at* (or *to* or *in*) *the house* (or *office* or *shop*) *of*
cousin, -e [kuzɛ̃, kuzin] m., f. *cousin*
descendre [desɑ̃:dr] *to descend, get out; take* (or *bring*) *down*
famille [fami:j] f. *family*
garçon [garsɔ̃] m. *boy, waiter, bachelor*
grand'mère [grɑ̃mɛːr] f. *grandmother*
grand-père [grɑ̃pɛːr] m. *grandfather*
mari [mari] m. *husband*

monter [mɔ̃te] *to mount, get in*
montrer [mɔ̃tre] *to show*
non [nɔ̃] *no* (opposed to *yes*)
oncle [ɔ̃:kl] m. *uncle*
ou [u] *or*
*****oui** [wi] *yes*
parent, -e [parɑ̃, parɑ̃:t] m., f. *relative*
petite-fille [pətitfiːj] f. *granddaughter*
petit-fils [pətifis] m. *grandson*
quand [kɑ̃] *when*
tante [tɑ̃:t] f. *aunt*
ville [vil] f. *city, town*

en automobile [otɔmɔbil] f. *in an automobile*
en voiture [vwatyːr] f. *in a carriage; All aboard!*

A. 1. Notre famille est grande. 2. J'ai un cousin et deux
nɔtrə famij ɛ grɑ̃ːd.   ʒe œ̃ kuzɛ̃ e dø
cousines à la campagne. 3. Mes cousins sont les enfants de
kuzin a la kɑ̃paɲ.   me kuzɛ̃ sɔ̃ lez‿ɑ̃fɑ̃ d
mon oncle et de ma tante. 4. Ma tante est la sœur de mon
mɔ̃n‿ɔ̃ːkl e d ma tɑ̃ːt.   ma tɑ̃ːt ɛ la sœr də mɔ̃
père. 5. Mon père et sa sœur sont les enfants de mon
pɛːr.   mɔ̃ pɛr e sa sœːr sɔ̃ lez‿ɑ̃fɑ̃ d mɔ̃
grand-père et de ma grand'mère. 6. Mon cousin et mon frère
grɑ̃pɛːr e d ma grɑ̃mɛːr.   mɔ̃ kuzɛ̃ e mɔ̃ frɛːr
sont les petits-fils de mon grand-père. 7. Ma grand'mère
sɔ̃ le ptifis də mɔ̃ grɑ̃pɛːr.   ma grɑ̃mɛr

---

[1] Note that **chez** is a preposition, and must have an object. The English *at* (or *to* or *in*) and also *of* are included in the meaning of **chez**.

accompagne sa fille et le mari de sa fille chez leurs cousins.
akɔ̃paɲ sa fiːj e l mari d̥ sa fiːj ʃe lœr kuzɛ̃.

8. Vos parents de la campagne sont-ils chez votre père? 9. Oui.
vo parɑ̃ d la kɑ̃paɲ sɔ̃t‿il ʃe vɔtrə pɛːr? wi.

Nous montrons la ville à nos parents. 10. J'accompagne votre
nu mɔ̃trɔ̃ la vil a no parɑ̃. ʒakɔ̃paɲ vɔtrə

fils chez sa tante. 11. Cette tante a trois enfants, deux petits
fis ʃe sa tɑ̃ːt. sɛt tɑ̃·t a trwɑz‿ɑ̃fɑ̃, dø pti

garçons et une petite fille. 12. Montons-nous en voiture ou
garsɔ̃ e yn pətit fiːj. mɔ̃tɔ̃ nu ɑ̃ vwatyːr u

en automobile? 13. Quelle automobile? 14. L'automobile de
ɑ̃n‿ɔtɔmɔbil? kɛl ɔtɔmɔbil? lɔtɔmɔbil də

cet homme-là. 15. Non, nous montons en voiture. 16. Quand
sɛt ɔm la. nɔ̃, nu mɔ̃tɔ̃ ɑ̃ vwatyːr. kɑ̃

la voiture arrive devant la porte de la maison de ma tante,
la vwatyr ariv dəvɑ̃ la pɔrt də la mɛzɔ̃ d ma tɑ̃ːt,

nous descendons.
nu desɑ̃dɔ̃.

B. 1. My sister. 2. My other sister. 3. My uncle. 4. My cousins (*m. and f.*). 5. His mother. 6. Her mother. 7. His aunt. 8. Her aunt. 9. Her other aunt. 10. His wife. 11. Her husband. 12. His children. 13. Our table. 14. Our tables. 15. Your brother. 16. Your brothers. 17. Their pens. 18. This man. 19. This man and that man. 20. These men and those men. 21. That tall man. 22. That hand. 23. That other pencil. 24. That pencil. 25. Which chair? 26. Which chairs? 27. Which bed? 28. Which beds? 29. What a boy! 30. What girls!

C. 1. Do your uncle and your cousins arrive at your brother's house in a carriage or in an automobile? 2. Does his aunt give her book to the children? 3. No, but she gives a pen and a pencil to her son. 4. When your grandmother accompanies the children to their father's home, does she get out of the carriage? 5. Yes, and she enters the house with her granddaughters. 6. What a boy! When I give your brother a notebook, he sells his paper to another pupil. 7. This little girl speaks French. 8. Which little boys are finishing their lessons? 9. Their relatives do not sell their houses. 10. That girl in front of the window in the dining-room is my brother's wife's sister. 11. Where does your cousin's husband choose his books? 12. Are you speaking of your children? 13. Is that city large or small? 14. Does he give his ink to this pupil? 15. Do you accompany your brother to your son's house?

D. 1. Note that double consonants are generally pronounced as one, as in **arriver, accompagner, ville.** 2. Turn to the Introduction (p. 8), and study the tongue position for the sounds [d], [t], [l], [n], [ɲ]. Practice these sounds carefully. 3. Watch the lip position and the tongue position for [y]. This is not a difficult sound, but it requires practice because it is not found in English. 4. Notice that **ou** in **cousin** is not pronounced like **ou** in **oui.** The latter is the semi-consonant sound (see p. 7). 5. Note the **e** in the first syllable of **descendre.** See p. 21. 6. Divide the words of the vocabulary into syllables and account for each letter.

LESSON VI

REVIEW

A. 1. Give the four forms of the definite article, and tell when each is used. Illustrate. 2. Give the two forms of the indefinite article. 3. Review the nouns of the first five lessons, noting well the gender of each and using with each the proper form of the definite article and of the indefinite article. 4. How is the feminine of an adjective regularly formed? 5. What is the feminine of an adjective ending in mute **e** in the masculine, such as **jeune** or **autre?** 6. How is the plural of a noun or of an adjective regularly formed?

Le Château d'Azay le Rideau

La Place de la Concorde, Paris

LESSON VI

7. Do any of the cardinal numerals change their forms for gender or number? 8. When a pronoun refers to a masculine noun and a feminine noun, what form is used? When it refers to three feminine nouns and a masculine noun, as *they*, meaning *my mother, my father, my sister,* and *my aunt?* 9. What are the meanings of **il donne?** Of **nous choisissons?** Of **vous vendez?** 10. How is a verb usually made negative? 11. How is interrogation commonly expressed when the subject is a personal pronoun (other than the first person singular)? How may interrogation be expressed when the subject is something else, such as a noun or a possessive pronoun? 12. How is the possessive case of a noun expressed? The dative case? 13. What happens when **de** precedes the different forms of the definite article? When **à** precedes? 14. How many conjugations of regular verbs are there? What is the infinitive ending of each? 15. How many principal parts has a French verb? What are they? 16. From which ones is the present indicative tense derived? How? 17. Give the forms, and tell what determines the use of each form, of (a) the possessive adjectives, (b) the interrogative adjectives, (c) the demonstrative adjectives. Illustrate.

B. *Answer in French:* 1. Avez-vous une maison à la campagne? 2. Est-ce que votre maison est grande ou petite? 3. Le salon est-il au rez-de-chaussée? 4. À quel étage se trouvent les chambres à coucher? 5. Où est la salle à manger? 6. Avez-vous un tableau dans votre chambre? 7. Est-ce que la chaise est devant la fenêtre? 8. Où sont les livres de votre père? 9. Jean n'est-il pas à l'école? 10. Le maître parle-t-il aux élèves? 11. Parle-t-il français ou anglais? 12. Avez-vous un crayon? 13. Montrez-moi votre crayon. 14. Avez-vous un frère? 15. Votre petit frère est-il à l'école aussi? 16. A-t-il son livre à la main? 17. Quel est ce livre? 18. Parlez-vous français à l'école? 19. Vos parents vendent-ils leur maison? 20. Ma tante est-elle chez mon frère?

C. 1. Where is the room with two beds? 2. It is on the second floor. 3. Show me your brother and sister. 4. They are not at school; they are at my grandfather's in the country. 5. Do you give your little brother the books on the shelves in the library? 6. Does not your brother's wife choose her paper in that shop? 7. My uncle and aunt and their children are getting into a carriage. 8. When our automobile arrives before the school, we get out. 9. The children are entering the classroom. 10. That tall girl is one of his sisters, and this little girl is his other sister. 11. Where is my ink? Isn't it on the teacher's desk? 12. We are finishing our French lessons. 13. Doesn't he show her husband the picture? 14. I hear Mary in the dining-room; she is talking English with her teacher. 15. To which boys does she give the pens? 16. I am giving this book to the tall man and that book to my uncle. 17. Three of my sister's children are at school. 18. My paper, pen, ink, and books are on the table downstairs.

D. 1. State the rules for syllabication. 2. When is **e** mute? 3. When is mute **e** pronounced in prose? 4. When is a vowel nasal? 5. When **n** or **m** nasalizes a preceding vowel, is the nasalizing consonant ever pronounced? (Note **mon encre**). 6. Which consonants are generally pronounced when final? 7. What is meant by elision? When a vowel is elided, how is the preceding consonant pronounced? (**l'enfant**) 8. What is the usual pronunciation of **a? e? i? o? u? ai?** 9. Can you recall (a) three words in which **a** is pronounced [ɑ]? (b) A word in which **oi** is pronounced [wɑ]? (c) A word in which **ai** is pronounced [e]? (d) A word in which **ou** is pronounced [w]? 10. Pronounce **é, è, ê, à, aî, où, ç, c** before **e**, **c** before **i**, **g** before **e**, **th**, **ch**, **gn**, **qu**, single **s** between vowels, **e** followed in the same syllable by a pronounced consonant (**derrière, avec**). 11. What effect upon pronunciation has the addition of **s** for the inflection of a verb, noun, or adjective? Pronounce **donne, donnes; table, tables; petit,**

petits. 12. Pronounce the following verb-endings: **-er, -ez, -e, -es, -ent, -ons, -ant.** 13. Pronounce: **femme, et, tu es, il est, bas, pas, classes, trois, crayon, rayon, quatre, cinq, cinq livres, cinq hommes, la fenêtre, une fenêtre, fils, fille, ville, famille, descendre.** 14. Transcribe Exercise B, above.

LESSON VII

18. Partitive. A partitive expresses a part of a whole, indefinite as to quantity and indefinite as to identity.

Thus, the expression *some books* means (1) a part of all existing books; (2) it does not state how many books, so it is indefinite as to quantity; (3) it does not state which books, so it is indefinite as to identity. *Three books*, while a part of a whole and indefinite as to identity, is not a partitive because it is definite as to quantity. *Those books* is not a partitive because it is definite as to identity.

19. Regular Partitive Construction. A noun in partitive construction is regularly preceded by **de** and the definite article:

 du pain *some bread*   **de la** viande *some meat*
 des hommes *some men*   **de l'**encre *some ink*

The expression of the partitive (usually *some* or *any*) is often omitted in English, but rarely in French:

 He has books and paper. Il a **des** livres et **du** papier.

20. Partitive Pronoun. The pronoun that replaces the partitive noun is **en** [ã]. It regularly stands before the verb, and must be expressed in French if there is a verb, although it is often omitted in English:

 Avez-vous des pommes? J'**en** ai. *Have you any apples? I have (some).*

21. Pronominal Adverbs. 1. **En** is often equivalent to the preposition **de** (*of, from,* etc.) and a pronoun in the third person:

 Il a trois livres et son frère **en** a cinq. *He has three books and his brother has five (of them).*

2. **Y** is sometimes used to mean *there* when the place referred to has already been mentioned. It is less emphatic than **là** (*there*):

> Est-il à l'école? Il **y** est. *Is he at school? He is (there).*

Y is sometimes equivalent to **à** (*at, to,* etc.), or some other preposition of position (such as **dans** or **sur**), and a pronoun in the third person. However, it very rarely refers to persons:

> Je pense à ma leçon. J'**y** pense. *I am thinking of my lesson. I am thinking of it.*

Notice that these two forms regularly stand before the verb. They are used in French although the equivalent may sometimes be omitted in English.

22. Distinction between il y a [ilja] (*there is, there are*) **and voilà** (*there is, there are*). The above expressions are not synonymous. The first merely states the existence of a thing, while the second points out an object to be looked at. Both may be accompanied by adverbial expressions of place. The difference may be rendered in English by stressing the *verb* for **il y a**, and the *adverb* for **voilà**:

> **Are** *there any apples?* Y a-t-il des pommes?
> **There** *are some apples (look at them).* Voilà des pommes.

EXERCISE VII

apporter [apɔrte] *to bring*
assiette [asjɛt] f. *plate*
bonne [bɔn] f. *maid(servant)*
café [kafe] m. *coffee*
chaque [ʃak] *each*
couteau [kuto] m. *knife*
cuiller [kyjɛːr] f. *spoon*
désirer [dezire] *to want, desire*
dîner [dine] *to dine*
dîner [dine] m. *dinner*
eau [o] f. *water*

encore [ãkɔːr] *yet, still, again*
fourchette [furʃɛt] f. *fork*
fruit [frɥi] m. *fruit*
lait [lɛ] m. *milk*
légume [legym] m. *vegetable*
pain [pɛ̃] m. *bread, loaf of bread*
penser [pãse] *to think*
place [plas] f. *place, seat, space*
pomme [pɔm] f. *apple*
pomme de terre [pɔm də tɛːr] f. *potato*
pour [puːr] *for; in order to*(+ infinitive)

LESSON VII

soir [swaːr] m. *evening*
sucre [sykr] m. *sugar*
tasse [tɑːs] f. *cup*
terre [tɛːr] f. *earth*
thé [te] m. *tea*
verre [vɛːr] m. *glass*
viande [vjɑ̃ːd] f. *meat*
vin [vɛ̃] m. *wine*

à la maison *at home, (to) home*
encore un (deux, trois, etc.) *one (two, three,* etc.) *more*
encore (+ a partitive) *some more*
s'il vous plaît [sil vu plɛ] *please, if you please*

A. 1. Nous dînons à la maison ce soir. 2. Nous entrons
    nu   dinɔ̃ a la mɛzɔ̃ sə swaːr.   nuz‿ɑ̃trɔ̃
dans la salle à manger. 3. Quand nous y entrons, le dîner
dɑ̃ la sal a mɑ̃ʒe.   kɑ̃   nuz‿i ɑ̃trɔ̃, lə dine
est sur la table. 4. Il y a à chaque place une assiette, un couteau,
ɛ syr la tabl.   ilja a ʃak   plas yn asjɛt, œ̃ kuto,
des fourchettes, des cuillers, et un verre. 5. Désirez-vous de
de furʃɛt,   de kyjɛːr,   e œ̃ vɛːr.   dezire vu   d
la viande et des légumes? 6. Un petit morceau de viande et
la vjɑ̃ːd e de legym?   œ̃ pti mɔrso d vjɑ̃ːd e
deux pommes de terre, s'il vous plaît. 7. La bonne apporte
dø   pɔm   də tɛːr, sil vu plɛ.   la bɔn apɔrt
de l'eau et du vin quand nous en désirons. 8. Elle donne à
də lo e dy vɛ̃ kɑ̃   nuz‿ɑ̃ dezirɔ̃.   ɛl dɔn a
chaque enfant un morceau de pain et un verre de lait. 9. Ils
ʃak   ɑ̃fɑ̃ œ̃ mɔrso d pɛ̃ e œ̃ vɛr d(ə)lɛ.   il
désirent du café au lait, mais nous n'en donnons pas aux
dezir dy kafe o lɛ, mɛ nu nɑ̃ dɔnɔ̃   paz‿o
petits enfants. 10. En désirez-vous une tasse? 11. Pour le
ptiz‿ɑ̃fɑ̃.   ɑ̃ dezire vu yn tɑːs?   pur lə
dîner je désire du café, mais mon frère désire du thé avec du
dine ʒə dezir dy kafe, mɛ mɔ̃ frɛr dezir dy te avɛk dy
sucre. 12. Voilà du sucre pour le thé. 13. J'en donne encore
sykr.   vwala dy sykrə pur lə te.   ʒɑ̃ dɔn ɑ̃kɔr
un morceau à mon frère. 14. La bonne apporte aux enfants
œ̃ mɔrso a mɔ̃ frɛːr.   la bɔn apɔrt oz‿ɑ̃fɑ̃
encore du pain. 15. Elle apporte aussi des fruits: des pommes.
ɑ̃kɔr dy pɛ̃.   ɛl apɔrt osi de frɥi: de pɔm.

16. Elle en donne une à chaque enfant. 17. Les pommes
ɛl ã dɔn yn a ʃak ãfã.   le pɔm
sont-elles sur la table? 18. Elles y sont, je pense.
sɔ̃t‿ɛl   syr la tabl?   ɛlz‿i sɔ̃, ʒə pã:s.

B. 1. Some ink. 2. Some children. 3. Some meat.
4. Some milk. 5. Some glasses. 6. Some coffee. 7. Some
potatoes. 8. Some paper. 9. Some pens. 10. Some chalk.
11. Have you any ink? 12. I have (some). 13. I haven't any.
14. Isn't she at school? 15. She is (there). 16. Are you
thinking of your lessons? 17. I am thinking of them. 18. Have
you any books? 19. I have (some). 20. My brother has
five (of them). 21. Is there any bread on the table? 22. There
is (some). 23. Has he any bread? 24. He has two pieces
(of it). 25. There is the dining-room; my brother is entering (into) it.

C. 1. Is your father at home? 2. No, he is at my aunt's.
3. Is he bringing your aunt a book? 4. He is bringing two
to my uncle, I think. 5. Has he any on his table? 6. There
are four more books on the shelf. 7. Are there any more
apples at home? 8. I have some at my father's home.
9. Where is your ink? There is my ink, on my desk. 10. He
is showing my wife another picture. (*Write* another *in
two ways.*) 11. We want some more bread. 12. Do they
want some meat and vegetables? 13. Have you any sugar
for your tea? Yes, I have. 14. Do you want some coffee
with milk? If you please. 15. Is your mother entering the
house? 16. She is entering my brother's house, and my
father is entering it also. 17. Are you finishing your lessons?
18. We are finishing two of them this evening. 19. We want
meat, bread, and wine. 20. Which maid gives some to your
brother?

D. 1. What is the sound of **s** when it is doubled? When it
is preceded or followed by a consonant? When it is initial?

When it is final and pronounced? (**fils**) 2. When has **s** the [z]-sound? 3. Apply the rule for semi-consonant **i** (p. 7), and divide **assiette** into syllables. What is the sound of the first **e**? Why? 4. Why isn't the **o** nasal in **bonne** and **pomme**? 5. What is the sound of the first **e** in **terre** and in **verre**? Why? 6. How many syllables are there in **viande** orthographically? Phonetically?

E. *Answer in French:* 1. Où dînons-nous ce soir? 2. Dans quelle pièce dînons-nous? 3. Quand nous y entrons, est-ce qu'il y a des assiettes sur la table? 4. La bonne apporte-t-elle de la viande et des légumes? 5. En désirez-vous? 6. Avez-vous un couteau et des fourchettes? 7. Le vin est-il dans le verre? 8. La bonne donne-t-elle du café aux enfants? 9. Donne-t-elle du pain et du lait aux enfants? 10. Désirez-vous du sucre?

LESSON VIII

23. Present Indicative of **aller** (*to go*), **faire** (*to do, to make*), and **voir** (*to see*).

je vais [ʒə ve] *I go* nous allons [nuz‿alɔ̃] *we go*
tu vas [ty va] *thou goest* vous allez [vuz‿ale] *you go*
il va [il va] *he goes* ils vont [il vɔ̃] *they go*

je fais [ʒə fɛ] *I do* nous faisons [nu fəzɔ̃] *we do*
tu fais [ty fɛ] *thou dost* vous faites [vu fɛt] *you do*
il fait [il fɛ] *he does* ils font [il fɔ̃] *they do*

je vois [ʒə vwa] *I see* nous voyons [nu vwajɔ̃] *we see*
tu vois [ty vwa] *thou seest* vous voyez [vu vwaje] *you see*
il voit [il vwa] *he sees* ils voient [il vwa] *they see*

Note 1. These are irregular verbs. In **aller,** only two forms can be derived: **allons** and **allez,** from **allant.** In **faire,** the singulars are regular, and the first person plural is derived from **faisant.** The other forms of these two verbs must be learned. In **voir,** the singulars are derived from the fourth principal part (**je vois**), and the plurals from the second principal part (**voyant**). Notice that in the third person plural **-oy-** becomes **-oi-** before a mute **e**. This is always true.

Note 2. The present participle of **faire, faisant,** is pronounced as if the first syllable were **fe-** [fə]. All forms derived from it have the same peculiarity in pronunciation.

24. Relative Pronouns qui [ki] and que [kə].

1. **Qui** (*who, which, that*) as a relative may be used as the subject of a verb, and refers to persons or things. It does not change its form for gender or number:

    L'homme **qui** est ici . . . *The man who is here . . .*
    Les hommes **qui** sont ici . . . *The men who are here . . .*
    La plume **qui** est sur la table . . . *The pen which is on the table . . .*
    Les plumes **qui** sont sur la table . . . *The pens which are on the table*

2. **Qui** (*whom*) as a relative may be used also as the object of a preposition, but then it refers only to persons:

    L'homme (les dames) à **qui** je parle . . . *The man (ladies) to whom I am speaking . . .*

3. **Que** (*whom, which, that*) as a relative may be used as the object of a verb or as a predicate nominative. It refers to persons or things, and is of both genders and both numbers:

    L'homme (les hommes) **que** je vais voir . . . *The man (men) whom I am going to see . . .*
    La leçon (les leçons) **que** je vais finir . . . *The lesson (lessons) which I am going to finish . . .*
    Le grand homme **qu'il** est . . . *The great man that he is . . .*

25. Interrogative Pronouns qui and que.

1. **Qui** (*who, whom*) as an interrogative refers only to persons, and may be used anywhere in the sentence and also absolutely:

    Qui (or **qui est-ce qui**) va à l'école? *Who is going to school?*
    Qui voyez-vous? *Whom do you see?*
    A **qui** parle-t-il? *To whom is he speaking?*
    Qui est-ce? *Who is it?*
    Un homme est à la porte? **Qui?** *A man is at the door. Who?*
    Je vois un homme. **Qui?** *I see a man. Whom?*

LESSON VIII

2. Que (*what*) as an interrogative never refers to persons. It may be used as the object of a verb or as a predicate nominative:

    Que voyez-vous? *What do you see?*
    Qu'est-ce? *What is it?*

EXERCISE VIII

aimer [ɛme] *to love, like*
après [aprɛ] *after, afterward*
aujourd'hui [oʒurdɥi] *today*
bicyclette [bisiklɛt] f. *bicycle*
bien [bjɛ̃] *well, very*
bonjour [bɔ̃ʒuːr] *good day, good morning*
cerise [səriːz] f. *cherry*
comme [kɔm] *as, like; how!*
comment? [kɔmɑ̃] *how?*
confiture [kɔ̃fityːr] f. *preserves, jam*
déjà [deʒa] *already*
déjeuner [deʒøne] *to lunch, breakfast*

déjeuner [deʒøne] m. *luncheon*
    petit—— *breakfast*
Français [frɑ̃sɛ] m. *Frenchman*
fromage [frɔmaːʒ] m. *cheese*
ici [isi] *here*
là [la] *there*
maintenant [mɛ̃tnɑ̃] *now*
matin [matɛ̃] m. *morning*
merci [mɛrsi] *thank you*
pied [pje] m. *foot*
toujours [tuʒuːr] *always, still*
très [trɛ] *very*

    à bicyclette, à pied *on a bicycle, on foot*
    Comment allez-vous? [kɔmɑ̃t‿ale vu] *How are you?*
    être debout [ɛtrə dbu] *to be standing (to be on one's feet)*
    être levé [ɛtrə lve] *to be up (out of bed)*
    le matin, le soir *in the morning, in the evening*
    tout de suite [tu t sɥit] *immediately, at once*

A. 1. Bonjour! Comment allez-vous? 2. Je vais très bien,
    bɔ̃ʒuːr!   kɔmɑ̃t‿ale vu?   ʒə ve trɛ bjɛ̃,
merci. 3. Êtes-vous déjà levé? 4. Nous allons tout de suite
mɛrsi.   ɛt vu deʒa lve?   nuz‿alɔ̃ tu t sɥit
entrer dans la salle à manger pour le petit déjeuner. 5. Le
ɑ̃tre dɑ̃ la sal a mɑ̃ʒe pur lə pti deʒøne.   lə
matin nous avons du café au lait et du pain. 6. Aimez-vous
matɛ̃ nuz‿avɔ̃ dy kafe o lɛ e dy pɛ̃.   ɛme vu
les confitures? 7. Quelle confiture? 8. Nous avons ici de la
le kɔ̃fityːr?   kɛl kɔ̃fityːr?   nuz‿avɔ̃z‿isi d(ə) la
confiture de cerises. 9. Je vais en donner à mon petit fils qui
kɔ̃fityr də sriːz.   ʒə vez‿ɑ̃ dɔne a mɔ̃ pti fis ki

est là devant la chaise. 10. Après le petit déjeuner il va toujours
ε la dvā la ʃεːz.   aprε lə pti deʒøne il va tuʒuːr
à l'école. 11. Les enfants y vont à pied ou à bicyclette. 12. Jean
a lekɔl.   lez‿āfā i vɔ̃(t‿)a pje u a bisiklεt.   ʒā
y va aujourd'hui en voiture avec son père. 13. Il est déjà
i va oʒurdɥi   ā vwatyːr avεk sɔ̃ pεːr.   il ε deʒa
debout devant la porte. 14. Voyez-vous la voiture? 15. Qu'allez-
dbu   dvā la pɔrt.   vwaje vu la vwatyːr?   kale
vous faire aujourd'hui? 16. Je vais voir mon frère qui est chez
vu fεr oʒurdɥi?   ʒə ve vwar mɔ̃ frεːr ki ε ʃe
ma cousine. 17. Après je vais au magasin que vous voyez
ma kuzin.   aprε ʒə vez‿o magazε̃ kə vu vwaje
quand vous allez à l'école. 18. Et que faites-vous? Qui allez-
kā   vuz‿alez‿a lekɔl.   e kə fεt vu?   ki ale
vous voir? 19. J'ai toujours mes leçons de français le matin.
vu vwaːr?   ʒe tuʒuːr me lsɔ̃ d frāsε lə matε̃.
20. Après nous allons déjeuner. 21. Comme les Français aiment
    aprε nuz‿alɔ̃ deʒøne.   kɔm le frāsε εm
le fromage, nous avons toujours du fromage avec du pain et
lə frɔmaːʒ, nuz‿avɔ̃ tuʒur dy frɔmaːʒ avεk dy pε̃ e
de la confiture pour le déjeuner. 22. Aimez-vous nos déjeuners?
d la kɔ̃fityːr pur lə deʒøne.   εme vu no deʒøne?
Oui.
wi.

B. 1. I go on foot. 2. He is going in a carriage. 3. Do they go in an automobile? 4. Aren't you going on a bicycle? 5. How is he? 6. We are very well, thank you. 7. Is she standing? 8. Does he want some cheese? 9. What are you doing? 10. Who sees the children? 11. Whom do you see? 12. What do you see? 13. The bread which they are making. 14. The pen which is on the table. 15. Who is going there?

C. 1. When the children see their teacher, they always speak French. 2. Are you going to be up after (the) breakfast? 3. I am going to [eat] breakfast now in my bed. 4. Do you want some bread and coffee with milk? 5. Do they not like our cherry preserves? 6. Do the French have cheese at (the) luncheon? 7. Today they are going to get into a carriage (in order) to go to the home of an aunt. 8. They don't always go (there) in the morning. 9. They are standing in front of the door. 10. I am going to give the little boys some chalk. 11. What are they going to do with it? (*with* = **de**) 12. What books is he going to give his sister? 13. What is he doing now? 14. There is the man whom you want to see. 15. There is a tall man at the store, who always speaks to their children. 16. Which lessons are you finishing now? 17. Do you like the men whom you see here? 18. What does he do there when they are making bread? 19. There is the book which I want. 20. As he is going to go there at once, I am going also.

D. 1. Note the pronunciation of **bien.** See p. 22. 2. Why is the **e** in **pied** pronounced [e]? 3. Pick out all the mute **e**'s in the vocabulary. Tell whether they are pronounced or not, and why. 4. Note the pronunciation of **j**. It always has this sound. 5. Divide the words of the vocabulary into their phonetic syllables, and pronounce them carefully.

E. 1. Comment allez-vous? 2. Êtes-vous déjà levé? 3. Que faites-vous ici? 4. Que fait votre fils? 5. Que voyez-vous là? 6. Qui voyez-vous? 7. Qu'allez-vous faire ce soir? 8. Où va votre frère? 9. Allez-vous déjeuner chez votre frère? 10. Comment allez-vous à l'école?

LESSON IX

26. Compound Tenses. 1. The third principal part of a French verb, the past participle, is used in forming all compound verb-forms.

In the first conjugation the past participle ends in **é**; in the second, in **i**; in the third, in **u**: donner, donn**é** [dɔne]; finir, fin**i** [fini]; vendre, vend**u** [vãdy]. In irregular verbs the past participle is often irregular: avoir, eu [y]; être, été [ete]; faire, fait [fɛ]; voir, vu [vy].

Avoir is used as the auxiliary to form the compound tenses of most verbs.

2. The past indefinite tense is the narrative past tense in conversational style. It is formed by adding the past participle to the present indicative tense of the auxiliary:

j'ai donné *I gave, have given*	nous avons donné *we gave, have given*
tu as donné *thou gavest, hast given*	vous avez donné *you gave, have given*
il a donné *he gave, has given*	ils ont donné *they gave, have given*

Thus also **j'ai fini, j'ai vendu, j'ai eu, j'ai été, j'ai fait, j'ai vu,** etc., etc.

Notice that this tense is equivalent to the English simple past as well as the English perfect. Just as **j'ai donné** means *I gave* as well as *I have given*, so **nous avons été** means *we have been* and also *we were*; **vous avez fait** means *you have done (made)* and also *you did (made)*; **ils ont vu** means *they have seen* and also *they saw*; etc.

27. Word Order. Rules of order that apply to the verb apply to the *auxiliary* in compounds. Thus, the *auxiliary* comes between the two parts of the negative: **il a été, il n'a pas été.** In inverted order the pronoun subject follows the *auxiliary*: **il a été, a-t-il été? Y** and **en** precede the *auxiliary*: **Il y a trouvé des livres. Il en a acheté six.**

28. Agreement. The past participle in a compound tense agrees in gender and number with a preceding direct object:

Quels livres a-t-elle achet**és**? Quelle plume avez-vous trouv**ée**? Voici les fleurs qu'il a vend**ues**.

However, there is no agreement with the partitive pronoun, **en:**

A-t-il acheté des plumes? Il en a acheté.

LESSON IX

29. Idiomatic Use of the **Present.** In French the present tense is used to express what has been true and still is true. Thus, **Il est ici depuis une semaine** means *He has been here a week*, which implies *He still is here.* **Il parle depuis une heure** means *He has been speaking for an hour*, and implies *He still is speaking.*

EXERCISE IX

acheter [aʃte] *to buy*
ami, -e [ami] m., f. *friend*
beaucoup [boku] *much, many, very much, very many*
chose [ʃoːz] f. *thing*
cuisinier [kɥizinje] m. *cook*
cuisinière [kɥizinjɛːr] f. *cook*
depuis (que) [dəpɥi(kə)] *since*
difficulté [difikylte] f. *difficulty*
dix [dis, di] *ten*
fleur [flœːr] f. *flower*
heure [œːr] f. *hour, time, o'clock*
*****huit** [ɥit, ɥi] *eight*
jusqu'à [ʒyska] *to, up to, until, as far as*
livre [liːvr] f. *pound*
marché [marʃe] m. *market, bargain*
messieurs [mesjø] m. pl. *gentlemen*

monsieur [məsjø] m. *gentleman, Mr., sir*
neuf [nœf, nœ] *nine*
parce que [parsk(ə)] *because*
passer [pɑse] *to pass, to spend (time)*
personne [pɛrsɔn] f. *person*
plein, -e [plɛ̃, plɛn] *full*
préparer [prepare] *to prepare*
près de [prɛ d(ə)] *near*
presque [prɛsk] *almost*
rapporter [rapɔrte] *to bring back*
rencontrer [rɑ̃kɔ̃tre] *to meet*
saison [sɛzɔ̃] f. *season*
semaine [səmɛn] f. *week*
sept [sɛt, sɛ] *seven*
six [sis, si] *six*
tram(way) [tram(we)] m. *street car*
trouver [truve] *to find*

(à) bon marché *cheaply, cheap*
de retour [də rtuːr] *back*
il y a (followed by an expression of time) *ago*
Mais oui! Mais non! *Why yes! Why no!*
Nous voici. Nous voilà. *Here we are.*
tout à fait [tut‿a fɛ] *quite, entirely*

A. 1. Qu'est-ce que vous allez faire aujourd'hui? 2. Comme
    kɛs   kə vuz‿ale fɛr oʒurdɥi?   kɔm
la bonne a beaucoup à faire, nous allons au marché acheter
la bɔn a boku a fɛːr,   nuz‿alɔ̃z‿o marʃe aʃte
des choses pour le dîner. 3. Désirez-vous y aller? Oui, j'y
de ʃoːz   pur lə dine.   dezire vu i ale? wi, ʒi

vais avec vous. 4. Voilà un tramway qui va jusqu'au marché.
vez‿avɛk vu.   vwala œ̃ tramwe ki va ʒysko marʃe.
5. Il y a déjà neuf personnes dans le tram, et il y en a huit
   ilja deʒa nœ pɛrsɔn dɑ̃ lə tram, e iljɑ̃‿a ɥit
qui montent ici. 6. Nous allons trouver des places avec
ki mɔ̃·t isi.   nuz‿alɔ̃ truve de plas avɛk
difficulté; à cette heure le tram est presque toujours tout à
difikylte; a sɛt œːr lə tram ɛ prɛsk tuʒuːr tut‿a
fait plein. 7. Mais non; voilà deux places près de la porte.
fɛ plɛ̃.   mɛ nɔ̃; vwala dø plas prɛ d la pɔrt.
8. Il y en a beaucoup encore. 9. Voyez-vous ce monsieur qui
   iljɑ̃‿a boku ɑ̃kɔːr.   vwaje vu sə məsjø ki
est debout? 10. Voilà des messieurs que j'ai rencontrés il y a
ɛ dbu?   vwala de mesjø kə ʒe rɑ̃kɔ̃tre ilja
une semaine chez un ami. 11. Bonjour, messieurs. Com-
yn səmɛn ʃez‿œ̃n‿ami.   bɔ̃ʒuːr, mesjø.   kɔ-
ment allez-vous? 12. Nous voici au marché; nous allons
mɑ̃t‿ale vu?   nu vwasi o marʃe; nuz‿alɔ̃
descendre.
desɑ̃ːdr.

13. Nous sommes de retour à la maison depuis une heure.
    nu sɔm də rtuːr a la mɛzɔ̃ dəpɥiz‿yn œːr.
14. Nous avons été au marché. 15. Qu'est-ce que vous avez
    nuz‿avɔ̃z‿ete o marʃe.   kɛs kə vuz‿ave
fait au marché? 16. Nous y avons acheté six livres de viande,
fɛ o marʃe?   nuz‿i avɔ̃z‿aʃte si livrə d vjɑ̃ːd,
sept de pommes de terre, et une de fromage. 17. Nous y
sɛt də pɔm də tɛːr, e yn də frɔmaːʒ.   nuz‿i
avons passé une heure; mon frère a rapporté les choses que
avɔ̃ pase yn œːr; mɔ̃ frɛr a rapɔrte le ʃoːz kə
nous avons achetées. 18. Nous avons rapporté aussi des fleurs,
nuz‿avɔ̃z‿aʃte.   nuz‿avɔ̃ rapɔrte osi de flœːr,
que nous avons achetées à très bon marché. 19. Elles sont
kə nuz‿avɔ̃z‿aʃte a trɛ bɔ̃ marʃe.   ɛl sɔ̃
bon marché en cette saison parce qu'il y en a beaucoup.
bɔ̃ marʃe ɑ̃ sɛt sɛzɔ̃ pars kiljɑ̃‿a boku.
20. Maintenant la cuisinière va tout de suite préparer le dîner.
    mɛ̃tnɑ̃ la kɥizinjɛr va tu t sɥit prepare l dine.

B. 1. We are finding. 2. We have found. 3. Did we not find? 4. He is here. 5. He has been here. 6. He has been back an hour. 7. He was here a week ago. 8. Are these flowers cheap? 9. Which flowers did you buy? 10. Here are the flowers which I bought. 11. He found three of them. 12. Did you see any? 13. What have they done? 14. Which pen did he have? 15. Has he been at school? 16. He brought the books which I gave to the children. 17. Who is that gentleman? 18. They have chosen. 19. We did not hear. 20. Has he not finished? 21. Which books did you sell? 22. Did he speak to your sisters? 23. Did he show the knife to his family? 24. Did they dine at home?

C. 1. Did you have coffee with milk for (the) breakfast? 2. Yes, sir; and my mother gave the children some jam. 3. Where were you after breakfast this morning? 4. We have been in this room three hours. 5. We have finished our lessons now, and we are going to my grandfather's. 6. Which lessons have you finished? Your French lessons? 7. I prepared three of them; I had some difficulty. 8. Did your brother buy seven apples? 9. No, sir; he didn't buy seven, but he bought six. 10. I wanted eight; but the gentlemen whom I found at the store bought two for another boy. 11. I have wanted flowers since I saw some at the market. 12. Mr. Black gave some to my sister a week ago. 13. Did the cook prepare the meat which that man sold to your father? 14. Are you going to spend a week in the country? 15. This tram goes as far as the house which they have bought. 16. I like this house very much because it is near the city. 17. The library is quite full of the books which they have bought. 18. What did you find at the market when you met your aunt there? 19. Those ten things which you found on the table have been there for a week. 20. Which gentlemen did your father see in the city this morning?

D. 1. Notice the sound of **eu** in forms of **avoir**: [y]. 2. For the pronunciation of the numerals, see §104. Write in phonetic characters: *six apples, six other apples, six men, I have six.* 3. Notice (a) the irregular pronunciation of **monsieur;** (b) its plural, **messieurs;** (c) the [ɑ] in **passer;** (d) the irregular pronunciation of **tramway.** 4. Account for the different pronunciations for the masculine and the feminine (a) of the word for *full,* (b) of the word for *cook.* 5. Watch carefully the pronunciation of the vowels in **difficulté.** 6. Notice the sound [o] in **chose.** Can you account for it? See p. 29. 7. Why have we the sound [ɛ] in **personne?** In **pleine?** In **près?** In **presque?** In **saison?**

E. 1. Où êtes-vous? 2. Y êtes-vous depuis une heure? 3. Qu'avez-vous fait ce matin? 4. Que faites-vous depuis une semaine? 5. Où avez-vous été il y a une semaine? 6. Qui avez-vous vu à l'école? 7. Avez-vous préparé votre leçon de français? 8. Avez-vous eu de la difficulté? 9. Avez-vous acheté des fleurs? 10. Est-ce que vous aimez beaucoup ces pommes que nous avons achetées ce matin? 11. La cuisinière a-t-elle préparé le dîner? 12. Qu'est-ce qu'elle a préparé pour le dîner? 13. Avez-vous acheté trois crayons? 14. Votre frère en a-t-il trouvé? 15. Quels messieurs votre mère a-t-elle vus? 16. Est-ce que les fruits sont bon marché en cette saison? 17. L'école est-elle près de votre maison? 18. Quelles choses est-ce que l'homme a vendues? 19. Montrez-moi l'homme qui a parlé à votre frère. 20. Le tramway va-t-il jusqu'au marché?

LESSON X

30. Irregular Plurals. 1. Nouns ending in **s, x,** or **z,** and adjectives in **s** or **x,** remain unchanged in the plural: **fils, prix, nez; français,**[1] **heureux.**

2. Most nouns and adjectives[1] in **al** change **al** to **aux**: **cheval, chevaux; égal, égaux;** but **bals, fatals.**

[1] See footnote 1 opposite page.

3. Nouns and adjectives[1] in **au**, nouns in **eu**, and seven nouns in **ou**[2] add **x**: **couteau, couteaux; beau, beaux; cheveu, cheveux; genou, genoux.** The only common adjective in **eu, bleu,** adds **s**.

4. Note **œil, yeux; travail, travails** or **travaux.**

31. Irregular Feminines. 1. Many adjectives ending in a consonant double the final consonant before adding **e** for the feminine: **ancien, ancienne; gros, grosse; bon, bonne; gentil, gentille;** etc.

2. Note the following: **actif, active; blanc, blanche; sec, sèche; cher, chère; dernier, dernière; long, longue; heureux, heureuse; faux, fausse.**[3]

3. The following five adjectives have two masculine singular forms each, the second being used when a following noun modified begins with a vowel or mute **h**:

Masc. Sing.		Fem. Sing.	Masc. Plu.	Fem. Plu.
beau	bel	belle	beaux	belles
nouveau	nouvel	nouvelle	nouveaux	nouvelles
vieux	vieil	vieille	vieux	vieilles
fou	fol	folle	fous	folles
mou	mol	molle	mous	molles

Thus, **un beau livre, un bel homme, une belle dame, deux beaux hommes, deux belles dames.**

4. Only one cardinal numeral has a separate form for the feminine: **un** homme, **une** femme; but **deux** hommes, **deux** femmes.

---

[1] The feminine plural of adjectives is made regularly by adding **s** to the feminine singular: **français, française, françaises; heureux, heureuse, heureuses; beau, belle, belles; égal, égale, égales.**

[2] **bijou, caillou, chou, genou, *hibou, joujou, pou.**

[3] For further irregular feminines see the Appendix, p. 211.

Only two ordinal numerals have separate feminine forms: **premier, première; second, seconde.** The rest of them, ending in mute **e**, remain unchanged like any other adjective.

32. Position of Adjectives. 1. An adjective usually follows the noun it modifies: une ville française, une fleur blanche.

2. However, a noun is preceded by the following: (1) definite and indefinite articles, (2) possessive adjectives, (3) interrogative adjectives, (4) demonstrative adjectives, (5) cardinal and ordinal numerals, (6) some very common adjectives, such as **grand** (*tall, great*), **gros**, (*big*), **petit** (*small*), **beau** (*beautiful, fine*), **joli** (*pretty*), **vilain** (*ugly*), **jeune** (*young*), **vieux** (*old*), **ancien** (*former*), **bon** (*good*), **mauvais** (*bad*), **long** (*long*), **court** (*short*), **autre** (*other*), and others.

The position of an adjective sometimes depends on its meaning or emphasis: **un brave homme** (*worthy man*), **un homme brave** (*brave man*); **la maison blanche** (to distinguish one house from another), **sa blanche main** (an inherent quality, not a distinguishing feature).

EXERCISE X

actif, active [aktif, aktiːv] *active*
ancien, -ne [ɑ̃sjɛ̃, ɑ̃sjɛn] *old (former)*
beau, bel, belle [bo, bɛl] *beautiful, fine, handsome*
blanc, blanche [blɑ̃, blɑ̃ːʃ] *white*
bleu [bløː] *blue*
bon, bonne [bɔ̃, bɔn] *good, kind*
brave [braːv] *brave; worthy*
cher, chère [ʃɛːr] *dear*
cheval, chevaux [ʃəval, ʃəvo] m. *horse*
cheveu [ʃəvø] m. *hair*
court, -e [kuːr, kurt] *short*
dame [dam] f. *lady*
dernier, dernière [dɛrnje, dɛrnjɛːr] *last*

difficile [difisil] *difficult, hard*
facile [fasil] *easy*
fois [fwa] f. *time (occasion)*
genou [ʒənu] m. *knee*
gros, -se [gro, gro(ː)s] *big, bulky*
heureux, heureuse [œrø, œrøːz] *happy, glad*
joli [ʒɔli] *pretty*
long, longue [lɔ̃, lɔ̃ːg] *long*
madame [madam] f. *madam, Mrs., mistress*
mademoiselle [madmwazɛl] f. *Miss*
mauvais, -e [movɛ, movɛːz] *bad*
nouveau, nouvel, -le [nuvo, nuvɛl] *new*
œil, yeux [œːj, jø] m. *eye*

LESSON X

pauvre [poːvr] *poor*
pendant [pãdã] *during, for* (a time)
premier, première [prəmje, prəmjɛːr] *first*
que [kə] *that* (conjunction)

second, -e [səgõ, səgõːd] *second*
si [si] *so* (adv.); *if* (conj.)
vieux, vieil, -le [vjø, vjɛːj] *old*
vilain, -e [vilɛ̃, vilɛn] *ugly*

à cheval *on horseback, astride*
à la bonne heure! *Very well! Fine! Well and good!* (approval)
de bonne heure *early*
pas du tout [pɑ dy tu] *not at all*

A. 1. Monsieur votre père et madame votre mère vont-ils
  məsjø   vɔtrə pɛːr e madam vɔtrə mɛːr võt‿il
arriver ce matin? 2. Oui, mademoiselle; ils vont arriver de
arive sə matɛ̃?   wi, madmwazɛl;   il võt‿arive də
bonne heure. 3. J'ai rencontré un monsieur qui a vu mon
bɔn œːr.   ʒe rãkõtre œ̃ məsjø ki a vy mõ
père il y a une semaine, et j'ai parlé avec ce monsieur pen-
pɛːr ilja yn səmɛn, e ʒe parle avɛk sə məsjø   pã-
dant une heure. 4. Mon père est vieux, mais il est encore
dã(t‿)yn œːr. mõ pɛr ɛ vjø, mɛ(z‿)il ɛt‿ãkɔr
très actif. 5. Ma chère mère est active aussi. 6. Quand ils ar-
trɛz‿aktif. ma ʃɛr mɛr ɛt‿aktiːv osi.   kãt‿ilz‿a-
rivent chez nous, ils sont toujours heureux. 7. La première
riv ʃe nu, il sõ tuʒur œrø.   la prəmjɛr
fois que vous avez vu mon père, il a parlé à votre oncle de
fwa kə vuz‿ave vy mõ pɛːr, il a parle a vɔtr õːklə d
votre école. 8. Ses longs cheveux sont maintenant tout à fait
vɔtr ekɔl. se lõ ʃvø sõ mɛ̃tnã tut‿a fɛ
blancs. 9. Ma mère est vieille, mais elle est toujours belle.
blã.   ma mɛr ɛ vjɛːj, mɛ(z‿)ɛl ɛ tuʒur bɛl.
10. Ses yeux bleus sont si bons. 11. Voilà deux nouveaux ta-
sez‿jø blø sõ si bõ.   vwala dø nuvo   tableaux que ma mère a achetés la semaine dernière. 12. Dans un
blo kə ma mɛr a aʃte la smɛn dɛrnjɛːr.   dãz‿œ̃
des tableaux il y a une jolie jeune fille à cheval. 13. Dans le
de tablo ilja yn ʒɔli ʒœn fij a ʃval.   dã lə
second il y a une bonne dame qui a sur ses genoux une pauvre
zgõ   ilja yn bɔn dam ki a syr se ʒnu yn povrə

petite fille, qui n'est pas du tout heureuse. 14. Notre ancien
ptit fiːj, ki nɛ pɑ dy tu œrøːz.   nɔtr ɑ̃sjɛ̃
maître d'anglais aime beaucoup ces deux tableaux. 15. Ma
mɛtrə dɑ̃glɛ ɛm boku se dø tablo.   ma
mère va donner ces tableaux à l'école. 16. A la bonne heure!
mɛr va dɔne se tablo   a lekɔl.   a la bɔn œːr!

B. 1. A fine book. 2. A handsome man. 3. A beautiful lady. 4. The white house. 5. (Some) blue eyes. 6. A difficult lesson. 7. A big piece of bread. 8. Two old horses. 9. (The) last week (= the past week—*adjective follows noun*). 10. The last book on the shelf (= the last in a series—*adjective precedes noun*). 11. My old uncle. 12. My old (former) teacher. 13. A short shelf. 14. A bad boy. 15. An ugly city. 16. Three long lessons. 17. His first book. 18. Two poor old women (poor = indigent—*adjective follows noun*). 19. His poor old father (poor = worthy of pity—*adjective precedes noun*). 20. A brave man.

C. 1. Your good mother is going to give the poor girl some pencils. 2. The last time that I saw his aunt, she spoke of you. 3. What did you think when you heard your former teacher? 4. Mrs. Grant and Miss Mary are very happy because Mr. Grant has bought two fine black horses. 5. These lessons are not difficult; they are easy. 6. Did you buy that good meat for our dinner? 7. Which pretty blue plates did you choose for your son's wife? 8. Are you not upstairs? No, my poor old father likes the small room on the ground floor. 9. She spent two long weeks at her uncle's in the country. 10. Last week he sold his last books; he hasn't any at all now. 11. Do you want to accompany your brother? Very well; he is going to arrive early this morning. 12. Do you see that lady on horseback? She is not very young, but she is still very active. 13. She is going to be at my mother's house for three weeks. 14. Mrs. Legrand does much for the children of the poor (*plural*). What a worthy woman!

15. If he doesn't find his knives this evening, I am going to give him two more (of them). 16. He wants to give the poor woman a glass of milk; but she doesn't want any. 17. She has been at the little shop, where she bought some white bread. 18. She has made some coffee, and she is going to [eat] lunch at home.

D. 1. Compare the pronunciation of **ancien** with that of **bien**. 2. Why is the **e** of **votre** pronounced in A 1, but not in A 7? 3. Note that in **second, c** has the sound [g]. 4. Why must **t** be pronounced in **courte** although it is silent in **court**? Cf. **longue, mauvaise, seconde, vilaine,** etc. 5. Notice that the masculine and the feminine of *dear* are pronounced alike, but those of *last* and of *first* differently. 6. Can you state the rule for the liquid **l** as illustrated in the second form of the masculine singular and in the feminine of *old*? 7. Divide the word for *Miss* into syllables orthographically and phonetically, and note the differences. 8. Note the cases of "assimilation" in A 8, A 12, A 13, and E 13. Try to explain them (see p. 9). 9. Note that **d** when linked is pronounced [t], as in A 6.

E. 1. Qui va arriver chez vous aujourd'hui? 2. Est-ce qu'ils vont arriver le matin ou le soir? 3. Madame votre mère est-elle heureuse quand elle est chez son fils? 4. Les cheveux de monsieur votre père ne sont-ils pas tout à fait noirs? 5. Est-ce que votre père et votre mère sont toujours actifs? 6. Qu'est-ce qu'ils ont pensé la première fois qu'ils ont vu cette ville? 7. Y a-t-il des tableaux chez votre mère? 8. Qu'y a-t-il dans ces tableaux? 9. Qui aime les tableaux? 10. Qui est-ce qui a les yeux bleus? 11. Avez-vous les yeux noirs? 12. La première plume qu'il a achetée est-elle bonne? 13. La seconde plume [la zgɔ˙d plym] est-elle mauvaise aussi? 14. Avez-vous des chevaux noirs ou blancs? 15. Aimez-vous les bonnes pommes? 16. Quel est cet homme à qui vous avez parlé? 17. Votre maison est-elle près du tramway? 18. Où allez-vous à six heures? 19. Désirez-vous accompagner votre petite sœur à l'école? 20. Est-ce que vous trouvez cette leçon difficile?

LESSON XI

33. Irregular Partitive Construction. The partitive is expressed by **de** alone (without the definite article):

1. When a noun in partitive construction is the direct object of a negative verb:

> Il a **du** pain. *He has some bread.* Il n'a pas **de** pain. *He hasn't any bread.*
> J'ai acheté **de la** viande. *I bought some meat.* Je n'ai pas acheté **de** viande. *I didn't buy any meat.*

2. When a noun in partitive construction is preceded by an adjective:

> Nous avons trouvé **des** plumes. *We found some pens.* Nous avons trouvé **de** bonnes plumes. *We found some good pens.*

3. When an adjective is used substantively in partitive construction:

> Vous avez vendu de grandes pommes et **de** petites. *You sold large apples and small ones.*

4. When a noun in partitive construction follows an adverbial expression of quantity:

> Beaucoup **de** crayons (*many pencils*), trop **de** papier (*too much paper*), combien **d'**élèves? (*how many pupils?*), assez **de** journaux (*enough newspapers*), plus **de** pommes (*more apples*), etc.

(a) Two expressions of quantity, **bien** (*much, many*) and **la plupart** (*most, the majority*), are followed by **de** and the definite article: bien **du** papier (*much paper*), bien **des** hommes (*many men*); la plupart **des** *hommes* (*most men*).

(b) An expression of quantity is not necessarily followed by a partitive. Thus, *Many of the apples which I bought this morning* . . . becomes Beaucoup **des** pommes que j'ai achetées ce matin . . . Here **pommes** is definite as to identity, and the sense requires the definite article.

(c) **Plusieurs** (*several*) is purely an adjective, and is not followed by a partitive. Note that the word has only one form for masculine and feminine: **Plusieurs hommes, plusieurs femmes.**

34. Omission of Partitive Expression.

Whether the partitive be regular or irregular, the expression of the partitive is omitted if the preposition **de** immediately precedes: **J'ai du pain** (**du** expresses the partitive). *I have need of some bread* becomes **J'ai besoin de pain. Il a des livres.** (**des** expresses the partitive). *He has need of some books* becomes **Il a besoin de livres. Il a de grands livres** (**de** expresses the partitive). *He has need of some large books* becomes **Il a besoin de grands livres.**

In most other cases,[1] however, the partitive is expressed in French, whether expressed in English or not, and must be repeated before each noun modified: *He has brothers and sisters.* **Il a des frères et des sœurs.**

EXERCISE XI

an [ɑ̃] m. *year*
animal [animal] m. *animal*
année [ane] f. *year*
arbre [arbr] m. *tree*
argent [arʒɑ̃] m. *money, silver*
assez [ase] *enough*
banc [bɑ̃] m. *bench*
besoin [bəzwɛ̃] m. *need*
champ [ʃɑ̃] m. *field*
combien? [kɔ̃bjɛ̃] *how much (many)?*
content, -e [kɔ̃tɑ̃, kɔ̃tɑ̃ːt] *happy, pleased, contented, glad*
côté [kote] m. *side*
demain [dəmɛ̃] *tomorrow*
ensemble [ɑ̃sɑ̃ːbl] *together*

herbe [ɛrb] f. *grass*
jardin [ʒardɛ̃] m. *garden*
jouer [ʒwe] *to play*
jour [ʒuːr] m. *day*
journée [ʒurne] f. *day*
marchand [marʃɑ̃] m. *merchant*
parc [park] m. *park*
la plupart [plypaːr] f. *most, the majority*
plusieurs [plyzjœːr] *several*
quitter [kite] *to leave* (transitive)
rouge [ruːʒ] *red*
temps [tɑ̃] m. *time*
trop [trɔ, tro] *too, too much, too many*
vache [vaʃ] f. *cow*
vert, -e [vɛːr, vɛrt] *green*

[1] See §83, 6, c.

depuis quand? *or* **depuis combien de temps?** *how long?*
avoir besoin (de) *to need (to have need of)*
tous les jours [tu le ʒuːr] *every day*
de ce côté-ci *on this side;* **de ce côté-là** *on that side;* **de l'autre côté**
on the other side; **d'un côté** *on one side;* etc.

A. Presque tous les jours la bonne accompagne les enfants
  prɛskə tu le ʒuːr la bɔn akɔ̃paɲ lez‿ɑ̃fɑ̃
au parc qui est près de notre maison. Là ils rencontrent
o park ki ɛ prɛ d nɔtrə mɛzɔ̃. la il rɑ̃kɔ̃ːtr
beaucoup de leurs petits amis, et ils jouent ensemble. Il y a
boku d lœr pətiz‿ami, e il ʒu ɑ̃sɑ̃ːbl. ilja
de grands arbres et de petits, et des bancs. L'herbe est verte;
də grɑ̃z‿arbr e də pti, e de bɑ̃. lɛrb ɛ vɛrt;
5 et les fleurs bleues, blanches et rouges sont très jolies. La
  e le flœr blø, blɑ̃ːʃ e ruːʒ sɔ̃ trɛ ʒɔli. la
plupart des enfants qui passent la journée au parc sont petits.
plypar dez‿ɑ̃fɑ̃ ki pas la ʒurne o park sɔ̃ pti.

Depuis combien de temps êtes-vous dans cette ville? Nous y
dəpɥi kɔ̃bjɛ̃ d tɑ̃ ɛt vu dɑ̃ sɛt vil? nuz‿i
sommes depuis trois ans. Mais demain matin nous allons
sɔm dəpɥi trwaz‿ɑ̃. mɛ dəmɛ̃ matɛ̃ nuz‿alɔ̃
quitter la ville pour aller à la campagne. Mon père a donné
kite la vil pur ale a la kɑ̃paɲ. mɔ̃ pɛr a dɔne
10 de l'argent à la bonne pour aller chez notre grand'mère. Quand
  d larʒɑ̃ a la bɔn pur ale ʃe nɔtrə grɑ̃mɛːr. kɑ̃
la bonne va à la campagne, les enfants y vont aussi. Ils en
la bɔn va a la kɑ̃paɲ, lez‿ɑ̃fɑ̃ i vɔ̃t‿osi. ilz‿ɑ̃
sont bien contents. Nous y avons été l'année dernière, et
sɔ̃ bjɛ̃ kɔ̃tɑ̃. nuz‿i avɔ̃z‿ete lane dɛrnjɛːr, e
nous y avons beaucoup d'amis. Les champs vont être si jolis
nuz‿i avɔ̃ boku dami. le ʃɑ̃ vɔ̃t‿ɛtrə si ʒɔli
en cette saison. Mon grand-père a de beaux chevaux et des
ɑ̃ sɛt sɛzɔ̃. mɔ̃ grɑ̃pɛr a d bo ʃvo e de
15 vaches. Les enfants aiment beaucoup les animaux. Une fois
  vaʃ. lez‿ɑ̃fɑ̃ ɛm boku lez‿animo. yn fwa
j'ai vu un de mes cousins à cheval sur une vache. D'un côté
ʒe vy œ̃ d me kuzɛ̃ a ʃval syr yn vaʃ. dœ̃ kote

LESSON XI

de la maison il y a un jardin. Dans le jardin il y a beaucoup
d̦ la mɛzɔ̃   ilja œ̃ ʒardɛ̃. dɑ̃ l ʒardɛ̃ ilja boku
de choses, mais il n'y a pas de fleurs. Les fleurs sont de l'autre
d̦ ʃoːz,   mɛ(z‿)il nja pɑ d̦ flœːr.   le flœr sɔ̃   d loːtrə
côté de la maison. Quand ma grand'mère a besoin de pommes
kote d la mɛzɔ̃.   kɑ̃   ma grɑ̃mɛr   a b(ə)zwɛ̃ d̦ pɔm
de terre, elle ne va pas au marché parce qu'elle en a assez   20
də tɛːr, ɛl nə va pɑz‿o marʃe pars   kɛl ɑ̃n‿a ase
dans le jardin. Elle en a trop pour sa famille; elle en vend aux
dɑ̃ l ʒardɛ̃.   ɛl ɑ̃n‿a tro pur sa famiːj; ɛl ɑ̃ vɑ̃   o
marchands.
marʃɑ̃.

B. 1. I have some money. 2. They haven't any money.
3. We have enough money. 4. Have you some beautiful
flowers? 5. Some white cows. 6. How many horses? 7. Large
books and small [ones]. 8. Good little girls and bad [ones].
9. Too many of those apples. 10. Several times. 11. Many
of the trees that I saw. 12. Most merchants. 13. Some
grass. 14. Some beautiful grass. 15. Some green grass.
16. Much grass. 17. Much of the grass. 18. How much
money? 19. He has some meat. 20. Does he need some
milk? 21. Does he want some good milk? 22. He doesn't
want any milk. 23. There isn't any ink. 24. You have some
good white bread. 25. I saw some gentlemen.

C. 1. How much cheese did your cook buy this morning?
2. Do the merchants sell many potatoes? 3. I am going to
spend the day in the park which is behind that church.
4. Are your cousins glad when you bring flowers? 5. Most
children leave home (the house) early to go to school. 6. He
gave my sister red flowers. 7. There are large books and
small ones in my father's library. 8. He saw many horses
in the fields. 9. Three weeks ago we bought a great deal
of (much) chalk, but now we haven't any at all. 10. If you
go to my cousin's, you are going to see some ladies whom

you haven't yet met. 11. He isn't going to the country because he hasn't enough money. 12. How many weeks are they going to spend together in that old city? 13. On which side of the garden did they find flowers? 14. They always need milk because they have small children. 15. Does he play with big boys or small [ones]?

D. 1. Notice the sound of **oi** when it is nasal: [wɛ̃], as in **besoin.** 2. In the verb **jouer** notice that **ou** = [w] when the following letter is a pronounced vowel; otherwise **ou** = [u]: nous **jouons** [ʒwɔ̃], ils **jouent** [ʒu]. 3. The **o** in **trop** is [o] when the word occupies the stressed position, elsewhere [ɔ]: **Il en a trop** [tro], but **trop long** [trɔ lɔ̃].

E. 1. Où est-ce que la bonne accompagne les enfants? 2. Quand est-ce qu'elle accompagne les enfants au parc? 3. Où est le parc? 4. Qui est-ce qu'ils y rencontrent? 5. Qu'est-ce que votre père a donné à la bonne? 6. Où allez-vous demain matin? 7. En êtes-vous contents? 8. Avez-vous déjà été à la campagne? 9. Y a-t-il des animaux dans les champs? 10. Quels animaux votre grand-père a-t-il? 11. Qu'est-ce qu'il y a d'un côté de la maison? 12. Y a-t-il des fleurs dans le jardin? 13. Où sont les fleurs? 14. Votre grand'mère va-t-elle acheter des pommes de terre? 15. À qui est-ce qu'elle en vend? 16. Avez-vous de grands livres? 17. Votre frère a-t-il besoin de crayons? 18. Désirez-vous encore de la viande? 19. Les messieurs que nous avons rencontrés sont-ils maintenant à la maison? 20. Qu'avez-vous fait l'année dernière?

LESSON XII

REVIEW

A. 1. What is meant by a partitive? 2. How is the partitive regularly expressed? 3. When is it expressed otherwise? 4. Give three entirely different uses of the word **en**.

5. Explain two uses of the word **y**. 6. Give two English sentences to illustrate the difference between **voilà** and **il y a**. 7. Write the present indicative of **aller, faire, voir;** and give the meanings of each form. 8. Give the forms for the following:[1] (a) relative pronoun, subject of a verb and referring to a person; (b) relative pronoun, subject of a verb and referring to things; (c) relative pronoun, object of a preposition and referring to persons; (d) relative pronoun, object of a verb and referring to persons; (e) relative pronoun, object of a verb and referring to things; (f) interrogative pronoun, subject of a verb and referring to a person; (g) interrogative pronoun, object of a verb and referring to persons; (h) interrogative pronoun, object of a preposition and referring to persons; (i) interrogative pronoun, predicate nominative and referring to persons; (j) interrogative pronoun, out of construction and referring to persons; (k) interrogative pronoun, predicate nominative and referring to things; (l) interrogative pronoun, object of a verb and referring to things. 9. Write the past indefinite of **faire,** and give the meanings of each form. 10. Give the rule for the agreement of the past participle, and write three sentences to illustrate. 11. When is the French present used for the English perfect? Illustrate. 12. What is the normal position for an adjective qualifying a noun? 13. Give the common adjectives that regularly precede a noun modified.

B. *Account for the following forms:* 1. Ex. VII, A 3 and 18: **y**; 2. Ex. VII, A 10, 13 and 16: **en;** 3. Ex. VIII, A 15 and 17: **que;** 4. Ex. VIII, A 16 and 18: **qui;** 5. Ex. IX, A 10: **rencontrés;** 6. Ex. IX, A 13: **sommes;** 7. Ex. IX, A 17 and 18: **achetées;** 8. Ex. IX, E 4: **faites;** 9. Ex. IX, E 10: **que;** 10. Ex. IX, E 15: **vus;** 11. Ex. IX, E 18: **vendues;** 12. Ex. IX, E 19: **qui;** 13. Ex. XI, A l.4: **de** grands arbres

[1] See Appendix, pp. 216.

et **de** petits; 14. Ex. XI, A l.7: combien **de** temps; 15. Ex. XI, A l.18: **de** fleurs; 16. Ex. XI, A l.19: **de** pommes de terre.

C. *Oral:* 1. Some ink. 2. Some pupils. 3. Some chalk. 4. Some paper. 5. Some large spoons. 6. Beautiful plates. 7. Some more vegetables. 8. Three more cups. 9. Big red apples. 10. Two glasses of milk, please. 11. Young men and old. 12. Much bread. 13. I have enough. 14. He saw several. 15. Are they at home? 16. The gentlemen I saw. 17. The cherries which are on the table. 18. Who is that man? 19. What did they eat? 20. Whom did you see? 21. With whom are you talking? 22. My uncle and aunt have brought some. 23. You have chosen. 24. You have had. 25. You are making.

D. 1. How many apples did he eat? He ate six. 2. Are you entering the house? Yes, sir, we are entering it. 3. Has she been at school today? No, madam, she hasn't (been there). 4. Show me the flowers which you bought. I didn't buy any. 5. There is the man of whom my father spoke this morning. 6. There are books and pencils on my table in the library. 7. The Frenchman is going to leave the city at six o'clock tomorrow morning. 8. Good morning! How are you? How long have you been standing in front of that door? 9. In the morning I am always up early. 10. There is the jam which our cook made a week ago. 11. My friend has been back in the city nine days. 12. Do you want to see those beautiful white horses? Why no. 13. I am going to give your daughter the first flowers. Thank you, sir. 14. His uncle found these new books, and he at once spoke of them to Mrs. Black. 15. You and your sister have found the French lessons quite easy. 16. Are those new books very dear? No, they are cheap. 17. He has been here a week, but he hasn't yet prepared one lesson. 18. Don't you need

the books which you gave to the little boy? Not at all.
19. I want to spend two hours each day in the park. Very
well! 20. That old man spoke of fields and (of) flowers.

E. 1. The four words **cerise, ici, bicyclette, français,** illustrate the four cases in which **c** is pronounced [s]. Formulate the rule. 2. State the rule that applies to the final sound in **bien, combien, ancien.** See p. 22. 3. Pronounce:

pain	passer	cuiller	vilain	cuisinier
pied	œil	comment	vilaine	cuisinière
six	yeux	acheter	vieux	monsieur
dix	second	tramway	vieil	messieurs
parc	temps	longue	vieille	plusieurs
banc	besoin	premier	beaucoup	mademoiselle

LESSON XIII

35. Conjunctive Personal Pronouns. A conjunctive personal pronoun is one that is used with a verb as subject, direct object, or indirect object.

For the subject forms see Lesson II.

36. Object Forms:

Direct Objects		Indirect Objects	
me [mə] *me*	**nous** [nu] *us*	**me** [mə] *to (for) me*	**nous** [nu] *to (for) us*
te [tə] *thee*	**vous** [vu] *you*	**te** [tə] *to (for) thee*	**vous** [vu] *to (for) you*
le [lə] *him, it*	**les** [le] *them*	**lui** [lɥi] *to (for) him,*	**leur** [lœːr] *to (for) them*
la [la] *her, it*		*her,* or *it*	

37. Position. A conjunctive personal pronoun object usually stands before the verb of which it is the object (see §27); it precedes **voici** and **voilà**, also. If the verb is negative, **ne** precedes the pronoun object. Observe carefully the following examples:

> Il **le** trouve. Il **la (les)** trouve. Vous **m'**aimez. Il **nous (vous)** aime.
> Il **me** parle. Il **lui (nous, vous, leur)** a parlé. Je vais **les** donner à mon frère. Je vais **lui** donner des bonbons. Il ne **le** trouve pas. Je ne **lui** parle pas. **Les** voilà. **Me** voici. **Vous** voilà.

38. Reflexive Verbs. A verb is reflexive when its subject and an object (direct or indirect) are the same person or thing.

There is a special form for the reflexive pronoun *in the third person*: **se** [sə]. This form is masculine or feminine gender, singular or plural number, direct or indirect object. In the first and second persons, the usual object forms are used also as reflexives.

je **me** flatte	*I flatter myself*	nous **nous** flattons	*we flatter ourselves*
tu **te** flattes	*etc.*	vous **vous** flattez	*etc.*
il **se** flatte		ils **se** flattent	
elle **se** flatte		elles **se** flattent	

In the plural the reflexive form may have reciprocal value; thus **Nous nous voyons** may mean *We see each other*; **Ils se parlent** may mean *They speak to each other*, etc. (see §101).

39. Order. When a verb has two personal pronoun objects, both of them usually precede the verb. Their order is shown in the table below. **Y** and **en** are here included because they take the same position in the sentence as conjunctive personal pronoun objects.

me	le	lui	y	en
te	la	leur		
se	les			
nous				
vous				

N.B. Two forms in the same column cannot be used together, nor can a form in the first column be used with one in the third column.[1] The table, therefore, means that (1) a form in the first column precedes one in the second, (2) one in the second precedes one in the third, (3) any one in the first three columns precedes the one in the fourth, (4)

---

[1] See Lesson XIX, §51, 9.

any one in the first four columns precedes the one in the fifth.[1]

Il **me le** donne. Je **le lui** donne. Il **nous y** a vus. Il va **vous en** donner. Il **n'y en** a pas eu. Je ne **les y** ai pas vus. Ils **s'en** vont.

EXERCISE XIII

affaire [afɛːr] f. *thing, business*
bonbon [bɔ̃bɔ̃] m. *bonbon, candy*
carte [kart] f. *map, card*
chapeau [ʃapo] m. *hat*
chercher [ʃɛrʃe] *to seek, look for, (go and) get*
envoyer [ɑ̃vwaje] *to send*
étranger, étrangère [etrɑ̃ʒe, etrɑ̃ʒɛːr] *foreign;* m., f. *foreigner*
étudiant, -e [etydjɑ̃, etydjɑ̃ːt] m., f. *student*
étudier [etydje] *to study*
fatigué [fatige] *tired*
fort, -e [fɔːr, fɔrt] *strong*
gant [gɑ̃] m. *glove*
hier [jɛːr] *or* [ijɛːr] *yesterday*

idée [ide] f. *idea*
journal [ʒurnal] m. *newspaper*
langue [lɑ̃ːg] f. *language*
longtemps [lɔ̃tɑ̃] (*a*) *long (time)*
pays [pɛi] m. *country (political division, or district)*
quelque [kɛlk(ə)] *some* (limited), *a small quantity*
quelquefois [kɛlkəfwa] *sometimes*
rentrer [rɑ̃tre] *to re-enter, return home*
rue [ry] f. *street*
vacances [vakɑ̃ːs] f. pl. *vacation*
village [vilaːʒ] m. *village*
visiter [vizite] *to visit, inspect*
voyage [vwajaːʒ] m. *journey*

bien entendu [bjɛ̃n‿ɑ̃tɑ̃dy] *of course*
eh bien! [e bjɛ̃] *well!*
en ville *downtown, about town*
il y a+time expression+**que**+present tense=the present with **depuis** (see Lesson IX, §29).

A. —Où sont mes gants et mon chapeau?
    u sɔ̃ me gɑ̃ e mɔ̃ ʃapo?

—Je vais vous les donner tout de suite.
  ʒə ve vu le dɔne tu t sɥit.

—Merci bien! Quelquefois j'ai besoin de mes amis pour me
  mɛrsi bjɛ̃! kɛlkəfwa ʒe bzwɛ̃ d mez‿ami pur mə
chercher mes affaires.
ʃɛrʃe mez‿afɛːr.

—Vous êtes si fatigué; il y a longtemps que vous étudiez trop. 5
  vuz‿ɛt si fatige; ilja lɔ̃tɑ̃ kə vuz‿etydje tro.

---

[1] The use of three forms is usually avoided.

88   A FRENCH GRAMMAR

—Pendant mes vacances je vais faire un long voyage avec
pãdã   me vakɑ:s ʒə ve fɛr œ̃ lɔ̃ vwaja:ʒ avɛk
deux autres étudiants de langues étrangères.
døz‿otrəz‿etydjã d lã:g etrãʒɛ:r.

—Est-ce que vous allez visiter des pays étrangers?
ɛs kə vuz‿ale vizite de pɛi etrãʒe?

—Bien entendu! Mon ami a déjà acheté quelques grandes
bjɛ̃n‿ãtãdy! mɔ̃n‿ami a deʒa aʃte kɛlkə grã·d
10 cartes des pays que nous allons visiter, et il me les a apportées.
kart de pɛi kə nuz‿alɔ̃ vizite, e il mə lez‿a apɔrte.
Je les ai étudiées hier soir.
ʒə lez‿e etydje jɛr swa:r.

—Quelle bonne idée!
kɛl bɔn ide!

—Nous voilà dans la rue. Il y a beaucoup de magasins de
nu vwala dã la ry. ilja boku d magazɛ̃ də
chaque côté de la rue.
ʃak kote d la ry.

15 —Je désire entrer dans ce petit magasin pour acheter des
ʒə dezir ãtre dã sə pti magazɛ̃ pur aʃte de
bonbons. Ma petite sœur les aime beaucoup, et je lui en
bɔ̃bɔ̃. ma ptit sœr lez‿ɛm boku, e ʒə lɥi ã
rapporte presque toujours quand je vais en ville. L'année
rapɔrt prɛskə tuʒu:r kã ʒ vez‿ã vil. lane
dernière elle a passé cinq semaines chez sa tante dans un petit
dɛrnjɛ:r ɛl a pase sɛ̃ s(ə)mɛn ʃe sa tã:t dãz‿œ̃ pti
village; ma mère l'y a envoyée parce qu'elle n'est pas très forte.
vila:ʒ; ma mɛr li a ãvwaje pars kɛl nɛ pɑ trɛ fɔrt.
20 Eh bien! Je lui ai acheté des bonbons chaque semaine, et je
e bjɛ̃! ʒə lɥi e aʃte de bɔ̃bɔ̃ ʃak səmɛn, e ʒ(ə)
les lui ai envoyés.
le lɥi e ãvwaje.

—Je désire chercher quelques journaux pour mon père.
ʒə dezir ʃɛrʃe kɛlkə ʒurno pur mɔ̃ pɛ:r.
En voilà deux qu'il aime. Il ne les a pas encore vus aujourd'hui.
ã vwala dø kil ɛm. il nə lez‿a pɑz‿ãkɔr vy oʒurdɥi.

—Maintenant nous allons rentrer à la maison. Nous allons
  mɛ̃tnɑ̃   nuz‿alɔ̃   rɑ̃tre   a la mɛzɔ̃.   nuz‿alɔ̃
nous voir demain.
nu   vwar dəmɛ̃.

B. 1. I choose it. 2. He sells them. 3. He gives me a book. 4. I gave him a book. 5. I didn't give them a book. 6. I choose it for her. 7. He bought it for me. 8. I didn't buy him any paper. 9. He sent me some. 10. He sold me ten. 11. I sent him there. 12. He shows us some. 13. There aren't any. 14. I have brought them to you. 15. Doesn't he want any? 16. I am thinking of it(**y**). 17. I am going to give them to you. 18. He wants to send it to her. 19. You met them there. 20. They brought back some for me. 21. He chooses some for himself. 22. I am going to buy myself three. 23. We are going to see each other tomorrow. 24. Here we are.

C. 1. When are they going to buy you those flowers? 2. I don't need any now; my brother sent me some yesterday. 3. The teacher has given us difficult lessons. 4. We have been studying them for a long time, and we are tired. 5. Where are the papers which he gave me? There they are on the chair. 6. When we visit foreign countries, we speak foreign languages. 7. You need some maps; I am going to get some for you. 8. He has some (a few) fine horses, but he thinks that he hasn't yet enough. 9. Sometimes we return home early, but sometimes we return at ten o'clock. 10. I chose two hats, and he sent them to me. 11. Do you like this candy (*pl.*)? I find it very good. 12. On which side of the street did you see them? 13. Are you going downtown today? Of course. 14. Well, do you want to accompany my sister to a store? Why yes. Very well! 15. I am going there at once; afterward I want to look for some gloves.

D. 1. In **chercher,** why is the first **e** pronounced [ɛ] and the second [e]? 2. See **y,** p. 35, and account for the pronunciation of **envoyer, voyage, pays.** 3. In **fatigué** and **langue**, what is the purpose of **u**? 4. Note the difference in the masculine and the feminine of **étranger, étudiant, fort.** 5. Divide the words of the vocabulary into syllables, and account for each letter.

E. 1. Que cherchez-vous? 2. Qui vous les donne? 3. Depuis quand êtes-vous si fatigué? 4. Qu'allez-vous faire pendant vos vacances? 5. Quels pays allez-vous visiter? 6. Quelles langues étrangères parlez-vous? 7. Qu'est-ce que votre ami vous a apporté? 8. Qu'est-ce que vous en avez fait? 9. Qu'est-ce qu'il y a de chaque côté de la rue? 10. Où désirez-vous entrer? 11. Qu'est-ce que vous désirez acheter dans ce magasin? 12. À qui est-ce que vous donnez des bonbons? 13. Où est-ce que votre petite sœur a passé plusieurs semaines l'année dernière? 14. Votre sœur est-elle bien forte? 15. Pour qui est-ce que vous achetez ces journaux? 16. Qu'est-ce que vous allez faire maintenant?

LESSON XIV

40. Être as Auxiliary. 1. The verb **être** is used as the auxiliary to form the compound tenses of

(1) Most intransitive verbs expressing motion:[1]

Je **suis** arrivé. *I arrived.* or *I have arrived.*
Il **est** venu. *He came.* or *He has come.*

---

[1] In this class may be mentioned **aller** (*to go*), **arriver** (*to arrive*), **descendre** (*to go down*), **entrer** (*to go in*), **monter** (*to go up*), **partir** (*to go away, set out, leave*), **rentrer** (*to re-enter, return (home)*), **retourner** (*to return, go back*), **revenir,** p. p.: **revenu** (*to return, come back*), **sortir** (*to go out*), **tomber** (*to fall*), **venir** p. p.: **venu** (*to come*), etc. Note that some of these verbs may be used transitively, and are then conjugated with **avoir** (unless used reflexively): **J'ai descendu ma malle,** *I brought down my trunk*; etc.

Among exceptions (conjugated with **avoir**) are **marcher** (*to walk*), **courir** p. p.: **couru** (*to run*), **voyager** (*to travel*), **voler,** (*to fly*) **sauter** (*to jump*), **grimper** (*to climb*), **passer** (*to pass*).

(2) Most intransitive verbs expressing change of state:[1]

Je **suis** devenu avocat. *I became (have become) a lawyer.*
Il **est** mort. *He died (has died).*

(3) All reflexive (or reciprocal) verbs:[2]

Je me **suis** levé. *I rose (have risen).* Literally, *I raised myself.*
Il s'**est** flatté. *He flattered (has flattered) himself.*[3]

2. The verb **être** is used also as the auxiliary to form the passive voice, as in English:

L'homme **est** trouvé.[4] *The man is found.*
Le livre **a été** écrit par son frère. *The book was written by his brother.*

41. Agreement. 1. When **être** is the auxiliary and the verb is not reflexive, the past participle agrees in gender and number with the subject.

This rule applies to compound tenses of non-reflexive verbs conjugated with **être,** and also to the passive voice:

Elle est allé**e**. Ils sont venu**s**. Ils sont devenu**s** avocats. Elles sont mort**es**. La femme est trouvé**e**. Les livres ont été écrit**s**.

2. In compound tenses of reflexive verbs, the first rule for the agreement of past participles applies (see Lesson IX, §28). The past participle agrees with the reflexive object if that object is direct; it may agree with some other preceding direct object. It does not agree if there is no preceding direct object:

Elle s'est levé**e**. Ils se sont flatté**s**. Quels gants s'est-elle acheté**s**?
But: Elle s'est acheté des gants. Ils se sont parlé.

---

[1] Examples: **devenir**, p. p.: **devenu** *(to become)*, **mourir**, p. p.: **mort** *(to die)*, **naître**, p. p.: **né** *(to be born)*, etc. Exceptions: **mûrir** *(to ripen)*, **grandir** *(to grow large)*, etc.

[2] Also: **rester** *(to remain)*, **demeurer** (when it means *to remain*), and **arriver** (when it means *to happen* as well as when it means *to arrive*).

[3] Note that we say   Je lui **ai** acheté des gants, but Je me **suis** acheté des gants. Why?

[4] See next lesson: **On** (§42, 2).

3. Observe carefully the agreement in the following:

je suis arrivé(e)	nous sommes arrivé(e)s
tu es arrivé(e)	vous êtes arrivé(e)(s) [1]
il est arrivé	ils sont arrivés
elle est arrivée	elles sont arrivées
je me suis levé(e)	nous nous sommes levé(e)s
tu t'es levé(e)	vous vous êtes levé(e)(s) [1]
il s'est levé	ils se sont levés
elle s'est levée	elles se sont levées
je me suis parlé [2]	nous nous sommes parlé
tu t'es parlé	vous vous êtes parlé
il s'est parlé	ils se sont parlé
elle s'est parlé	elles se sont parlé

[1] The agreement with **vous** is logical: masculine or feminine singular, masculine or feminine plural, although the verb-form is always second person plural.

[2] *I talked to myself*, etc.

EXERCISE XIV

après-demain [aprɛdmɛ̃] *the day after tomorrow*
avant-hier [avãt‿jɛːr] *the day before yesterday*
bientôt [bjẽto] *soon*
se coucher [sə kuʃe] *to go to bed, lie down*
demander [dəmãde] *to ask (for)*
devenir [dəvniːr] p.p. **devenu** [dəvny] *to become*
dire [diːr] p.p. **dit** [di] *to say*
donc [dɔ̃(ːk)] *so, then, therefore*
faire (with infinitive) *to have (done) i. e. to cause*
lettre [lɛtr] f. *letter*
lever [ləve] *to raise*
se lever [sə lve] *to rise*
malade [malad] *sick*
médecin [mɛtsɛ̃] m. *doctor, physician*

midi [midi] m. *noon*
mourir [muriːr] p.p. **mort** [mɔːr] *to die*
nouvelles [nuvɛl] f. pl. *news*
nuit [nɥi] f. *night, darkness*
partir [partiːr] *to leave* (intransitive), *depart, set out, start out*
réponse [repɔ̃ːs] f. *reply, answer*
rester [rɛste] *to remain, stay*
retourner [rəturne] *to return* (= *go back*)
revenir [rəvniːr] p.p. **revenu** [rəvny] *to return* (= *come back*)
sortir [sɔrtiːr] *to go out*
tomber [tɔ̃be] *to fall*
venir [vəniːr] p.p. **venu** [vəny] *to come*
vers [vɛːr] *towards, at about* (*time*)

LESSON XIV 93

tout à coup [tut‿a ku]
tout d'un coup [tu˘dœ̃ ku]   *suddenly, all at once*
faire venir *to call, send for, have (cause to) come*

A. Madame Foulard, l'amie de ma sœur, est tombée malade
  madam fulaːr, lami d ma sœːr, ɛ tɔ̃be   malad
tout d'un coup il y a quelques semaines. Avant-hier j'ai
tu dœ̃ ku ilja kɛlkə smɛn.   avãt‿jɛːr ʒe
envoyé une lettre à Chicago pour demander à ma sœur des
ãvwaje yn lɛtr a ʃikago pur dəmãde a ma sœːr de
nouvelles de Madame Foulard. Voici la réponse qui est arrivée
nuvɛl   də madam fulaːr. vwasi la repɔ̃ːs ki ɛt‿arive
ce matin: 5
s matɛ̃:

J'ai eu une lettre du mari de mon amie. Je suis partie tout
 ʒe y yn lɛtrə dy mari d mɔ̃n‿ami. ʒə sɥi parti tu
de suite pour Chicago. En y arrivant je suis allée chez
t sɥit pur ʃikago. ãn‿i arivã   ʒə sɥiz‿ale ʃe
mon amie. La bonne m'a fait entrer, et nous sommes montées
mɔ̃n‿ami. la bɔn ma fɛt‿ãtre, e nu sɔm   mɔ̃te
au premier où j'ai trouvé Madame Foulard bien malade.
o prəmje u ʒe truve madam fular bjɛ̃ malad.
En m'entendant entrer, elle a levé les yeux vers moi et elle 10
ã   mãtãdãt‿ãtre,   ɛl a lve lez‿jø vɛr mwa e ɛl
m'a dit: «Il y a deux jours que je suis comme vous me voyez.
ma di: « ilja dø ʒuːr kə ʒ sɥi kɔm vu m vwaje.
Avant-hier, bientôt après le dîner, je suis tombée malade.
 avãt‿jɛːr, bjɛ̃to aprɛ l dine, ʒə sɥi tɔ̃be malad.
Je me suis couchée et mon mari a fait venir deux médecins.
ʒə m sɥi kuʃe e mɔ̃ mari a fɛ vnir dø mɛtsɛ̃.
Ils sont venus tout de suite. Mon mari est resté près de mon
il sɔ̃ vny tu t sɥit. mɔ̃ mari ɛ rɛste prɛ d mɔ̃
lit pendant la nuit, et ma mère est venue le matin. Vers midi 15
li pãdã   la nɥi, e ma mɛr ɛ vny lə matɛ̃. vɛr midi
je me suis levée. Mon mari est sorti et ma mère est retournée
ʒə m sɥi lve. mɔ̃ mari ɛ sɔrti e ma mɛr ɛ rturne
chez elle. Quand mon mari est rentré le soir, il m'a trouvée
ʃez‿ɛl.   kã   mɔ̃ mari ɛ rãtre l swaːr, il ma truve

encore au lit. Depuis ce temps-là, je n'ai pas quitté ma
ãkɔr o li. dəpɥi s tã la, ʒə ne pɑ kite ma
chambre.»
ʃã:br.»

20 Je suis donc restée chez Madame Foulard. Elle est morte
ʒə sɥi dɔ̃(k) rɛste ʃe madam fulaːr. ɛl ɛ mɔrt
hier. Je vais revenir à la maison après-demain.
jɛːr. ʒə ve rəvnir a la mɛzɔ̃ aprɛ dmɛ̃.

B. 1. *Continue:* I go to bed, etc. 2. *Continue:* I have gone to bed, etc. 3. *Continue:* I have gone, etc. 4. *Continue:* I did not arrive, etc. 5. *Continue:* Did I not get up?, etc. 6. She has become. 7. She raised one hand. 8. She has risen. 9. You have remained. 10. I came back. 11. He went back. 12. You went out. 13. They have fallen. 14. They (*f.*) have come. 15. They have asked. 16. We have departed. 17. They have died. 18. I have him enter. 19. You have me go out. 20. You sent for the doctor.

C. 1. My little sister fell in the street this morning. 2. When my mother arrived, my brother and sister went out. 3. The doctor set out about noon, and returned about six o'clock. 4. How long (During how much time) did your sisters stay in that country? 5. My friend (*f.*) is going to arrive here the day after tomorrow to spend her vacation with us. 6. We don't always go to bed early, but last night we went to bed at nine o'clock. 7. Sometimes we get up at about noon. 8. I asked him [for] some good gloves, and he showed me some. 9. The day before yesterday I bought some beautiful flowers and sent them to her. 10. I bought myself some candy; I like it very much. 11. A few days ago I sent him a letter; the reply arrived this morning. 12. Have you had any news of my friend? My uncle told me she died last week. 13. When did your brothers arrive? They haven't come yet. 14. When I came back, I found them at home. 15. They set out during the night and returned after noon.

La Chapelle du Château d'Amboise

La Place de la Bastille, Paris

D. 1. Note the nasal in **bientôt.** Since this word is a compound, **-ien** is treated as a final group. In the same word, account for the close **o,** [o]. 2. Watch the mute **e**'s in **venir, devenir, revenir, lever, retourner, demander.** 3. What opens the first **e** in **let're**? In **rester**? In **nouvelles**? 4. Note the somewhat irregular pronunciation of **médecin.** 5. Account for the devocalization (see p. 9) in **que je suis** (A l.11).

E. 1. Qui est Madame Foulard? 2. À qui avez-vous envoyé une lettre? 3. Qu'est-ce que vous lui avez demandé? 4. Quand est-ce que la réponse est arrivée? 5. Qui a envoyé une lettre à votre sœur? 6. Quand est-elle partie? 7. En arrivant à Chicago, où est-elle allée? 8. Comment a-t-elle trouvé son amie? 9. Où l'a-t-elle trouvée? 10. Quand est-ce que Madame Foulard est tombée malade? 11. Qui est resté près de son lit pendant la nuit? 12. Qui est arrivé le matin? 13. Monsieur Foulard a-t-il fait venir des médecins? 14. Est-ce que Madame Foulard est toujours malade? 15. Quand est-ce que votre sœur va revenir?

LESSON XV

42. Indefinite Pronoun on. 1. The pronoun **on** is equivalent to the indefinite value of *one, somebody, people, we, you, they*:[1]

One can see that he is sick. On peut voir qu'il est malade.
Somebody is coming. On vient.
People talk too much. On parle trop.
We haven't that construction in English. On n'a pas cette construction en anglais.
You can't always tell. On ne peut pas toujours le dire.
They speak French in France. On parle français en France.

---

[1] Note that **on** is always third person singular; therefore the verb is alway third person singular.

2. This construction often takes the place of an English passive when the agent is not expressed, as does also the reflexive:

That isn't done. On ne fait pas cela. Cela ne se fait pas.

43. General Noun. It is necessary to distinguish carefully between the partitive, which expresses an indefinite part of a whole, and the general noun, which refers to a whole class. The general noun is preceded by the definite article:

He bought books (some books). Il a acheté des livres.
Books (all books, books as a class) are expensive. **Les** livres sont chers.

44. Definite Article for **Possessive.** 1. The definite article often replaces the possessive adjective before a noun expressing a part of the body or an article of clothing when there is no ambiguity as to the possessor:

Il a mis la main dans la poche. *He put his hand in* **his** *pocket.*
J'ai mal à la tête. *I have a pain in* **my** *head.*

2. Possession may often be expressed by an indirect object:

Je **me** suis cassé le bras. *I broke* **my** *arm (the arm (belonging) to me).*
Je **lui** ai lavé les mains. *I washed* **his** *hands.*

EXERCISE XV

assis, -e [asi, asiːz] *seated, sitting*
bras [bra] m. *arm*
casser [kɑse] *to break*
commencer [kɔmɑ̃se] *to begin*
courir [kuriːr] p.p. **couru** [kury] *to run*
cri [kri] m. *cry*
se demander [sə dmɑ̃de] *to wonder*
enfin [ɑ̃fɛ̃] *finally, at last*
examiner [ɛgzamine] *to examine*
figure [figyːr] f. *face; figure*
grimper [grɛ̃pe] *to climb*

joie [ʒwa] f. *joy, delight*
laver [lave] *to wash*
marcher [marʃe] *to walk, to march, to go, to move*
Marthe [mart] *Martha*
mettre [mɛtr] p.p. **mis** [mi] *to put (on)*
on [ɔ̃] *one, somebody,* etc.
peine [pɛn] f. *pain, trouble*
pleurer [plœre] *to weep, cry*
porter [pɔrte] *to carry, wear*
pourquoi [purkwa] *why*

LESSON XV

puisque [pɥisk(ə)] *since* (causal conj.)
quelque chose[1] [kɛlkə ʃoːz] *something*
répondre [repɔ̃ːdr] *to answer*
se retourner [sə rturne] *to turn around*
sauter [sote] *to jump*

tant [tɑ̃] *so much, so many*
tête [tɛːt] f. *head*
vif, vive [vif, viːv] *lively, quick, keen*
vite [vit] *quick(ly)*

Qu'y a-t-il? Qu'est-ce qu'il y a? *What's the matter?*
Qu'a-t-il (elle)? Qu'avez-vous? *What ails him (her), you?*

A. Nous nous sommes levés de bonne heure. Nous nous
   nu nu sɔm ləve d bɔn œːr. nu nu
sommes fait du café, et nous sommes sortis bientôt après le
sɔm fɛ dy kafe, e nu sɔm   sɔrti bjɛ̃to aprɛ lə
petit déjeuner. Nous avons marché vite; les enfants ont couru
pti deʒøne. nuz‿avɔ̃ marʃe vit; lez‿ɑ̃fɑ̃ ɔ̃ kury
et sauté de joie. Quand nous sommes arrivés au parc, nous
e sote d ʒwa. kɑ̃ nu   sɔmz‿arive o park, nu
nous sommes assis sur des bancs, et les enfants ont joué sur
nu sɔmz‿asi syr de bɑ̃, e lez‿ɑ̃fɑ̃ ɔ̃ ʒwe syr 5
l'herbe derrière nous. Après quelque temps je me suis retourné·
lɛrb dɛrjɛr nu. aprɛ kɛlkə tɑ̃ ʒə m sɥi r(ə)turne·
Je me suis demandé: Qu'est-ce que les enfants sont devenus,
ʒə m sɥi dmɑ̃de: kɛs kə lez‿ɑ̃fɑ̃ sɔ̃ dəvny,
puisqu'on ne les entend pas? Tout à coup j'ai entendu un
pɥiskɔ̃ n lez‿ɑ̃tɑ̃ pa?   tut‿a ku ʒe ɑ̃tɑ̃dy œ̃
grand cri derrière les arbres. Quand j'y suis arrivé j'ai demandé
grɑ̃ kri dɛrjɛr lez‿arbr. kɑ̃ ʒi sɥiz‿arive ʒe dmɑ̃de
à mon fils: «Qu'est-ce qu'il y a? Pourquoi est-ce que ta sœur 10
a mɔ̃ fis: «kɛs   kilja? purkwa ɛs kə ta sœr
pleure? Qu'a-t-elle?» Il m'a répondu: «Marthe a grimpé
plœːr?   katɛl?»   il ma repɔ̃dy: «mart a grɛ̃pe
dans cet arbre et elle est tombée.» Je l'ai portée chez un
dɑ̃ sɛt‿arbr e ɛl ɛ tɔ̃be.» ʒə le porte ʃez‿œ̃
médecin, qui l'a examinée. Enfin il a dit: «Monsieur, la petite
mɛtsɛ̃, ki la ɛgzamine. ɑ̃fɛ̃ il a di: «məsjø, la ptit
s'est cassé le bras.» Elle a pleuré longtemps, mais enfin je lui
sɛ kase lə bra.» ɛl a plœre lɔ̃tɑ̃,   mɛ ɑ̃fɛ̃ ʒə lɥi

---

[1] Although **"chose"** is feminine, **"quelque chose"** is neuter; it never requires any agreement of an adjective or of a past participle.

15 ai lavé la figure, je lui ai mis son chapeau sur la tête, et nous
   e lave la figy:r, ʒə lɥi e mi sɔ̃ ʃapo   syr la tɛ:t, e nu
sommes rentrés à la maison en automobile. La journée a
  sɔm   rɑ̃tre   a la mɛzɔ̃ ɑ̃n‿otɔmɔbil.   la ʒurne a
commencé bien, mais vous voyez comment elle a fini. Les en-
  kɔmɑ̃se   bjɛ̃, mɛ   vu vwaje kɔmɑ̃   ɛl a fini. lez‿ɑ̃-
fants nous font quelquefois tant de peine. Ils sont si vifs, et
  fɑ̃   nu   fɔ̃   kɛlkəfwa tɑ̃   d̥ pɛn.   il sɔ̃ si vif, e
vite quelque chose est arrivé. Maintenant Marthe va rester
  vit kɛlkə   ʃoz ɛt‿arive.   mɛ̃tnɑ̃   mart va rɛste
20 à la maison pendant quelques semaines.
   a la mɛzɔ̃   pɑ̃dɑ̃   kɛlkə   smɛn.

B. 1. What's the matter? 2. What's the matter with them? 3. Somebody is arriving. 4. Something has happened. 5. She has gone. 6. She has walked. 7. They have climbed. 8. We have run. 9. I wash my face. 10. He is standing. 11. I am sitting on the bench. 12. She is very lively. 13. What did he answer them? 14. The lesson has been written[1] quickly. (*Write three ways.*) 15. Are children happy? 16. Is meat expensive? 17. Did he speak to you? 18. Did he talk to himself? 19. Do they speak French in (**à**) New York? 20. Do you like apples? 21. We found apples at the market. 22. I washed his face. 23. He washed his hands. 24. Did she run so quickly? 25. He has his hat on his head.

C. 1. They met (each other) in the street and went to school together. 2. I gave him some milk, and afterward I prepared myself some coffee. 3. That lesson has not yet been prepared. 4. The old lady has her grandson and her granddaughter on her knees. 5. Why did you give him so much money? 6. They (*indefinite*) sometimes ran and jumped. 7. Did you put your hat on your head? 8. Did you

---

[1] p. p.: **écrit**.

put his new hat on his head? 9. Books and good paper are expensive. 10. I bought him good books, paper, several pens, a few pencils and some ink. 11. People need friends in order to be happy. 12. He jumped on his old black horse and set out for the city. 13. One sometimes wonders why one isn't happy when one has so many good friends. 14. They are not standing on the other side of the street; they are sitting on the bench in the garden. 15. Of course, they are too tired to (**pour**) remain standing so long. 16. In what foreign language did they talk to each other? 17. Those gentlemen arrive every day at noon, and they always bring us something. 18. He put the books on the table and left the house.

D. 1. Note the back a [ɑ] in **casser**. 2. When is **x** pronounced [gz] as in **examiner**? (See p. 34). 3. Account for [s] in **casser**, [k] and [s] in **commencer**, [ɛ] in **examiner** (syllabicate this word), [ɛ] in **peine**, [w] in **pourquoi**, [o] and [z] in **chose**, [ɛ] in **tête**.

E. 1. Quand vous êtes-vous levés? 2. Où êtes-vous allés après le petit déjeuner? 3. Qu'est-ce que les enfants ont fait? 4. Qu'avez-vous entendu? 5. Qu'avez-vous demandé à votre fils? 6. Qu'est-ce que votre fille a fait? 7. Où l'avez-vous portée? 8. Qui l'a examinée? 9. Qu'est-ce qu'il a dit enfin? 10. Votre fille a-t-elle pleuré? 11. Comment êtes-vous rentrés à la maison? 12. Pourquoi n'êtes-vous pas restés dans le parc?

LESSON XVI

45. Comparison. 1. The comparative of an adjective or an adverb is generally formed by placing **plus** (*more*) or **moins** (*less*) before the positive form:

grand (*tall*), plus grand (*taller*), moins grand (*less tall* or *not so tall*)
vite (*quickly*), plus vite (*more quickly*), moins vite (*less quickly* or *not so quickly*)

Some adjectives and some adverbs have irregular comparatives:

> bon (*good*), meilleur (*better*, adj.); bien (*well*), mieux (*better*, adv.)

2. The superlative is formed by placing the definite article before the comparative. Before an adjective the article agrees in gender and number:

> grand, plus grand, **le** plus grand; grande, plus grande, **la** plus grande; grand(e)s, plus grand(e)s, **les** plus grand(e)s; bonnes, meilleures, **les** meilleures. [1, 2, 3]

Before an adverb the definite article is always **le**:

> vite, plus vite, **le** plus vite; bien, mieux, **le** mieux.

3. Observe the following:

> Il est **aussi** grand **que** son frère. (*as tall as*)
> Il est venu **aussi** vite **que** son frère. (*as quickly as*)
> Il n'est **pas si** grand **que** son frère. (*not so tall as*)
> Il est **moins** grand **que** son frère. (*less tall than = not so tall as*)
> Il est **plus** grand **que** son frère. (*taller than*)

Following **plus** or **moins**, **de** replaces **que** to express *than* before a numeral when the numeral is one of the terms of the comparison:

> Il a plus **de** vingt livres. *He has more than twenty books.*
> Il a mangé plus **de** trois pommes. *He ate more than three apples.*
> But: Il a mangé plus **que** trois hommes. *He ate more than three men.*

4. After a superlative, *in* is expressed by **de**:

> la plus grande ville **de** France *the largest city in France*

46. Position of Adverbs. 1. An adverb that modifies a verb generally follows as closely as possible after the verb;

---

[1] The possessive adjective may replace the article: **son meilleur ami.**

[2] The article must not be omitted if the superlative follows the noun modified: **l'homme le plus fort.**

[3] Notice that there can be no distinction in French between *the larger* and *the largest*, or between *the better* and *the best*.

in a compound, after the auxiliary.[1] The position is not absolutely fixed: an adverb may come at the beginning or at the end of a sentence; in most cases it is not correct to place an adverb between the subject and the verb:

> Il parle souvent de vous. *He often speaks of you.*
> Il a souvent parlé de vous. *He has often spoken of you.*
> Parle-t-il souvent de vous? *Does he often speak of you?*
> Il parle quelquefois de vous. Quelquefois il parle de vous. Il parle de vous quelquefois. *He sometimes speaks of you.*

2. An adverb precedes an adjective or an adverb which it modifies:

> Il est très malade. *He is very sick.*
> Il parle trop vite. *He speaks too fast.*

[1] These ten adverbs never come between an auxiliary and a past participle, but follow the past participle in a compound verb-form: ici (*here*), là (*there*), ailleurs (*elsewhere*), partout (*everywhere*), hier (*yesterday*), aujourd'hui (*today*), demain (*tomorrow*), autrefois (*formerly*), tôt (*early*), tard (*late*). Ex.: Il est arrivé tard.

EXERCISE XVI

avant [avã] *before* (time)
départ [depaːr] m. *departure*
voyager [vwajaʒe] *to travel*
dimanche [dimãːʃ] m. *Sunday*
lundi [lœ̃di] m. *Monday*
mardi [mardi] m. *Tuesday*
mercredi [mɛrkrədi] m. *Wednesday*
jeudi [ʒødi] m. *Thursday*
vendredi [vãdrədi] m. *Friday*
samedi [samdi] m. *Saturday*

*onze [ɔ̃ːz] *eleven*
douze [duːz] *twelve*
treize [trɛːz] *thirteen*
quatorze [katɔrz] *fourteen*
quinze [kɛ̃ːz] *fifteen*
seize [sɛːz] *sixteen*
dix-sept [dissɛt] *seventeen*
dix-huit [dizɥit] *eighteen*
dix-neuf [diznœf] *nineteen*
vingt [vɛ̃] *twenty*

dimanche *next* (or *last*) *Sunday*
le dimanche *any* (or *every*) *Sunday*
huit jours *a week*
quinze jours *two weeks*
à l'église [egliːz] f. *at church, to church*
à l'étranger *abroad*
au revoir [o rvwaːr] *good-bye* (*till we meet again*)

de mon (son, notre, etc.) **mieux** *my (his, our,* etc.*) best*
donner la main à *to shake hands with*
faire (rendre) visite (f.) **à** *to visit*
se mettre+à+infinitive *to begin*

A. Il y a quinze jours notre maître de langues nous a dit:
  ilja kɛz ʒuːr nɔtrə mɛtrə d lãːg nuz‿a di:
Si vous étudiez bien le français, nous allons voyager à l'étranger.
  si vuz‿etydje bjɛ̃ lə frãsɛ, nuz‿alɔ̃ vwajaʒe a letrãʒe.
Nous nous sommes donc mis à étudier de notre mieux; le
  nu nu sɔm dɔ̃(k) miz‿a etydje də nɔtrə mjø; lə
maître dit qu'il est content de nous. Ma sœur, qui est déjà
  mɛtrə di kil ɛ kɔ̃tã d nu. ma sœːr, ki ɛ deʒa
5 aussi grande que ma mère, étudie depuis longtemps; mais mon
  osi grãˑd kə ma mɛːr, etydi dəpɥi lɔ̃tã; mɛ mɔ̃
frère, qui est le meilleur élève de sa classe, parle aussi bien que
  frɛːr, ki ɛ l mɛjœr elɛv də sa klɑːs, parl osi bjɛ̃ k
ma sœur. Quelquefois je pense qu'il parle mieux. Je suis
  ma sœːr. kɛlkəfwa ʒə pɑ̃s kil parl mjø. ʒə sɥi
moins grand que mon frère, mais il y a plus de douze semaines
  mwɛ̃ grã k mɔ̃ frɛːr, mɛ(z‿)ilja ply d duz səmɛn
que j'étudie le français, et je commence à le parler aussi.
  kə ʒetydi lə frãsɛ, e ʒə kɔmɑ̃ˑs a l parle osi.
10 Comme nous aimons beaucoup la France, le français et les
  kɔm nuz‿ɛmɔ̃ boku la frãːs, lə frãsɛ e le
Français, nous sommes bien heureux d'aller en France. Dans
  frãsɛ, nu sɔm bjɛ̃n‿œrø dale ã frãːs. dã
huit jours nous allons quitter notre pays. Avant notre départ
  ɥi ʒuːr nuz‿alɔ̃ kite nɔtrə pɛi. avã nɔtrə depaːr
nous avons beaucoup à faire. Demain, dimanche, nous allons à
  nuz‿avɔ̃ boku a fɛːr. dəmɛ̃, dimãːʃ, nuz‿alɔ̃z‿a
l'église. Lundi, mardi et mercredi nous allons passer la journée
  legliːz. lœ̃di, mardi e mɛrkrədi nuz‿alɔ̃ pɑse la ʒurne
15 dans les magasins, parce que nous avons besoin de beaucoup
  dã le magazɛ̃, pars kə nuz‿avɔ̃ bəzwɛ̃ d boku
de choses pour le voyage. Le jeudi nous allons toujours faire
  d ʃoːz pur lə vwajaːʒ. lə ʒødi nuz‿alɔ̃ tuʒuːr fɛr

visite à ma grand'mère. En la quittant nous allons lui donner
vizit a ma grãmɛːr.   ã la kitã   nuz‿alɔ̃ lɥi dɔne
la main et lui dire «Au revoir!» pour les quatorze semaines de
la mɛ̃ .e lɥi dir   o rvwaːr pur le katɔrz səmɛn də
nos vacances. Vendredi nous allons partir pour New-York,
no vakãːs.   vãdrədi nuz‿alɔ̃   partir pur   nu jɔrk,
et samedi nous allons quitter New-York pour la France.   20
e samdi nuz‿alɔ̃   kite   nu jɔrk pur la frãːs.

B. 1. *Count from 1 to 20.* 2. *Write and pronounce the names of the days of the week.* 3. He speaks better. 4. She speaks best. 5. They are better. 6. He (**ce**) is the taller of the two. 7. These books are as good as those books. 8. He stays as long as his brother. 9. These flowers are not so beautiful (*two ways*). 10. He has more money than you. 11. I have more than you. 12. You bought more than one hat. 13. She (**ce**) is the liveliest girl in school. 14. He answered very quickly. 15. Here is the largest school in the city.

C. 1. She died more than two weeks ago. 2. He (**ce**) is not the tallest boy in school, but he (**ce**) is the best pupil in his class. 3. They came [on] Monday and are going to leave [on] Friday. 4. She always stays at home on Thursday. 5. Did you shake hands with my friend? 6. We shook hands with each other. 7. Did you visit them when you went to New York? 8. He has not finished his lessons, but he has done his best. 9. When did you begin to (**à**) study (the) French? 10. How long has your brother been traveling abroad? 11. He told me something, but I am not going to tell (it to) you. 12. Who washed his face and hands the most quickly? 13. A week before our departure we bought many things. 14. Haven't you sometimes wondered why they didn't come? 15. We have seen them, and now we are going to leave. Good bye!

D. 1. Note the pronunciation of **jeudi, dix-sept, dix-huit, dix-neuf.** 2. Why is the mute **e** in **mercredi** and in **vendredi** pronounced, while in **samedi** it is silent? 3. Can you tell why **eu** is pronounced [ø] in **mieux,** but [œ] in **pleurer**? (See p. 23). 4. Note the devocalization of [z] in **douze semaines** (A l.8) and of [d] in **beaucoup de choses** (A l.16). Can you explain? 5. Note that the **h** of **huit** is aspirate, and does not permit linking or elision; hence **dans huit jours** [dā ɥi ʒuːr], but **dans une semaine** [dāz‿yn səmɛn]. **Onze** is treated as if it began with aspirate **h: les onze hommes** [le ɔ̃z ɔm].

E. 1. Votre maître de français est-il content de vous? 2. Qu'est-ce qu'il vous a dit? 3. Depuis quand est-ce que vous étudiez le français? 4. Parlez-vous français? 5. Est-ce que votre sœur parle mieux que votre frère? 6. Est-ce que vous êtes plus grand que votre frère? 7. Où allez-vous voyager? 8. Quand est-ce que vous allez partir? 9. Aimez-vous le français? 10. Votre grand'mère reste-t-elle à la maison le jeudi? 11. Qu'est-ce que vous allez faire jeudi? 12. Qu'est-ce que vous avez fait dimanche dernier?

LESSON XVII

47. Imperfect Indicative. Forms: The imperfect indicative is formed by adding to the stem of the present participle the endings **-ais, -ais, -ait, -ions, -iez, -aient**:

donner, donnant, je donnais, etc.;   finir, finissant, je finissais, etc.;
vendre, vendant, je vendais, etc.;   être, étant, j'étais, etc.;
aller, allant, j'allais, etc.;   faire, faisant, je faisais,[1] etc.;
voir, voyant, je voyais, etc.

The imperfect stem of **avoir** is irregular: **ayant, j'avais,** etc.

je donnais [dɔnɛ], faisais [fəzɛ]   nous donnions [dɔnjɔ̃], faisions [fəzjɔ̃]
tu donnais [dɔnɛ], faisais [fəzɛ]   vous donniez [dɔnje], faisiez [fəzje]
il donnait [dɔnɛ], faisait [fəzɛ]   ils donnaient [dɔnɛ], faisaient [fəzɛ]

[1] See §23, Note 2.

LESSON XVII

48. Meanings of Imperfect Indicative. The imperfect, one of the past tenses, has special uses. It expresses

1. A progressive or continued past:

   Il chantait quand je suis arrivé. *He was singing when I arrived.*
   Il parlait pendant trois heures. *He spoke (continued to speak, kept on speaking) for three hours.*

2. A repeated or habitual past:

   Il la voyait tous les dimanches. *He saw her every Sunday.*
   Je lui parlais quelquefois. *I used to speak to him sometimes.*

3. A descriptive past:

   Il était malade hier. *He was sick yesterday.*

4. A past tense[1] after **if** (expressing a condition on which something depends):

   S'il allait . . *If he went (or were to go or should go) . .*
   But: Il est allé. *He went.*

49. Idiomatic Use of the **Imperfect.** In French the imperfect tense is used to express what had been true and still was true. Thus, **Il était ici depuis une semaine** means *He had been here a week,* which implies *He still* **was here.** **Il parlait depuis une heure** means *He had been speaking for an hour,* and implies *He still* **was speaking.**

---

[1] This means such English forms as *if he gave, if he were to give, if he should give,* but does not include *if he has given,* which is translated **s'il a donné.**

EXERCISE XVII

alors [alɔːr] *then (at that time)*
(s')arrêter [arɛte] *to stop*
bottine [bɔtin] f. *(high) shoe, boot*
chemise [ʃəmiːz] f. *shirt*
commander [kɔmãde] *to order, command*
confiserie [kɔ̃fizri] f. *confectionery*
course [kurs] f. *errand, race, course*
cravate [kravat] f. *neck-tie*
faux-col [fokɔl] m. *collar*
glace [glas] f. *ice; mirror*
hélas! [elɑːs] *alas!*
malle [mal] f. *trunk*
mouchoir [muʃwaːr] m. *handkerchief*
paire [pɛːr] f. *pair*
pardessus [pardəsy] m. *overcoat*

payer [pɛje] *to pay (for)*
peu [pø] *little, not much, few, not many*
se porter *to be (well, ill,* etc.*)*
robe [rɔb] f. *dress*
route [rut] f. *road, way*
sac [sak] m. *sack, (hand)bag, valise*
sorte [sɔrt] f. *sort, kind*
soulier [sulje] m. *(low)shoe, oxford*
souvent [suvɑ̃] *often*
tout, tous [tu], **toute, toutes** [tut] *all*
travailler [travaje] *to work*
se trouver *to be* (location, etc.)
vêtement [vɛtmɑ̃] m. *garment*

    en route *on the way; let's go!*
    et ainsi de suite [e ɛ̃si d̥ sɥit] *and so forth, et cetera*
    faire une malle *to pack a trunk*
    Nous voilà partis! *We're off!*

A. Nous voilà en route pour New-York. J'étais si fatigué
    nu vwala ɑ̃ rut pur nu jɔrk. ʒetɛ si fatige
hier que ma grand'mère a pensé que j'allais tomber malade.
jɛːr kə ma grɑ̃mɛr a pɑ̃se kə ʒalɛ tɔ̃be malad.
Nous travaillions beaucoup depuis trois jours pour nous pré-
nu travaijɔ̃ boku dəpɥi trwɑ ʒuːr pur nu pre-
parer pour le voyage. Lundi nous avons acheté des vêtements:
pare pur lə vwajaːʒ. lœ̃di nuz‿avɔ̃z‿aʃte de vɛtmɑ̃:
5 des pardessus, des chapeaux, des souliers, des chemises, des
de pardəsy, de ʃapo, de sulje, de ʃmiːz, de
faux-cols, des mouchoirs, des cravates, et ainsi de suite. Ma
fokɔl, de muʃwaːr, de kravat, e ɛ̃si d̥ sɥit. ma
mère s'est acheté plusieurs robes et une paire de bottines.
mɛr sɛt‿aʃte plyzjœr rɔb e yn pɛr də bɔtin.
Les marchands nous ont montré toutes sortes de choses. Enfin
le marʃɑ̃ nuz‿ɔ̃ mɔ̃tre tut sɔrt də ʃoːz. ɑ̃fɛ̃
mon père a payé toutes les choses que nous avions achetées,
mɔ̃ pɛr a pɛje tut le ʃoːz kə nuz‿avjɔ̃z‿aʃte,
10 et les marchands les ont envoyées chez nous. Nous nous
e le marʃɑ̃ lez‿ɔ̃t‿ɑ̃vwaje ʃe nu. nu nu
sommes arrêtés à une confiserie qui se trouvait près des grands
sɔmz‿arɛte a yn kɔ̃fizri ki sə truvɛ prɛ de grɑ̃
magasins, et nous avons commandé des glaces. Hélas! On
magazɛ̃, e nuz‿avɔ̃ kɔmɑ̃de de glas. elɑːs! ɔ̃
nous a dit qu'il n'y en a pas, en France, comme nous les aimons.
nuz‿a di kil njɑ̃n‿a pɑ, ɑ̃ frɑ̃ːs, kɔm nu lez‿ɛmɔ̃.

Mardi nous avons acheté des sacs et des malles: un sac pour
mardi nuz‿avɔ̃z‿aʃte de sak e de mal: œ̃ sak pur
chaque personne et deux malles pour la famille. Alors
ʃak pɛrsɔn e dø mal pur la famiːj.   alɔr
nous avons fait nos malles. Quelle affaire! Enfin nous avons
nuz‿avɔ̃ fɛ no mal.   kɛl afɛːr!   ɑ̃fɛ̃ nuz‿avɔ̃
fini, mais très peu avant l'heure du dîner. Mercredi nous avons
fini, mɛ trɛ pø avɑ̃ lœr dy dine. mɛrkrədi nuz‿avɔ̃
fait des courses et encore des courses. Vers le soir nous sommes
fɛ de kurs e ɑ̃kɔr de kurs.   vɛr lə swaːr nu sɔm
rentrés à la maison, bien fatigués; et nous nous sommes couchés
rɑ̃tre a la mɛzɔ̃, bjɛ̃ fatige; e nu nu sɔm kuʃe
de bonne heure. Après notre visite chez grand'mère jeudi,
d bɔn œːr. aprɛ nɔtrə vizit ʃe grɑ̃mɛr ʒødi,
nous avons fait nos sacs. Enfin nous voilà partis, mais
nuz‿avɔ̃ fɛ no sak. ɑ̃fɛ̃ nu vwala parti, mɛ
nous avons eu bien de la peine ces derniers jours-ci.
nuz‿avɔ̃z‿y bjɛ̃ d la pɛn se dɛrnje ʒur si.

B. 1. He was making. 2. They used to choose. 3. We kept on talking. 4. You were going. 5. I saw him often. 6. I have seen him often. 7. She used to have. 8. He was giving. 9. They used to sell. 10. We were finishing. 11. I used to be. 12. If you were. 13. He had been here an hour. 14. They had been seeking for some time.

C. 1. He was showing me the little trunk that his father bought him yesterday. 2. The pencils and paper were on the little boy's desk in the classroom. 3. There were seventeen grown people (large persons) and eleven children in the church when we entered. 4. How long had your uncle and his friends been there when they heard the news? 5. We used to choose candy, but now we choose flowers. 6. My sister was not quite well yet when she left for the city. 7. Why were they remaining at your sister's so long? 8. In that little white house on the other side of the street there used to be a family of eight people. 9. When I saw them for the first time, they were getting out of a big red automobile. 10. When I was little I used to want an automobile; now I want two black horses and a carriage. 11. Each morning he found in front of his house an old man, who spoke to him as he went out. 12. How do you like those green apples I brought you yesterday? 13. I prefer (like better) the red cherries which one finds at market now. 14. The biggest boy in our street has more books than my two brothers; he has more than twenty. 15. I used to meet him almost every day when I was spending my vacation in the country. 16. They sent them to her to (**pour**) tell her that they weren't going to be back before ten o'clock. 17. He wasn't so strong as his brother, but he used to get up early to work in the fields before breakfast. 18. He told his father that he was going to visit his friends that day.

D. 1. In **hélas,** why is **a** pronounced [ɑ]? 2. Explain the pronunciation of **payer** and of **travailler.** 3. Account for the pronunciation of every **s** and **c** in the vocabulary. 4. Account for every vowel. 5. Read **A** from the transcription, noticing especially the treatment of the mute **e,** liaisons, and assimilation.

E. 1. Êtes-vous toujours à la maison? 2. Étiez-vous fatigué hier? 3. À qui avez-vous fait visite? 4. Qu'est-ce qu'elle a pensé en vous voyant? 5. Pourquoi étiez-vous si fatigué? 6. Pourquoi avez-vous acheté toutes ces choses? 7. Est-ce que tous les enfants de votre famille vont en France pour les vacances? 8. Où êtes-vous entrés avant de retourner à la maison? 9. Où est-ce que cette confiserie se trouvait? 10. Qu'est-ce que vous avez commandé? 11. Est-ce qu'on mange toutes sortes de glaces en France? 12. Quand avez-vous fait vos malles? 13. Avez-vous fini de bonne heure? 14. Qu'avez-vous fait avant-hier? 15. Quand allez-vous arriver à New York?

LESSON XVIII
REVIEW

A. 1. Give the forms of the conjunctive personal pronouns used (a) as subject, (b) as direct object, (c) as indirect object. 2. Give the table for the order of pronoun objects before the verb, and tell what it means. 3. What is a reflexive verb? 4. With what classes of verbs is **être** used as the auxiliary to form the compound tenses? 5. With what does the past participle agree (a) when **avoir** is the auxiliary? (b) When the verb is reflexive? (c) When **être** is the auxiliary in the compound tense and the verb is not reflexive? (d) When the verb is passive? 6. How does the general noun differ in meaning from the partitive? 7. When may the definite article replace the possessive adjective? 8. How do the past indefinite and the imperfect tenses differ in meaning?

B. *Divide into syllables and transcribe,* accounting for each step:* 1. oiseau, 2. redemander, 3. apprendre, 4. craindront, 5. meuble, 6. toussez, 7. monnaie, 8. montagne, 9. évêque, 10. Montpellier, 11. importun, 12. accident, 13. commençons, 14. Phèdre, 15. sec, 16. mettons, 17. jetez, 18. douleur, 19. moine, 20. foin, 21. autel, 22. plein, 23. pleine, 24. gigot, 25. moyen, 26. rayonnante, 27. chanson, 28. pacifiste, 29. cycliste, 30. pince.

C. 1. I spoke to John. 2. She spoke to me. 3. They sent some to me. 4. He used to bring them to her. 5. I did not see them. 6. We were going to sell it to them. 7. I flatter myself. 8. He flatters me. 9. He flatters himself. 10. They flattered us. 11. They flattered themselves. 12. They bought them for me. 13. They bought themselves some. 14. She got up. 15. You got up. 16. He raised his hand. 17. I found his

---
* Disregard the sign of length [ː].

hat. 18. There she is. 19. Here are two. 20. There aren't any. 21. There wasn't any. 22. She has come. 23. We have become. 24. They have walked. 25. They have died. 26. She has become. 27. We remained. 28. Books are expensive. 29. I like books. 30. I was buying books. 31. As tall as a man. 32. Not so good as this candy. 33. More than six books. 34. More books. 35. The best book in the library. 36. Much more quickly. 37. I like it better. 38. He speaks best. 39. He isn't here. 40. He has been here a week. 41. He was here a week ago. 42. He was here all last week. 43. He had been here two weeks. 44. He was playing and we were talking. 45. He arrived as we were leaving. 46. We used to finish early. 47. She cried and cried and cried. 48. If I had them!

D. 1. Were you going to leave the store at once? Of course. 2. When I was downtown a week ago, I ordered an overcoat, two hats, low shoes and collars. 3. I wonder why they haven't arrived. What has become of them? (What have they become?) 4. We had been studying a long time when they began to study. 5. Sometimes he used to buy several papers from (à) that poor old woman in the street. 6. How many students were there at school when you were there? 7. Am I going to need gloves for my journey? Yes, sir; more than one pair. 8. A foreign language is not easy for pupils who have always spoken English. 9. When did your teacher show you that map? Shortly (little) before our departure for France. 10. While his brother was packing the bags the day before yesterday, John suddenly got up and left the room. 11. As we went to bed at about eleven o'clock last night, we didn't want to get up before six o'clock this morning. 12. Why did she begin to cry all at once? The doctor brought her news of her friend who is ill. 13. If he is too tired, I am going to have him remain until tomorrow.

14. What is the matter? What ails Martha? Something has happened. 15. We shook hands and said, "Good-bye." 16. I want to finish all my lessons before dinner; I am doing my best. 17. Since when has he been abroad? He isn't abroad; he has been back three days. 18. Our children used to play together all (the) day (*f.*) when they were smaller.

LESSON XIX

50. Disjunctive Pronouns. A personal pronoun not used directly with a verb as subject, direct object, or indirect object, is a disjunctive pronoun. The forms are

moi [mwa] *I, me*	**nous** [nu] *we, us*
toi [twa] *thou, thee*	**vous** [vu] *you*
lui [1][lɥi] *he, him*	**eux** [ø] *they, them* (masculine)
elle [ɛl] *she, her*	**elles** [ɛl] *they, them* (feminine)

51. Uses of Disjunctive Pronouns:

1. After a preposition:

   Il est parti avec **moi.** *He set out with me.*

2. In the predicate:

   C'est **lui.** *It is he.*

   Ce is used as a grammatical subject to anticipate a logical subject noun or pronoun in the predicate. When the noun or pronoun in the predicate is third person plural, the verb is generally third person plural: C'est moi. C'est nous. C'est vous. But: Ce **sont** eux (elles) or C'est eux (**elles**).—C'est mon ami. But: Ce **sont** mes amis.

3. Absolutely:

   Qui a fait cela? **Lui.** *Who did that? He.*
   Qui avez-vous vu? **Lui.** *Whom did you see? Him.*

4. After a comparative, the verb being omitted:

   Il est plus âgé que **moi.** *He is older than I (am).*

---

[1] Note that **lui** as a conjunctive pronoun is masculine or feminine; as a disjunctive pronoun, masculine only.

5. In a compound subject or object, which may be summed up in one conjunctive form:

Lui et **moi** (nous) sommes partis. *He and I left.*
Il (nous) a vu(s) mon frère et **moi**. *He saw my brother and me.*
Je parle à **vous** et à **lui**. *I am speaking to you and to him.*

6. For emphasis (generally repeated by a conjunctive):

Moi je ne sais pas. *Or:* Je ne sais pas, **moi**. *I don't know.*
Lui parle. *He* is talking.

7. Compounded with **même**:

Je l'ai fait **moi-même**. *I did it myself.*

8. As a subject which is separated from its verb by anything other than **ne** or a conjunctive personal pronoun object:

Lui seul est arrivé. *He alone has arrived.*
Moi qui vous parle les ai vus. *I who am speaking to you saw them.*

9. To avoid the coming together of a form in the first column and one in the third column, or of two forms in the same column, of the table given in Lesson XIII, §39:

Il nous a présentés à **lui**. *He introduced us to him.*
Elle s'est présentée à **moi**. *She introduced herself to me.*

10. To explain a conjunctive object or a possessive that is ambiguous:

Je lui parle (*to him* or *to her*). Je lui parle à **lui** (*to him*). Je lui parle à **elle** (*to her*).
Je l'entends (*him* or *her*). Je l'entends **lui** (*him*). Je l'entends **elle** (*her*).
Voilà son livre (*his* or *her*). Voilà son livre à **lui** (*his*). Voilà son livre à **elle** (*her*).

EXERCISE XIX

approcher (de) [aprɔʃe] *to approach*
bateau [bato] m. *boat*
chauffeur [ʃofœːr] m. *chauffeur*
chemin de fer [ʃəmɛ̃ d̥ fɛːr] m. *railroad*
conducteur [kɔ̃dyktœːr] m. *conductor*
descendre *to put up* (*at a hotel*)
s'écrier [ekrie] *to shout, cry out*
s'embarquer [ɑ̃barke] *to set sail, go on board*

LESSON XIX

fleuve [flœːv] m. *(large) river*
gare [gaːr] f. *(railway) station*
hôtel [ɔtɛl] m. *hotel*
inviter [ɛ̃vite] *to invite*
liberté [libɛrte] f. *liberty*
libre [libr] *free, unengaged*
mer [mɛːr] f. *sea*
monde [mɔ̃ːd] m. *world; people*
paquebot [pakbo] m. *steam-boat*
puis [pɥi] *then (afterward)*
quai [ke] m. *quai, wharf, platform (of a station)*
se rendre [rɑ̃ːdr] *to go (betake oneself)*
statue [staty] f. *statue*
tard [taːr] *late* (adv.)
taxi(mètre) [taksi(mɛtr)] m. *taxicab*
wagon [vagɔ̃] m. *(railway) coach*

à côté de *beside*
en pleine mer *on the open sea*
tout le monde *everybody;* **beaucoup de monde** *many people;* etc.

A. Après sept heures, dans un wagon de chemin de fer, nous approchons de la ville de New-York. Mes parents en sont contents, et moi aussi. Arrivés à la gare, le conducteur s'écrie: «New-York! Tout le monde descend!» Mon frère et moi nous sommes à New-York pour la première fois. 5
Il y a beaucoup de monde dans la gare, et nous avons de la difficulté à trouver un taxi. Enfin en voilà un qui est libre, mais il n'y a pas assez de place pour toute la famille. Le chauffeur m'invite à monter à côté de lui. Nous descendons dans un hôtel, pour y passer la nuit. Comme mon frère désire 10 sortir, c'est lui qui accompagne ma mère. Je suis trop fatigué, moi; je me couche donc de bonne heure.

Le matin nous sommes tous [tus] levés avant six heures. Nous faisons beaucoup de courses; et puis, vers midi, nous nous rendons sur le quai pour nous embarquer sur le paque- 15 bot. À deux heures le bateau quitte le quai et descend le fleuve. Un peu plus tard nous voyons la statue de la Liberté et avant la nuit nous sommes en pleine mer.

B. 1. Who is it? I. 2. In front of them. 3. I am taller than he. 4. He and I saw them. 5. You and I saw them. 6. You and she saw them. 7. He spoke to me. 8. He spoke to you and me. 9. I saw him and her. 10. Did you see her? 11. Did you see him or her? I saw *her.* 12. You gave me *his* book. I want *her* book. 13. It is I — he — she — we — you — they. 14. He arrived with her. 15. You like it, but *I* don't like it. 16. I cry out. 17. You cried out. 18. We cry out. 19. They went on board. 20. He goes (betakes himself) to the station.

C. 1. Who is that man beside your father? Is it your brother? Why yes, it is he. 2. Do you want to order some clothes for them? No; they want to do it themselves. 3. There were some people in front of the door when she came in. 4. My sister and I are now on the way to (for) New York. 5. Do you often see him and his mother together? 6. Who paid [for] those shoes, you or he? It was he who paid [for] them. 7. How long have you been traveling? Who? I? *I'm* not traveling. 8. What were you doing last Tuesday when my friends stopped at your house? 9. There were so many people at the station that I didn't see you. 10. We got out of the taxi in front of the store, and we walked to the church. 11. I wonder why there weren't more people on the boat. 12. He who has so often seen them, what does he think of (**de**) them? 13. We sent for the doctor, who said that they were very sick. 14. They put up at that large hotel and stayed there a long time. 15. Everybody was returning late; we had much difficulty in finding (**à** + *infinitive*) a carriage that was free.

D. 1. Combien de temps avez-vous passé en chemin de fer? 2. Est-ce la première fois que vous visitez New-York? 3. Est-ce qu'il y avait beaucoup de monde à la gare? 4. Êtes-vous allés à pied jusqu'à l'hôtel? 5. Est-ce que vous y êtes restés longtemps? 6. Êtes-vous sortis le soir? 7. Qui est-ce qui a accompagné madame votre mère? 8. Et vous, qu'avez-vous fait? 9. Vous êtes-vous levés tard le matin? 10. Pourquoi? 11. Où vous êtes-vous rendus vers midi? 12. Quand vous êtes-vous embarqués? 13. À quelle heure le paquebot a-t-il quitté le quai? 14. Qu'avez-vous vu en quittant New-York? 15. Où étiez-vous avant la nuit?

E 1 Account for the pronunciation of **i** in **écrier.** 2. Note that **hôtel** is pronounced with an open **o** [ɔ] in spite of the circumflex. 3. Note the [e] in **quai.** See p. 18. 4. **Tous,** when it is an adjective, is pronounced [tu]; when a pronoun, [tus].

LESSON XX

52. Future. The future tense is derived from the infinitive. The future stem is regularly the whole infinitive (minus **e** in verbs ending in **-re**); the endings are the same as in the present indicative of **avoir.** Thus, to **donner-, finir-, vendr-,** we add **-ai, -as, -a, -ons, -ez, -ont.**

The future stem of irregular verbs may be irregular, but the endings never vary: **avoir, j'aurai** [ʒɔre], *etc.*; **être, je serai** [ʒə sre], *etc.*; **aller, j'irai** [ʒire], *etc.*; **faire, je ferai** [ʒə fre], *etc.*; **voir, je verrai** [ʒə vɛre], *etc.*

je donnerai [ʒə dɔnre], *I shall give*   nous donnerons [nu dɔnrɔ̃], *we shall give*
tu donneras [ty dɔnra], *thou wilt give*   vous donnerez [vu dɔnre], *you will give*
il donnera [il dɔnra], *he will give*   ils donneront [il dɔnrɔ̃]; *they will give*

j'aurai [ʒɔre]   nous aurons [nuz‿ɔrɔ̃]   je ferai [ʒə fre]   nous ferons [nu frɔ̃]
tu auras [ty ɔra]   vous aurez [vuz‿ɔre]   tu feras [ty fra]   vous ferez [vu fre]
il aura [il ɔra]   ils auront [ilz‿ɔrɔ̃]   il fera [il f(ə)ra] ils feront [il f(ə)rɔ̃]

53. Conditional. The conditional stem is always the same as the future stem. The endings are the same as those of the imperfect indicative. Thus:

j'irais [ʒirɛ], *I should go*   nous irions [nuz‿irjɔ̃], *we should go*
tu irais [ty irɛ], *thou wouldst go*   vous iriez [vuz‿irje], *you would go*
il irait [il irɛ], *he would go*   ils iraient [ilz‿irɛ], *they would go*

54. Conditional Sentences. 1. A condition expressed in English in the present or future, is expressed in French in the present indicative. The result is then generally expressed in the future, possibly in the present or the imperative, as the sense requires:

If he **arrives** *early, I shall see him.* S'il **arrive** de bonne heure, je le **verrai**.
If he **is** *not sick, he is at school now.* S'il n'**est** pas malade, il **est** à l'école en ce moment.
If you **have** *time, finish your lessons.* Si vous **avez** le temps, **finissez** (Lesson XXIII) vos leçons.

2. A condition expressed in English in the past tense[1] is expressed in French in the imperfect indicative. The result is then in the conditional:

If he **were** *here, I should go.* S'il **était** ici, je **partirais**.
If he **came** *(were to come, should come),* **would you speak** *to him?* S'il **venait**, lui **parleriez**-vous?

3. The verb in either clause, or in both, may be compounded as the sense requires, the auxiliaries following the rules of sequence:

If he **leaves**, *he* **will have finished** *his lessons.* S'il **part,** il **aura fini** ses leçons.
If he **has come**, *I shall speak to him.* S'il **est arrivé,** je lui **parlerai**.
If he **has gone,** *he* **has finished** *his lessons.* S'il **est parti,** il **a fini** ses leçons.
If he **had been** *here, he* **would have done** *it.* S'il **avait été** ici, il l'**aurait fait**.

4. Note that neither the future nor the conditional may be used in a conditional *if*-clause. However, when *if* means *whether*, it may be followed by any tense that the sense requires:

I wonder if (whether) he will come. Je me demande s'il viendra.
I wondered if (whether) he would come. Je me demandais s'il viendrait.

55. Future after **Quand.** After certain conjunctions, especially **quand** (*when*), the future tense is used in French

[1] See p. 105, note.

if the idea is future, although the English may use the present:

I shall speak to him when I see him. Je lui parlerai quand je le **verrai.**

EXERCISE XX

d'abord [dabɔːr] *first* (adv.)
beurre [bœːr] m. *butter*
cabine [kabin] f. *cabin*
calme [kalm] *calm*
Charles [ʃarl] *Charles*
chocolat [ʃɔkɔla] m. *chocolate*
continuer [kɔ̃tinɥe] *to continue*
garçon [garsɔ̃] m. *waiter, steward*
gracieux, gracieuse [grasjø, grasjøːz] *graceful, gracious*
s'habiller [abije] *to dress*
là-bas [laba] *down there, yonder*
magnifique [maɲifik] *magnificent*
mal [mal] *badly;* m. *illness, evil*
matinal [matinal] *up early*
moment [mɔmɑ̃] m. *moment*
mouette [mwɛt] f. *gull*

oiseau [wazo] m. *bird*
par [paːr] *by, through, during, on* (a day)
Philippe [filip] *Philip*
pont [pɔ̃] m. *bridge; deck*
prêt [prɛ] *ready*
se promener [prɔmne] *to take a walk or ride*
que . . ! *how . . !* (Note order of sentence in Ex. A.)
seulement [sœlmɑ̃] *only* (adv.)
suivre [sɥiːvr] *to follow*
temps [tɑ̃] m. *weather*
toilette [twalɛt] f. *toilet*
se tromper [trɔ̃pe] *to be mistaken*
vague [vag] f. *wave*
vent [vɑ̃] m. *wind*

A. —Bonjour, Charles! Qu'allons-nous faire aujourd'hui?

—D'abord, je vais me lever, faire ma toilette, et m'habiller. Après nous verrons.

—Quel temps magnifique! Si le beau temps continue, nous n'aurons pas le mal de mer.

—Êtes-vous prêt, Philippe? Désirez-vous vous promener sur le pont avant le petit déjeuner?

—Oui, j'aimerais tant sortir un moment. Que la mer est calme! S'il y avait du vent, il y aurait des vagues. Comme c'est beau!

—Voyez-vous ces oiseaux là-bas? Si je ne me trompe pas, ce sont des mouettes. On me dit qu'elles suivent les bateaux pendant trois ou quatre jours quelquefois. Elles sont si gracieuses!

15 —Maintenant nous descendrons à la salle à manger. Qu'est-ce que le garçon nous donnera à manger? Moi je commanderai seulement du chocolat, du pain et du beurre.

—Ce sera assez pour moi aussi. Voilà notre père et notre mère qui entrent.

20 —Bonjour, mes enfants! Déjà levés? Vous êtes matinaux. Qu'est-ce qu'il y a? Vous n'êtes pas malades?

—Nous ne désirions pas rester dans notre cabine par un si beau temps, mon père. Nous allons passer cette belle journée sur le pont. Quand vous aurez fini, vous nous y 25 trouverez. Au revoir!

B. 1. I shall finish. 2. He has finished. 3. We shall have finished. 4. You were finishing. 5. They would finish. 6. They used to sell. 7. They would sell. 8. If he works, I shall work. 9. If he went, I should go. 10. What would they do? 11. Whom will you see? 12. If he has left, I shall remain. 13. If he had left, I should have remained. 14. We should go. 15. He will stop. 16. We shall have stopped. 17. If they stop. 18. If you stopped. 19. We were approaching. 20. He would invite.

C. 1. When will the steamer arrive at the wharf? 2. If the sea is calm tomorrow, we shall be glad. 3. He would dress, if he weren't so sick. 4. When you go[1] to France, will your brother go (there) too? 5. When we buy many things at the store, we have them sent home. 6. When he arrived in (à) New York, his friends were already there. 7. If you were stronger than he, you would finish more quickly. 8. If he doesn't arrive before noon, he will not see them. 9. I should like some chocolate, white bread and good butter. 10. How he likes horses! How fine his horses are! 11. Did everybody leave the station to go to the hotel? 12. Will you have good cabins on the steamer? 13. If I had (the) time, I should accompany you. 14. Will dinner be ready when we go[1] down? 15. He told me that I should be seasick, but he was mistaken. 16. We shall go up on deck immediately after luncheon. 17. The gull is a very graceful bird. 18. Would they have gone on board if there had been wind and waves?

D. 1. Est-ce que vos parents se sont levés les premiers ce matin? 2. Qu'est-ce que vous et Philippe avez fait d'abord? 3. Y avait-il du monde sur le pont quand vous y êtes montés? 4. Vous êtes-vous promenés longtemps sur le pont? 5. Si vous aviez trouvé des jeunes filles sur le pont, est-ce que vous leur auriez parlé? 6. Si vous entrez dans la salle à manger, est-ce que le garçon vous donnera quelque chose à manger? 7. Qu'est-ce qu'on vous a donné pour le petit déjeuner ce matin? 8. Qu'est-ce que votre père a dit en entrant? 9. Où désirez-vous passer cette belle journée? 10. S'il y avait eu du vent, seriez-vous restés dans votre cabine?

LESSON XXI

56. Some Uses of Prepositions. 1. The preposition **chez** means *at the house (office, shop) of, to the house* (etc.) *of*. It governs a personal object.

> Je suis chez mon frère. *I am at my brother's.*
> Je suis allé chez vous. *I went to your house (office, shop).*
> J'ai acheté ce chapeau chez Marshall Field. *I bought this hat at Marshall Field's.*

2. The preposition *in* (ordinarily **dans:** dans la maison) is expressed by **à** in certain fixed expressions. These must be learned by observation:

> à la campagne *in the country*, à l'école *in school*, à la main *in his (her, my,* etc.*) hand*, au mois de *in the month of*, etc.

[1] Tense?

3. With names of cities, *in* or *to* is expressed by **à,** and there is usually no article:

à Paris, à New-York, etc. But: à la Nouvelle Orléans, au Havre.

4. With feminine singular names of countries, continents, large islands, and provinces, *in* or *to* is expressed by **en,** and there is then no article:

en France, en Chine, en Europe, en Sicile, en Picardie.

But if the name is masculine singular, or masculine or feminine plural, **à** is used with the definite article:

au Canada, au Mexique, aux États-Unis.

If the name has an adjectival qualifier, **dans** is used with the article:

dans l'Amérique du Sud, dans la France méridionale.

5. After a superlative, *in* is expressed by **de.** This rule takes precedence over all others:

le meilleur élève de la classe, la plus belle ville de France, la plus belle église de Paris, le plus grand homme du Canada, etc.

6. Note: en été [ete] m. (*summer*), en automne [otɔn] m. or f. (*autumn*), en hiver [ivɛːr] m. (*winter*). But: au printemps [prɛ̃tã] m. (*spring*).

7. With the interrogative pronoun **qui,** **de** denotes relationship, **à** denotes ownership:

De qui est-il le fils? *Whose son is he?*
À qui est cette maison? *Whose house is this?*

8. With an expression of time, **dans** (*in*) means *at the end of*, **en** (*in*) means *during*:

He will leave in two hours (i. e. *at the end of two hours*): Il partira **dans** deux heures.
He will do it in two hours (i. e. *it will take him two hours*): Il le fera **en** deux heures.

The use of prepositions is largely idiomatic in all languages. The student is advised to watch prepositions closely.

LESSON XXI

57. Idiomatic Uses of Avoir. Note the following: **avoir chaud**[1] [ʃo], *to be warm*; **avoir froid**[1] [frwɑ] *to be cold*; **avoir faim** [fɛ̃], *to be hungry*; **avoir soif** [swaf], *to be thirsty*; **avoir peur** [pœːr], *to be afraid;* **avoir raison** [rɛzɔ̃], *to be right*; **avoir tort** [tɔːr], *to be wrong*; **avoir sommeil** [sɔmɛːj], *to be sleepy*; **avoir besoin** [bəzwɛ̃] (**de**), *to need*; **avoir dix ans** [diz‿ɑ̃], etc., *to be ten (etc.) years old*; **avoir mal à la tête (aux dents,** etc.) [mal a la tɛːt (o dɑ̃)], *to have a headache (toothache, etc.)*.

> Quel âge avez-vous? J'ai vingt ans. Avez-vous chaud? Non, j'ai froid. Mon frère a faim.

58. Impersonal Verbs. 1. **Faire** is used in impersonal expressions of the weather:

> Il fait chaud. *It is warm.* Il fera froid. *It will be cold.* Il faisait doux. *It was mild.* Fait-il du vent? *Is it windy?* Il fait beau (temps). *It is fine.* Il fait mauvais (temps). *The weather is bad.* Il fait sombre. *It is dark.* Quel temps fait-il? *How is the weather?*

2. There are also a great many purely impersonal verbs in French:

> Il neige (*snows*). Il pleut (*rains*). Il gèle (*freezes*). Il grêle (*hails*), etc.

EXERCISE XXI

Angleterre [ɑ̃ɡlətɛːr] f. *England*
demeurer [dəmœre] *to live (dwell)*
États-Unis [etaz‿yni] m. pl. *United States*
exemple [ɛɡzɑ̃ːpl] m. *example*
faible [fɛːbl] *weak*
gens [ʒɑ̃] *people (individuals)*
  jeunes gens *young men*
histoire [istwaːr] f. *story, history*
Indes [ɛ̃ːd] f. pl. *India*
lendemain [lɑ̃dmɛ̃] m. *the next day*

malheur [malœːr] m. *misfortune*
nation [nɑsjɔ̃] f. *nation*
orage [ɔraːʒ] m. *storm*
remarquer [rəmarke] *to notice*
rouler [rule] *to roll*
silence [silɑ̃ːs] m. *silence*
sud [syd] m. *south*
surlendemain [syrlɑ̃dmɛ̃] m. *the second day following*
voisin, -e [vwazɛ̃, vwazin] *near, contiguous;* m. f., *neighbor*

  par exemple *for example*
  passer sous [su] **silence** *to pass over in silence*

---
[1] Not used of inanimate objects or impersonally.

A. Nous avons quitté notre pays samedi. C'est aujourd'hui vendredi. Nous arriverons à Plymouth, en Angleterre, demain matin; et le soir nous serons à Cherbourg [ʃɛrbuːr], en France. Mon frère et moi nous serons les enfants les plus
5 heureux du monde quand nous y arriverons.

Le lendemain de notre départ il a fait très beau; mais le surlendemain il a fait mauvais. Pendant la nuit le vent s'était levé; il y a eu un orage, et le paquebot roulait. Le matin je désirais sortir; mais quand j'ai levé la tête, j'ai
10 remarqué que j'étais faible comme un petit enfant. J'avais chaud, puis j'avais froid; j'avais mal à la tête; et pendant deux jours, je n'avais pas du tout faim. Je pensais que tout irait bien une fois que je serais sur le pont. Mais comment y arriver? C'était le mal de mer! Quel malheur! Mais
15 assez de cette histoire; nous allons passer ces quelques jours sous silence.

Il y a sur le paquebot des gens de presque toutes les nations. Par exemple, dans une des cabines voisines il y a un monsieur et sa femme qui demeurent au Canada; ils sont en route
20 pour aller visiter leurs fils qui demeurent à Bombay [bɔ̃bɛ], aux Indes. De l'autre côté il y a deux jeunes gens qui vont dans l'Amérique du Sud où demeurent leurs parents; ils ont passé sept ans aux États-Unis, et ils désirent voir la France avant de retourner chez eux. À table à côté de moi
25 il y a une dame qui retourne en Italie; et ainsi de suite.

B. 1. I am hungry. 2. We were thirsty. 3. You will be sleepy. 4. Aren't you afraid? 5. Were you cold? 6. Is it cold today? 7. They are warm. 8. It wasn't warm yesterday. 9. The weather is fine. 10. How old is he? 11. My brother is eleven years old. 12. In his garden. 13. In one's hand. 14. In Paris. 15. In England. 16. In Canada. 17. In the United States. 18. In South America. 19. In summer. 20. In spring.

C. 1. Do you see that child yonder? Whose daughter is she? 2. There are people who think that they are always right, but everybody is wrong sometimes. 3. How much money will you need in order to spend three or four weeks in Paris? 4. Your friend's little son will be five years old the day after tomorrow. 5. They arrived in Canada a week ago, and the next day they left for the United States. 6. If you do not eat enough, you will be hungry before noon. 7. Whose is that large book that you have in your hand? 8. In spring there are always many flowers in his mother's garden. 9. He lives in Paris, the largest city in France. 10. He is never satisfied: in spring he is afraid of (the) storms, in summer it is too hot, in autumn (the) classes begin after the long vacation, in winter it is too cold. 11. We had been working for several hours and we were very warm. 12. They sometimes used to go for a walk in the park in the evening. 13. We have seen all sorts of birds, but the gull is the most graceful of all. 14. Will the steward bring me some more meat if I tell him that I am hungry? 15. First we washed our hands, then we put on our gloves. 16. He is not very well; he has had a headache since yesterday. 17. Those two young men will set sail for foreign lands. 18. There are more beautiful things in France than in the United States.

D. 1. Quel jour de la semaine est-ce aujourd'hui? 2. Quel jour est-ce que c'était hier? 3. Quel jour est-ce que ce sera demain? 4. Où est-ce que vous arriverez demain matin? 5. Et demain soir? 6. Avez-vous eu des orages pendant votre voyage? 7. Est-ce que vous avez eu le mal de mer? 8. Êtes-vous resté longtemps au lit? 9. Est-ce qu'il y a seulement des Français sur le paquebot? 10. Où allez-vous? 11. Et la dame qui est à côté de vous à table où va-t-elle? 12. Où demeurent ces deux jeunes gens qui ont passé sept ans aux États-Unis?

E. 1. Notice the back **a** [ɑ] in **nation** (see p. 17). Also the [s]-sound for the **t** (see p. 32). 2. Notice that the final **d** is pronounced in **sud**.

LESSON XXII

59. Present Subjunctive. The present subjunctive is formed by adding to the stem of the present participle the endings **-e, -es, -e, -ions, -iez, -ent.**

In irregular verbs there is often an irregular present subjunctive stem; this stem occurs in the three singulars and in the third plural, the other two forms taking the stem of the present participle. Only three verbs (**être, faire, pouvoir**) carry the change throughout the tense.

The endings never vary except in **avoir** and **être**.

je donne [dɔn] (*give*)	finisse [finis] (*finish*)	fasse [fas] (*make*)
tu donnes [dɔn]	finisses [finis]	fasses [fas]
il donne [dɔn]	finisse [finis]	fasse [fas]
nous donnions [dɔnjɔ̃]	finissions [finisjɔ̃]	fassions [fasjɔ̃]
vous donniez [dɔnje]	finissiez [finisje]	fassiez [fasje]
ils donnent [dɔn]	finissent [finis]	fassent [fas]

je sois [swa] (*be*)	aie [ɛ] (*have*)	aille [aːj] (*go*)	voie [vwa] (*see*)
tu sois [swa]	aies [ɛ]	ailles [aːj]	voies [vwa]
il soit [swa]	ait [ɛ]	aille [aːj]	voie [vwa]
nous soyons [swajɔ̃]	ayons [ɛjɔ̃]	allions [aljɔ̃]	voyions [vwaijɔ̃]
vous soyez [swaje]	ayez [ɛje]	alliez [alje]	voyiez [vwaije]
ils soient [swa]	aient [ɛ]	aillent [aːj]	voient [vwa]

60. Uses of the Subjunctive. The subjunctive is used in a dependent clause after

1. Expressions of willing:

Je désire qu'il **finisse** son ouvrage. *I want him to finish his work.*
Où voulez-vous que j'**aille**? *Where do you want me to go?*

2. Expressions of emotion (joy, sorrow, fear,[1] surprise, etc.):

> Je suis heureux que vous **soyez** ici. *I am glad that you are here.*
> Cela m'étonne qu'il **ait** fait cela. *I am surprised that he has done that.*

3. Expressions of necessity:

> Il faut que nous lui **parlions**. *We must speak to him.* (*It is necessary that we speak to him.*)

4. Certain conjunctions (**bien que,** *although*; **quoique** *although*; **afin que,** *in order that*; **pour que,** *in order that*; etc.):

> Il y sera bien qu'il **soit** malade. *He will be there although he is sick.*
> Je le ferai pour que vous me **laissiez** tranquille. *I shall do it so that you will leave me alone.*

61. Sequence of Tenses. There being a reason for a subjunctive, the present subjunctive is used in the dependent clause if the verb in the independent clause is present or future; otherwise the imperfect subjective (Lesson XXV) is used.

This rule is observed in literary French, but in conversational style the imperfect subjunctive is never used. Consequently, the present subjunctive is used after any tense if a subjunctive cannot be avoided. The tense may be retained by compounding:

> J'étais heureux qu'il ait été ici. *I was glad he[2] was here.*

---

[1] If both clauses are affirmative, a pleonastic (meaningless) **ne** is inserted before the subjunctive following an expression of fear: J'ai peur qu'il **ne** me voie. *I am afraid he will see me.*

[2] Notice that the conjunction *that* (**que**) cannot be omitted as in English.

EXERCISE XXII

allumette [alymɛt] f. *match*
assurer [asyre] *to assure*
avril [avril] m. *April*
bien que [bjɛ̃ k(ə)] *although*

car [kaːr] *for* (conj.), *because*
cloche [klɔʃ] f. (*large*) *bell*
confortable [kɔ̃fɔrtabl] *comfortable*
débarquer [debarke] *to land*

décider [dɔside] *to decide*
déclarer [deklare] *to declare*
douane [dwan] f. *custom-house*
douanier [dwanje] m. *custom-house official*
entre [ɑ̃:tr] *between, among*
expliquer [ɛksplike] *to explain*
il faut [fo] *it is necessary*
formalité [fɔrmalite] f. *formality*
gai [ge] *gay, cheerful*
Henri [ɑ̃ri] *Henry*
machine [maʃin] f. *machine, engine*
naturellement [natyrɛlmɑ̃] *naturally*
nécessaire [nesesɛ:r] *necessary*

officier [ɔfisje] m. *official*
passeport [paspɔ:r] m. *passport*
pension [pɑ̃sjɔ̃] f. *boarding-house*
poser [poze] *to put, ask (a question)*
question [kɛstjɔ̃] f. *question*
(se) réveiller [revɛje] *to awaken*
sembler [sɑ̃ble] *to seem*
simple [sɛ̃:pl] *simple, mere*
singulier, singulière [sɛ̃gylje, sɛ̃gyljɛ:r] *strange, funny, singular*
sonner [sɔne] *to sound, ring*
tabac [taba] m. *tobacco*
train [trɛ̃] m. *train*
wagon-lit [vagɔ̃li] m. *sleeping car*

à bord [a bɔ:r] m. *on board*
bien à vous [bjɛ̃‿a vu] *yours truly*
de la sorte *thus, in this (or that) way*
être bien *to be comfortable*

Paris, le 9 Avril, 1923.

Mon cher Henri:—

Enfin nous voilà en France! Nous sommes arrivés à Cherbourg avant-hier vers six heures du soir. Les officiers fran-
5 çais sont venus à bord pour examiner nos passeports. Puis nous avons débarqué. Naturellement il est nécessaire qu'on passe par la douane, mais c'est une simple formalité pour la plupart des gens. Le douanier nous a posé trois questions: «Avez-vous quelque chose à déclarer? Vous n'avez pas d'al-
10 lumettes? Pas de tabac?» Et c'était fini.

Bien que les wagons-lits français soient très confortables, nous sommes restés à Cherbourg jusqu'au lendemain. Mon père a dit: «Je ne désire pas que nous fassions le voyage la nuit; il y a tant de jolies choses à voir entre Cherbourg et
15 Paris.» Je suis bien content qu'il en ait décidé de la sorte.

Hier matin, dimanche, quand je me suis réveillé, les cloches sonnaient. Il y avait beaucoup de monde qui allait à l'église. Il était nécessaire que nous soyons à la gare à dix heures, car le train partait à cette heure. Que les wagons et la machine nous semblaient singuliers! Mais il faut que je vous explique cela une autre fois. Je vous assure que les trains français marchent vite. Nous avons passé par plusieurs villes et beaucoup de petits villages. Vers cinq heures nous sommes arrivés à Paris. Que Paris est beau! Nous sommes heureux que nous soyons venus en France en cette saison. Bien qu'il fasse encore un peu froid, tout est gai. L'herbe est verte, et il y a déjà beaucoup |de fleurs. Nous demeurons dans une pension, où nous serons très bien.

Il faut que je finisse; nous allons sortir voir Paris!

Bien à vous,

Charles.

B. 1. *Continue:* Bien que je vende, etc. 2. *Continue:* Pour que je me réveille, etc. 3. *Continue:* Il faut que j'aille, etc. 4. *Continue:* Est-elle contente que je les choisisse? etc. 5. *Continue:* Désire-t-elle que je sois ici? etc. 6. I want him to go (that he go). 7. You want him to do it. 8. They want you to have it. 9. We want them to be there. 10. I am glad that he is doing it. 11. Are you glad that he has done it? 12. Although he finishes it . . . 13. Although he has finished it . . . 14. It is necessary that he go. 15. It is necessary that they go.

C. 1. Although he goes to the hotel every evening, I shall not see him. 2. I am glad that we have not yet sailed. 3. Do you want the little boy's sister to be here before noon? 4. Although he awoke early, he has not yet dressed. 5. I woke them early so that (**pour que**) they may be downstairs before breakfast. 6. I want him to be ready when I arrive at his house. 7. What a misfortune that they aren't yet here! 8. How glad I am that the weather is so fine! 9. I am not afraid that he will finish before my departure. 10. Although he is hungry, he will give you a piece of his bread. 11. If I am not mistaken, they were walking over there an hour ago.

12. If the weather were cold, we should remain here another week. 13. Everybody began to shout when the boat approached the wharf. 14. Although he went to bed late last night, he has already risen and gone out. 15. If you want him to go with me, you must (it is necessary that you) awaken him at once.

D. 1. Quel jour de la semaine êtes-vous arrivés à Cherbourg? 2. À quelle heure avez-vous débarqué? 3. Êtes-vous partis tout de suite pour Paris? 4. Faut-il que tout le monde passe par la douane? 5. Les douaniers français, qu'est-ce qu'ils ont demandé? 6. Est-ce que les wagons-lits français sont confortables? 7. Pourquoi êtes-vous restés à Cherbourg jusqu'au lendemain? 8. Qu'avez-vous entendu en vous réveillant? 9. Est-ce que les trains français marchent vite? 10. Comment trouvez-vous Paris? 11. Est-ce qu'il fait déjà chaud? 12. Où demeurez-vous à Paris?

E. 1. Account for the different values for **x** in **exemple** and **expliquer**. See p. 34. 2. Notice the vowel sound in **gai**. 3. Because of the **s** preceding, the **t** in **question** has the [t]-sound. Cf. **nation**. 4. Note that, contrary to the rule, the final **c** in **tabac** is silent.

LESSON XXIII

62. Imperatives. The French verb has three imperatives: the second person singular (familiar), the first person plural, and the second person plural (polite). The forms are generally the same as the corresponding forms of the present indicative, except that the **s** of the **es** ending of a second person singular is dropped.[1] There is no subject expressed.

Pres. Ind.:	tu donnes	nous donnons	vous donnez
Imperative:	donne (*give*)	donnons (*let us give*)	donnez (*give*)

[1] This **s** is retained, however, before **y** or **en**: **Envoies-y. Donnes-en.**

| Pres. Ind.: | tu finis | nous finissons | vous finissez |
| Imperative: | finis (*finish*) | finissons (*let us finish*) | finissez (*finish*) |

| Pres. Ind.: | tu vends | nous vendons | vous vendez |
| Imperative: | vends (*sell*) | vendons (*let us sell*) | vendez (*sell*) |

In **avoir** and **être,** the imperatives are taken from the present subjunctive. In the other irregular verbs that we have studied, they are taken from the present indicative:

avoir:	aie	ayons	ayez
être:	sois	soyons	soyez
aller:	va[1]	allons	allez
faire:	fais	faisons	faites
voir:	vois	voyons	voyez

63. Position and Order of Personal Pronoun Objects.

1. Personal pronoun objects follow an *affirmative* imperative:

Donnez-lui[2] des livres. Donnez-les à votre frère. Donnez-en à Robert.

2. When there are several pronoun objects after an affirmative imperative, the order is the usual order of the English:

Donnez-le-nous. [2] (*Give* **it to us.**) Donnez-la-leur. (*Give* **it to them.**)
Envoyez-l'y. (*Send* **him there.**) Donnons-les-lui. (*Let's give* **them to him.**)

En always comes last in order of verb and pronoun object:

Donnez-m'en (*Give* **me some.** Not *Give* **some to me.**) Va-t'en (*Go away.*)

3. **Me** and **te** change to **moi** and **toi** when last in order of verb and pronoun object (i. e. except before **y** or **en**):[3]

Donnez-moi du pain. Donnez-le-moi. Lève-toi.

---

[1] Note the omission of the **s**: **tu vas: va.** But **Vas-y.**

[2] Except where there is elision, personal pronoun objects after an affirmative imperative are joined to each other and to the verb by hyphens.

[3] Although the table for the order of pronoun objects before the verb (§39) does not apply to pronoun objects after the verb, it still holds true that two forms in the same column of that table or a form in the first column and a form in the third column cannot be used together: *Introduce me to them.* **Présentez-moi à eux.**

4. Personal pronoun objects precede a negative imperative in the usual order (See §39):

> Ne le leur donnez pas. Ne me le donnez pas. Ne m'en donnez pas.
> N'y va pas. Ne t'en va pas. Ne te lève pas. N'en donne pas
> à Robert.

64. Present Subjunctive as Imperative.

There being no imperative form in the third person, a command in the third person is expressed by the present subjunctive, generally introduced by **que**. Personal pronoun objects always precede:

> Que tous les enfants **aient** des livres! *Let all the children have books!*
> Qu'ils **soient** ici demain! *Let them be here tomorrow!*
> Qu'il me le **donne**! *Let him give it to me!*
> Qu'elle s'en **aille**! *Let her go away!*
> **Vivent** les États-Unis! *Hurrah for the United States!* Literally: *Let the United States live!*

EXERCISE XXIII

allons! [alɔ̃] *come (now)!*
américain, -e [amerikɛ̃, amerikɛn] *American*
arc [ark] m. *arch*
attention [atɑ̃sjɔ̃] f. *care, attention*
avenue [avny] f. *avenue*
Champs-Élysées [ʃɑ̃z‿elize] fine avenue in Paris
coin [kwɛ̃] m. *corner*
compter [kɔ̃te] *to count, intend*
cour [kuːr] f. *court, yard*
à droite [drwat] *on (to) the right*
étoile [etwal] f. *star*
à gauche [goːʃ] *on (to) the left*
laisser [lese] *to leave, let*
large [larʒ] *broad, wide*

monument [mɔnymɑ̃] m. *monument, public building*
nom [nɔ̃] m. *name*
perdre [pɛrdr] *to lose, waste*
place [plas] f. *public square*
prier [prie] *to pray, beg, request*
promenade [prɔmnad] f. *walk, ride*
quartier [kartje] m. *quarter, district*
rayon [rɛjɔ̃] m. *ray*
regarder [rəgarde] *to regard, look (at), watch*
tourner [turne] *to turn, go around*
tout [tu] *entirely, quite, very* (adv.)
traverser [travɛrse] *to cross*
triomphe [triɔ̃ːf] m. *triumph*
vue [vy] f. *view, sight*

s'attendre à [atɑ̃ːdr] *to expect*
donner sur *to open upon, look out upon*
n'est-ce pas? [nɛs pa] *Is it not so?* (May repeat any verb in any tense.)
Soyez tranquille! [trɑ̃kil] *Don't worry!*

Le Château de Chaumont

L'Arc de Triomphe de l'Étoile, Paris

LESSON XXIII

—Bonjour, ma chère mère! Comment allez-vous ce matin?

—Très bien, merci. Aimez-vous votre chambre, Philippe?

—Mon frère et moi nous avons une belle chambre qui donne sur la cour. Mais nous ne comptons pas y passer beaucoup de temps. Nous ne désirons pas perdre nos journées à Paris; il faut que nous voyions tant de choses. Allons, Charles! N'êtes-vous pas encore prêt?

—Pas tout à fait. Donnez-moi ma cravate, s'il vous plaît.

—Où est-elle donc? Je ne la vois pas.

—La voilà sur la table à droite. Donnez-la-moi. Merci. Regardez! Ne dirait-on pas que j'ai besoin de nouveaux gants? Mère, achetez-m'en quand vous irez en ville, je vous en prie.

—Très bien, mon fils. Laissez-moi vos gants pour que je voie quelle sorte vous aimez. Donnez-les-moi.

—Au revoir, chère mère! Nous allons sortir.

—Où irons-nous d'abord? Descendons cette rue jusqu'au coin, tournons à gauche, et puis traversons le pont. Regardez ces bateaux. Comme ils marchent vite, n'est-ce pas? Quelle belle vue sur le fleuve!

—Montons cette large avenue. Je me demande quelle est cette église. Entrons un moment. Mais, c'est une église américaine! Je ne m'attendais pas à en trouver à Paris.

—Nous sommes tout près des Champs-Élysées; c'est un quartier où demeurent beaucoup d'Américains.

—Nous voilà arrivés à l'arc de Triomphe de l'Étoile. Quel joli monument et quelle jolie place! Mais pourquoi est-ce qu'on lui a donné ce nom d'Étoile?

—Voyez toutes ces avenues qui commencent ici. Comptez-les. Il y en a douze. Ce sont les rayons d'une étoile.

—Voilà un monsieur qui nous parle. Qu'est-ce qu'il dit?

—Il dit: «Qu'on fasse attention aux automobiles!» Il y a trop d'automobiles dans cette avenue. Ne la traversons pas.

—Soyez tranquille! Je ferai bien attention. Retournons maintenant à la pension. Nous avons fait une très bonne promenade, n'est-ce pas?

B. 1. Let's take a walk (*two ways*). 2. Be here at noon. 3. Pay (make) attention. 4. Finish your lessons. 5. Let's finish them. 6. Give me some bread. 7. Give me some. 8. Give it to me. 9. Don't give me any. 10. Don't give me any bread. 11. Don't give it to me. 12. Show it to them. 13. Don't show it to them. 14. I showed it to him. 15. He showed it to us. 16. Show it to us. 17. Don't show it to us. 18. Send him there (**y**). 19. Don't send him there. 20. Speak to him of it.

C. 1. Our lessons are not very long; let's finish them this evening. 2. If it is necessary that you go there, go at once. 3. Get up, wash your hands, and dress. 4. Don't go to bed before nine o'clock. 5. Where did he put my matches? Give them to me. 6. If you have his pen, give it to him. 7. He doesn't need any tobacco. Don't give him any. 8. We haven't any meat. Bring us two pounds. 9. Do you see that gentleman? Speak to him. 10. Show them our passports; it is necessary that they see them. 11. Take care! Don't leave them on the table. 12. Do French trains go fast? 13. Go into the yard and stay there until (the) evening. 14. There is the church we saw yesterday. Let's enter (into) it. 15. Look at that man with the birds. Let's count them. 16. Turn to the right and enter the park. 17. We haven't much time; let's not waste it. 18. Don't worry! You will have a good room that looks out upon a beautiful garden.

D. 1. Est-ce que votre chambre donne sur la rue? 2. Comptez-vous passer beaucoup de temps dans votre chambre? 3. Pourquoi pas? 4. Votre frère était-il prêt avant vous? 5. Qu'est-ce qu'il demande à madame votre mère?

6. Où est-ce que vous êtes allés? 7. Est-ce que les rues sont larges à Paris? 8. Est-ce qu'il y a de belles vues? 9. Qu'est-ce que vous avez vu en montant l'avenue? 10. Est-ce que vous vous y attendiez? 11. À quelle place êtes-vous arrivés? 12. Qu'est-ce qu'il y a sur cette place? 13. Combien d'avenues y a-t-il qui commencent là? 14. Faut-il qu'on fasse attention aux automobiles? 15. Comptez-vous faire encore une promenade à la Place de l'Étoile?

LESSON XXIV

REVIEW

A. 1. Account for the use of the disjunctive pronouns in the following passages: **moi** (XIX, l.3); **moi** (1.5); **lui** (1.9); **lui** (1.11); **moi** (1.12); **moi** (XX, 1.16); **moi** (1.18); **eux** (XXI, 1.24); **moi** (1.24).

2. Explain the use of **en** in XIX, ll.2, 7, 18; XXI, ll.2 and 4; XXIII, ll.12, 23, 30.

3. Explain the use of every preposition governing a proper noun in XXI, A.

4. Account for the following: **de** (XIX, ll. 6 and 14); **du** and **des** (XX, l. 9); **des** (l. 12); **du** (l. 17); **de** (XXI, l. 15); **des** (XXII, l. 8); **d'** (l. 9); **de** (ll. 10 and 14); the absence of the partitive sign in **nouveaux gants** (XXIII, l. 11.)

5. Account for the following verb-forms: **avait** (XX, l. 9); **aurait** (XX, l. 9); **désirions** (l. 22); **aurez** (l. 24); **était** (XXI, l. 8); **désirais** (l. 9); **ai levé** (l. 9); **étais** (l. 10); **avais** (l. 10); **étais** (l. 14); **sont venus** (XXII, l. 5); **passe** (l. 7); **soient** (l. 11); **sommes restés** (l. 12); **fassions** (l. 13); **ait** (l. 15); **suis** (l. 16); **sonnaient** (l. 17); **soyons** (l. 18); **explique** (l. 21); **soyons** (l. 25); **fasse** (l. 26); **finisse** (l. 29); **irez** (XXIII, l. 12); **voie** (l. 15); **fasse** (l. 32); **soyez** (l. 34).

6. Can you explain why we say **Nous sommes partis de la ville,** but **Nous avons quitté la ville?**

B. 1. In front of him. 2. In front of her. 3. I am speaking to him. 4. I was speaking to her. 5. They will walk more rapidly than I. 6. He would do it himself. 7. He and I were finishing. 8. If he is here, I shall be glad. 9. If he were here, I should be glad. 10. In New York. 11. In England. 12. In South America. 13. In Canada. 14. In the United States. 15. In school. 16. The best in the world. 17. In Europe. 18. In America. 19. In winter. 20. In spring. 21. I am warm. 22. He was cold. 23. We shall be hungry. 24. You would be thirsty. 25. If they were afraid. 26. He has been right. 27. You are wrong. 28. We were sleepy. 29. Although he reads books. 30. He is sixteen years old. 31. How old is he? 32. He had a headache. 33. It is warm. 34. Although it is cold. 35. It will be fine. 36. It was windy. 37. Be here early. 38. Let's be there at six o'clock. 39. Let's go there together. 40. Speak to him. 41. Although I have spoken to him. 42. Don't speak to him. 43. I am glad he is here. 44. I am not afraid that he has come. 45. I want him to go. 46. Show it to me. 47. Show me some. 48. Show them to him. 49. Don't show them to me. 50. Don't show him any. 51. He is approaching, isn't he? 52. He was dressing, wasn't he? 53. They have gone on board, haven't they? 54. They will count the money, won't they? 55. You would look at them, wouldn't you?

C. 1. Although he alone has arrived, they will not be afraid. 2. If he doesn't like the room which looks out on the garden, let him look for another. 3. Beside him on the table there were good red apples. 4. If the boat travels fast, we shall be on the open sea before seven o'clock. 5. Were there many people at the hotel where you lived when you were here last year? 6. Although we invited the whole family, we shall have enough room for others. 7. Is it necessary that he see them this morning? 8. If he is hungry, give him some. 9. Don't worry! It won't be cold tomorrow. 10. The bells were ringing when we entered the church. 11. If they hadn't any chocolate, I should say, "Bring us some good hot tea and a few pieces of bread." 12. We were crossing a wide avenue when he let fall his coat. 13. In a corner of his father's room he found some money, which we had been looking for for some time. 14. The children have been playing an hour in the yard behind the school. 15. I told him that if it wasn't too warm we should go there on foot. 16. When did you land in France? It was yesterday, wasn't it? 17. Naturally, I don't want you to have all the best candy; give them some too. 18. When you are free I shall bring them to you, in order that you may see that we have been working this summer. 19. How warm it is today and how calm the sea is! 20. The officers used to stay on deck all night when there was a storm. 21. Although one doesn't always see them, there are five which have been there since yesterday. 22. Although candy is dear, he ordered five pounds for the children. 23. First he must wash his hands; then his mother will give him something to (à) eat. 24. Is it you who want him to sell his house to the men we met yesterday? 25. Whose are those beautiful flowers that arrived an hour ago? 26. Let him be there when I arrive if he wants to see me. 27. You like French hats and French dresses, don't you? 28. Take care; don't awaken him. 29. On the right there were vegetables, on the left there were beautiful flowers and green trees. 30. Americans like ice cream, but there are very few French [people] who eat it.

LESSON XXV

65. Past Definite. Forms. The past definite tense is always derived from the fifth principal part, which is the first person singular of this tense.

When the infinitive ends in **-er,** the fifth principal part ends in **-ai;** the endings of the past definite are then **-ai, -as, -a, -âmes, -âtes, -èrent.**

When the infinitive of a regular verb ends in **-ir** or **-re,** the fifth principal part ends in **-is;** the endings of the past definite are then **-is, -is, -it, -îmes, -îtes, -irent.**

The fifth principal part of an irregular verb may end in **-ai** or **-is,** the rest of the tense following regularly; or it may end in **-us,** in which case the endings of the past definite are **-us, -us, -ut, -ûmes, -ûtes, -urent.**

je donnai [dɔne]	je finis [fini]	je fus [fy] (être)
tu donnas [dɔna]	tu finis [fini]	tu fus [fy]
il donna [dɔna]	il finit [fini]	il fut [fy]
nous donnâmes [dɔnam]	nous finîmes [finim]	nous fûmes [fym]
vous donnâtes [dɔnat]	vous finîtes [finit]	vous fûtes [fyt]
ils donnèrent [dɔnɛːr]	ils finirent [finiːr]	ils furent [fyːr]

From **vendis** [vãdi] (vendre), **eus** [y] (avoir), **allai** [ale] (aller), **fis** [fi] (faire), **vis** [vi] (voir), form the whole past definite.

66. Imperfect Subjunctive. Forms. To form the imperfect subjunctive of any verb, drop the last letter of the fifth principal part (**i** or **s**), then except in the third person singular insert **-ss-** and add the endings of the present subjunctive. In the third person singular, after having dropped the last letter of the fifth principal part, circumflex the vowel and add **t:**

je donna*i*	je fini*s*	je fu*s*
je donnasse [dɔnas]	je finisse [finis]	je fusse [fys]
tu donnasses [dɔnas]	tu finisses [finis]	tu fusses [fys]
il donnât [dɔna]	il finît [fini]	il fût [fy]
nous donnassions [dɔnasjɔ̃]	nous finissions [finisjɔ̃]	nous fussions [fysjɔ̃]
vous donnassiez [dɔnasje]	vous finissiez [finisje]	vous fussiez [fysje]
ils donnassent [dɔnas]	ils finissent [finis]	ils fussent [fys]

67. Uses of Past Definite and Imperfect Subjunctive.

1. The past definite is the *literary past narrative* tense. Since the student is not producing literature when he is writing exercises, he will never use the past definite tense. He must continue to use the past indefinite for the past narrative, and the imperfect indicative to express the special values as explained in Lesson XVII (§48).

2. The imperfect subjunctive, derived from the past definite, is likewise a literary tense and must not be used by the student. See §61.

3. Since the student will constantly meet these two tenses in his reading, it will be well for him to learn them. As both tenses are invariably derived from the fifth principal part, the learning of them requires no great effort.

EXERCISE XXV

A.[1] Après sept heures dans un wagon de chemin de fer, nous arrivâmes à la ville de New-York. Mes parents en étaient contents, et moi aussi. Arrivés à la gare, le conducteur s'écria: «New-York! Tout le monde descend!» Mon frère et moi nous étions à New York pour la première fois. Il y avait beaucoup de monde dans la gare, et nous eûmes de la difficulté à trouver un taxi. Enfin nous en trouvâmes un qui était libre, mais il n'y avait pas assez de place pour toute la famille. Le chauffeur m'invita à monter à côté de lui. Nous descendîmes dans un hôtel pour y passer la nuit. Comme mon frère désirait sortir, ce fut lui qui accompagna ma mère. J'étais trop fatigué, moi; je me couchai donc de bonne heure.

[1] Note—This exercise is that of Lesson XIX re-written in the past tense to illustrate the use of the past definite. Study the exercise carefully, noticing the difference between the past definite (or past indefinite) and the imperfect.

Le matin nous fûmes tous levés avant six heures. Nous fîmes beaucoup de courses, et puis vers midi nous nous rend mes sur le quai pour nous embarquer sur le paquebot. À deux heures le bateau quitta le quai et descendit le fleuve. Un peu plus tard nous vîmes la statue de la Liberté, et avant la nuit nous fûmes en pleine mer.

B. Write the past definite and the imperfect subjunctive of **entendre, choisir, aller, avoir, voir.**

C. Re-write A, using the past indefinite as the narrative past tense.

LESSON XXVI

68. Derivation of Verb-Forms. The learning of irregular verbs, sometimes considered the most difficult part of the study of French, may be made comparatively simple by means of a scheme of derivation which has been given piecemeal in preceding lessons and which is here given in full for the convenience of the student. It will be well to master this scheme before attempting to learn further irregular verbs. There are generally forty-eight forms of a French verb, not including the compounds; these can be mastered by learning at the most eleven forms, often by learning only the principal parts.

69. I. The Infinitive. Verbs are divided into three conjugations according to the infinitive ending: First conjugation, donn-**er**; second conjugation, fin-**ir**; third conjugation, vend-**re**. Verbs having these infinitive endings may be regular or irregular.[1] Some irregular verbs end in **-oir.**

The Future. Stem: In regular verbs and in many irregular verbs the whole infinitive (less the mute **e** when the ending

---

[1] Only two verbs in **-er** are irregular: **aller** and **envoyer.**

LESSON XXVI

TABLE OF DERIVATION OF VERB-FORMS.

I INFINITIVE	II PRESENT PARTICIPLE	III PAST PARTICIPLE	IV 1st SING. PRESENT IND.	V 1st SING. PAST DEFINITE
Future Conditional	Plurals Present Indicative Plural Imperatives Imperfect Indicative Present Subjunctive	Compounds	Singulars Present Ind. Singular Imperative	Past Definite Imperfect Subjunctive

is **-re**) is used as the stem of the future. Irregular verbs may have an irregular future stem, which must be learned. The future stem always ends in **r**. Endings: The future endings are always the same as in the present indicative of **avoir: -ai, -as, -a, -ons, -ez, -ont.**

The Conditional. Stem: The stem of the conditional is always the same as the stem of the future. Endings: The conditional endings are always the same as those of the imperfect indicative: **-ais, -ais, -ait, -ions, -iez, -aient.**

Thus it will be noticed that the future and conditional can always be learned by learning the stem.

II. The Present Participle. In first and third conjugation regular verbs, the stem of the infinitive is also the stem of the present participle; second conjugation verbs insert **-iss-** before adding the ending. Irregular verbs may have an irregular stem. The ending of the present participle is always **-ant**.

Plurals Present Indicative. The three plurals of the present indicative are regularly derived by cutting off the ending (**-ant**) of the second principal part and adding the endings **-ons, -ez, -ent.** In irregular verbs the third plural is often irregular, the first and second plurals rarely.

Plural Imperatives. The plural imperatives are almost invariably the same as the first and second persons plural of the present indicative. **Avoir, être,** and **savoir** are exceptions.

Imperfect Indicative. The imperfect indicative is almost invariably formed by adding to the stem of the present participle the endings **-ais, -ais, -ait, -ions, -iez, -aient.** These endings are always used. The stem varies in **avoir, savoir, échoir.**

Present Subjunctive. The stem of the present subjunctive is usually the same as that of the second principal part.

When the stem of the present subjunctive is not the same as that of the present participle, the change occurs in the first, second, and third persons singular and in the third person plural; the first and second persons plural use the stem of the present participle. Only **être, faire** and **pouvoir** carry the change through the whole tense. Except in **avoir** and **être,** the endings are always **-e, -es, -e, -ions, -iez, -ent.**

III. The Past Participle. The endings of the past participle in the three conjugations are **-é, -i, -u.** These are added to the stem of the infinitive. An irregular verb may have an irregular past participle.

Compound Tenses. The compound tenses are formed by adding the past participle to the proper form of the proper auxiliary. **Être** is the auxiliary with (1) most intransitive verbs expressing motion (a few exceptions: **marcher, courir,** etc.), (2) most intransitive verbs expressing change of state (a few exceptions: **grandir, mûrir,** etc.), (3) all reflexive verbs, (4) the verbs *to remain* (**rester** and **demeurer**) and *to happen* (**arriver**). **Avoir** is used with other verbs.

The past participle in a compound tense agrees in gender and number with a preceding direct object, whether the auxiliary be **avoir** or **être.** There is no agreement, however, with the partitive pronoun **en.**

When **être** is the auxiliary and the verb is not reflexive, the past participle agrees in gender and number with the subject.

Passive Voice. The passive voice is formed by adding the past participle to the proper form of **être,** as in English. See the second rule for agreement above.

IV. First Singular of the Present Indicative. The fourth principal part has the following endings: first conjugation, **-e;** second conjugation, **-is;** third conjugation, **-s.** These are added to the stem of the infinitive. Irregular verbs may vary.

Singulars Present Indicative. The ending of the first person singular of the present indicative being **-e,** the other two are **-es** and **-e;** the first being **-is,** the others are **-is** and **-it;** the first being **-s,** the others are **-s** and **-t** (but this **t** is omitted if the stem ends in **c, d,** or **t**). Irregular verbs may have **-x, -x, -t,** or entirely irregular endings, as well as irregular stems.

Singular Imperative. The singular imperative is usually the same as the second person singular of the present indicative, except that **s** is dropped when the latter form ends in **-es,** also in **aller.** However, this **s** is retained before **y** or **en: Vas-y. Donnes-en.** A few irregular verbs have entirely different imperatives: **Avoir, tu as, aie; Être, tu es, sois; Savoir, tu sais, sache.**

V. First Singular of the Past Definite. The fifth principal part in the first conjugation ends in **-ai;** in the second and third conjugations, in **-is.** Some irregular verbs have the ending **-us.**

The stem remains the same throughout the tense. Three sets of endings are possible; the fifth principal part always determines the other forms: (1) **-ai, -as, -a, -âmes, -âtes, èrent;** (2) **-is, -is, -it, -îmes, -îtes, -irent;** (3) **-us, -us, -ut, -ûmes, -ûtes, -urent.** Note the similarity in the plural. Note also that the second and third sets of endings are alike except in the first letter.

Imperfect Subjunctive. To form this tense, drop the last letter of the fifth principal part (**i** or **s**), and in all except the third person singular insert **-ss-** and add the endings of the present subjunctive; but in the third singular, circumflex the vowel (**a, i,** or **u**) and add **t.**

Note 1. When the **i** is nasal (as in **venir** and **tenir**), the **n** which nasalizes must be retained throughout: **vins, vins, vint, vînmes, vîntes, vinrent; vinsse, vinsses, vînt, vinssions, vinssiez, vinssent.**

Note 2. The circumflex is not written in these two tenses when the diæresis occurs: **haïmes, haïtes; haït** (from **haïr**).

70. To illustrate, let us study the verb **aller.** We shall attempt to derive the tenses in order from the principal parts, and shall put in bold-face type the forms that cannot be derived and must therefore be learned.

Prin. Parts: **aller, allant, allé, je vais, j'allai.**
Pres. Ind.: Sing. from IV: je **vais,** tu **vas,** il **va**
          Plu. from II: nous allons, vous allez, ils **vont**
Imperatives: Sing. from IV: **va**
          Plu. from II: allons, allez
Imperfect Ind. from II: j'allais, tu allais, il allait, nous allions, vous alliez, ils allaient.
Future from I: j'**ir**ai, tu iras, il ira, nous irons, vous irez, ils iront
Cond. from I: j'**ir**ais, tu irais, il irait, nous irions, vous iriez, ils iraient
Past Def. from V: j'allai, tu allas, il alla, nous allâmes, vous allâtes, ils allèrent
Pres. Subj. from II: j'**aille,** tu ailles, il aille, nous allions,
                vous alliez, ils aillent (*Watch stem change.*)
Imperf. Subj. from V: j'allasse, tu allasses, il allât, nous allassions,
                 vous allassiez, ils allassent.

We note, then, that besides the principal parts (5)—only one of which differs from a regular verb of the first conjugation—we must learn the second (6) and third (7) persons singular and the third person plural (8) of the present indicative, the singular imperative (9), the future stem (10), and the present subjunctive stem (11). This is the most irregular verb in French.

Review the verbs **avoir, être, faire,** and **voir.**

For a summary of the three conjugations and **avoir** and **être,** see the Appendix, p. 228.

LESSON XXVII

71. Demonstrative Pronouns. Invariable forms: **ce** [sə], **ceci** [səsi], **cela** [səla] (familiarly shortened to **ça** [sa]); variable forms: **celui** [səlɥi] (masc. sing.), **celle** [sɛl] (fem. sing.), **ceux** [sø] (masc. plu.), **celles** [sɛl] (fem. plu.). To the variable forms may be added **-ci** or **-là**, thus: **celui-ci, celui-là,** etc.

72. Uses of ce. 1. **Ce** is rarely used as the subject of any verb but **être**. It is the grammatical subject of some form of the verb **être** when the logical subject following is a determinate noun [1] (or an adjective used as such) or a pronoun. It may mean *he, she, it, they, this, that, these, those:*

Qui est cet homme? C'est mon frère. *Who is that man? He is my brother.*
C'est moi qui ai parlé. *It was I who spoke.*
C'est une rusée. *She is a sly one.*
Regardez-les. Ce sont les miens. *Look at them. Those are mine.*
Ce sont[2] les hommes que vous cherchez. *They are the men you are seeking.*

2. **Ce** is used as the antecedent of a relative to express the English *what*, equivalent to *that which:*

Il me dit **ce que** vous faites. *He tells me what you do.*
Il m'a dit **ce qui** est arrivé. *He told me what happened.*

3. **Ce** is sometimes used to sum up what goes before:

Il a fait beaucoup de mal, c'est vrai. *He has done much harm, that is true.*
Il m'a dit que vous étiez parti, ce qui n'était pas vrai. *He told me that you had left, (that) which was not true.*
Ce qu'il ne sait pas, c'est que tu es ma sœur. *What he does not know, (it) is that you are my sister.*

73. Uses of ceci and cela. **Ceci** (*this*) and **cela** (*that*) are used to call attention to something not definitely named:

Ceci n'est pas à moi. *This (this thing—not named) is not mine.*
Envoyez-lui cela. *Send him that (that thing).*
Cela m'a fait beaucoup de peine. *That caused me much pain.*

---

[1] But: Elle est mère. Il est général. Il est malheureux.
[2] When the logical subject is third person plural, the verb is generally third person plural: C'est moi. C'est elle. C'est nous. C'est vous. But: Ce sont eux. Ce sont mes amis.

74. Uses of the Variable Forms. The variable form must, of course, agree in gender and number with the antecedent. The shorter form (without **-ci** or **-là**) must be followed by a relative or the preposition **de**:

> Celui qui parle est mon frère. *He (the one, that one) who is speaking is my brother.*
>
> Voici mes plumes et celles de mon frère. *Here are my pens and my brother's (those of my brother).*
>
> Montrez-moi ceux que vous avez achetés. *Show me the ones you bought.*

If neither **de** nor a relative follows, the longer form must be used:

> Donnez-moi une autre plume; je n'aime pas celle-ci. *Give me a different pen; I don't like this one.*

To distinguish between *this one* and *that one*, *these* and *those*, it is necessary to use the longer forms:

> J'ai acheté deux livres; celui-ci est un livre anglais, celui-là est un livre français. *I bought two books; this is an English book, that is a French book.*

Celui-là (**celle-là,** etc.) may mean *the former* and **celui-ci** (**celle-ci,** etc.) *the latter.* If the forms are used in two clauses, the one in which *the latter* occurs comes first, reversing the usual English order:

> J'ai deux frères, Jean et Robert; celui-ci (Robert) est médecin et celui-là (Jean) est avocat. *I have two brothers, John and Robert; the former (John) is a lawyer and the latter (Robert) is a doctor.*

Note—Since no form of **tout** can stand as the antecedent of a relative, the demonstrative must be inserted before a relative following *all*:

> Il m'a dit tout **ce** qu'il en savait. *He told me all that (all that which) he knew about it.*
>
> Nous avons vu tous **ceux** qui y étaient. *We saw all (those) who were there.*

75. partir (*to leave*)   partant parti [1]   je pars   je partis
   sortir (*to go out*)   sortant sorti [1]   je sors   je sortis
   dormir (*to sleep*)   dormant dormi   je dors   je dormis

From the above forms, derive the whole verb.

EXERCISE XXVII

acteur [aktœːr] m. *actor*
actrice [aktris] f. *actress*
affiche [afiʃ] f. *bill, placard*
annoncer [anɔ̃se] *to announce*
apprendre [aprɑ̃ːdr] *to learn*
attendre [atɑ̃ːdr] *to wait (for), expect*
bâton [batɔ̃] m. *stick*
billet [bijɛ] m. *ticket, note*
bois [bwa] m. *wood*
bureau [byro] m. *office*
coûter [kute] *to cost*
(se) dépêcher [depɛʃe] *to hurry*
écouter [ekute] *to listen (to)*
entr'acte [ɑ̃trakt] m. *intermission*
frapper [frape] *to knock, strike*
guichet [giʃɛ] m. *ticket window*
intéressant [ɛ̃terɛsɑ̃] *interesting*

matinée [matine] f. *morning; afternoon performance*
moderne [mɔdɛrn] *modern*
moyen [mwajɛ̃] m. *means*
ouvert [uvɛːr] *open*
parmi [parmi] *among*
pièce [pjɛs] f. *play; coin*
prochain [prɔʃɛ̃] *next*
queue [kø] f. *queue, tail, line*
(se) reposer [rəpoze] *to rest*
rideau [rido] m. *curtain*
scène [sɛn] f. *scene, stage*
signal [siɲal] m. *signal*
sonnette [sɔnɛt] f. *(small) bell*
théâtre [teɑtr] m. *theater*
voix [vwa] f. *voice*

   (billets) en location [lɔkasjɔ̃] f. *reserved (seats)*
   faire la queue *to stand in line*

A. Qu'est-ce que c'est que ceci? Je vais vous dire ce que c'est: c'est mon billet; nous allons au théâtre jeudi prochain. Nous avons vu les affiches qui annoncent une pièce moderne à l'Odéon, et "Andromaque" pour la matinée
5 au Théâtre-Français. Je pensais que nous trouverions celle-ci plus intéressante que celle-là. Nous sommes allés au bureau, mais le guichet n'était pas encore ouvert. Nous avons donc attendu pour avoir des billets, bien qu'ils coûtent plus cher en location: nous n'aimons pas à faire la queue.

[1] Auxiliary?

Après le déjeuner nous nous sommes dépêchés; le rideau était à deux heures. Nous sommes montés dans le tram, celui qui passe près du Louvre. En approchant du théâtre nous avons entendu les sonnettes, et nous avons vite trouvé nos places. On frappait déjà sur la scène avec un bâton de bois: c'est là (=cela est) le signal qu'on va tout de suite commencer.

Parmi les actrices nous avons aimé le mieux celle qui a joué Andromaque. Comme elle est belle! Et puis, quelle belle voix! Nous écoutions bien. Mon père nous a dit que pour ceux qui désirent apprendre le français c'est un des meilleurs moyens. Pendant les entr'actes tout le monde sort. Comme cela, on se repose un peu en marchant. Nous comptons retourner souvent à ce théâtre.

B. 1. I like this. 2. He bought that. 3. We brought this one (*look*). 4. They sold that one (*house*). 5. He is my brother. 6. What is it? 7. This hat and my father's (that of my father). 8. Your pen and my sister's. 9. This book and those we saw yesterday. 10. These ladies and those who will arrive tomorrow. 11. He told me all he had heard. 12. I invited all that I saw. 13. He sent me what I wanted. 14. He told me what happened. 15. Who are those two men? They are my friends. 16. He is sleeping. 17. He leaves. 18. He is going out. 19. He has slept. 20. He has left. 21. He was leaving. 22. They are going out. 23. We are sleeping. 24. We were sleeping. 25. Although he sleeps. 26. Although I am leaving. 27. We shall leave. 28. They would leave. 29. Let's go out. 30. Sleep.

C. 1. He told me you were working, which was what I desired. 2. My books and my sister's are all on the table. 3. I like this bread better than that which you bought yesterday. 4. Which apple do you want? The one which is on that table over there. 5. He lost all that he had.

6. When he arrives he will tell me all that is interesting. 7. This train goes faster than the one that started two hours ago. 8. That is more expensive than this. 9. Was it your uncle who told you that? 10. What he hasn't told me is what you paid for that hat 11. Give him that one (pencil), and send these to your sister. 12. I have seen Charles and Philip; the latter is now at home. 13. There are three books; this one is a French book, those are English books. 14. When they went out I was sleeping. 15. We approached the ticket window and asked for three tickets, which my cousin paid for. 16. When the curtain rose, the actor was striking the table with (**de**) his hand. 17. We had been resting only a few moments when they announced that you were leaving. 18. As I do not like to (**à**) stand in line, I always prefer (like better) reserved seats. 19. I listened to him while he spoke of his travels. 20. I hurried, but he arrived before me. 21. The next time I see him I shall tell (it to) him. 22. He stayed at home and worked all morning. 23. If the office is not open, I shall go back (there) tomorrow. 24. Of all the plays I have seen I like this one the best.

D. 1. Qu'est-ce que vous avez acheté? 2. Où les avez-vous achetés? 3. Quelle pièce joue-t-on au Théâtre-Français? 4. Aimez-vous à faire la queue? 5. Qu'est-ce que vous avez fait après le déjeuner? 6. Par quel tramway êtes-vous partis? 7. Qu'avez-vous entendu en approchant du théâtre? 8. Quel est le signal qu'on va commencer? 9. Quelle actrice avez-vous trouvée la meilleure? 10. Avez-vous bien écouté? Pourquoi? 11. Que fait-on pendant les entr'actes? 12. Comptez-vous retourner à ce théâtre?

LESSON XXVIII

76. Peculiarities of First-Conjugation Verbs. 1. If there is a mute **e** (see p. 12) in the last syllable of the stem of an infinitive of the first conjugation, the mute **e** must become an open **e** [ɛ] whenever there is a mute **e** in the following syllable, that is, in the three singulars and the third plural of the present indicative and of the present subjunctive, in the singular imperative, and throughout the future and the conditional. This is accomplished in some verbs by writing a grave accent (**è**), in others by doubling a following consonant. Note the changes in **acheter** [aʃte] and **appeler** [aple]:

Pres. Ind.:	j'achète [aʃɛt]	nous achetons [aʃtɔ̃]
	tu achètes [aʃɛt]	vous achetez [aʃte]
	il achète [aʃɛt]	ils achètent [aʃɛt]
	j'appelle [apɛl]	nous appelons [aplɔ̃]
	tu appelles [apɛl]	vous appelez [aple]
	il appelle [apɛl]	ils appellent [apɛl]
Pres. Subj.:	j'achète [aʃɛt]	nous achetions [aʃtjɔ̃]
	tu achètes [aʃɛt]	vous achetiez [aʃtje]
	il achète [aʃɛt]	ils achètent [aʃɛt]
	j'appelle [apɛl]	nous appelions [apljɔ̃] [apəljɔ̃]
	tu appelles [apɛl]	vous appeliez [aplje] [apəlje]
	il appelle [apɛl]	ils appellent [apɛl]
Sing. Imp.:	achète [aʃɛt]	
	appelle [apɛl]	
Future:	j'achèterai [aʃɛtre]	nous achèterons [aʃɛtrɔ̃]
	tu achèteras [aʃɛtra]	vous achèterez [aʃɛtre]
	il achètera [aʃɛtra]	ils achèteront [aʃɛtrɔ̃]
	j'appellerai [apɛlre]	nous appellerons [apɛlrɔ̃]
	tu appelleras [apɛlra]	vous appellerez [apɛlre]
	il appellera [apɛlra]	ils appelleront [apɛlrɔ̃]
Conditional:	j'achèterais [aʃɛtrɛ]	nous achèterions [aʃɛtriɔ̃]
	tu achèterais [aʃɛtrɛ]	vous achèteriez [aʃɛtrie]
	il achèterait [aʃɛtrɛ]	ils achèteraient [aʃɛtrɛ]
	j'appellerais [apɛlrɛ]	nous appellerions [apɛlriɔ̃]
	tu appellerais [apɛlrɛ]	vous appelleriez [apɛlrie]
	il appellerait [apɛlrɛ]	ils appelleraient [apɛlrɛ]

Notice **mener** [məne], je **mène** [mɛn]; **jeter** [ʒəte], je **jette** [ʒɛt]; etc.

2. If there is an acute **e** (**é**) in the last syllable of the stem of an infinitive of the first conjugation, the acute **e** becomes a grave **e** (**è**) wherever the stress falls upon it, that is, in the three singulars and the third plural of the present indicative and of the present subjunctive and in the singular imperative, but *not* in the future and the conditional:

céder [sede]: je cède [sɛd], tu cèdes [sɛd], il cède [sɛd], nous cédons [sedɔ̃], vous cédez [sede], ils cèdent [sɛd]; but je céderai [sedre], etc.

This change does not take place, however, in verbs like **créer,** in which no consonant follows the acute **e: je crée** [kre], etc.

3. Verbs in **-cer** or **-ger** change **c** to **ç** and **g** to **ge** (to retain the soft sound) immediately before an ending beginning with **a** or **o**:

commencer: nous commençons, je commençais, etc.
manger: nous mangeons, je mangeais, etc.

4. Verbs ending in **-oyer** or **-uyer** change **y** to **i** before a mute **e**:

employer: j'emploie, j'emploierai, etc.
ennuyer: il s'ennuie, etc.

Verbs ending in **-ayer** *may* change **y** to **i** before a mute **e**:

payer: je paye or je paie, etc.

Note—In irregular verbs, **oy** changes to **oi** and a mute **e** becomes an open **e** when there is a mute **e** in the following syllable:

voir, voyant: ils voient, bien que je voie, etc.
prendre, prenant: ils prennent, bien que je prenne, etc.

77. envoyer *(to send)* envoyant envoyé j'envoie j'envoyai
Fut. Stem: *Watch*
   enverr-   *vowel*
                change.

Le Palais du Louvre, Paris

Le Musée de Cluny, Paris

EXERCISE XXVIII

agréablement [agreabləmā] *agreeably*
ainsi [ɛ̃si] *thus*
appeler [aple] *to call*
argot [argo] m. *slang*
asseoir [aswaːr] p.p. **assis** [asi] *to seat*
autobus [otɔbys] m. *autobus*
boulevard [bulvaːr] m. *boulevard*
circulation [sirkylasjɔ̃] f. *traffic, communication*
collège [kɔlɛːʒ] m. *college*
connaître [kɔnɛːtr] *to know, be acquainted with*
écrire [ekriːr] *to write*
emplette [ɑ̃plɛt] f. *purchase*
employer [ɑ̃plwaje] *to use, employ*
espérer [ɛspere] *to hope*

historique [istɔrik] *historical*
latin [latɛ̃] *Latin*
mener [məne] *to lead, conduct, take*
moyen âge [mwajɛn‿aːʒ] m. *Middle Ages*
musée [myze] m. *museum*
objet [ɔbʒɛ] m. *object*
occupé [ɔkype] *busy, occupied*
Parisien [parizjɛ̃] *Parisian*
partie [parti] f. *part*
partout [partu] *everywhere*
peut-être [pøt‿ɛːtr] *perhaps*
à présent [prezɑ̃] m. *at present, now*
souterrain [sutɛrɛ̃] *underground*
système [sistɛːm] m. *system*
trottoir [trɔtwaːr] m. *sidewalk*

de temps en temps [də tɑ̃z‿ɑ̃ tɑ̃] *from time to time*
faire des emplettes *to shop*

A. Nous commençons à connaître assez bien Paris, parce que presque tous les jours mon père nous mène dans quelque quartier de la ville que nous n'avons pas encore visité. Les moyens de circulation sont si bons: des autobus, des tramways, et le Métro—c'est ainsi qu'on appelle le Métropolitain, le système des chemins de fer souterrains à Paris. Nous sommes donc si occupés que nous avons très peu de temps pour écrire des lettres; de temps en temps j'envoie des cartes à mes amis aux États-Unis, c'est tout ce que je fais à présent. Plus tard j'aurai peut-être plus de temps.

Ainsi, par exemple, hier nous sommes allés dans le quartier des écoles, qu'on appelle le Quartier Latin. C'est une des parties les plus anciennes de Paris. Nous avons visité la Sorbonne, le Collège de France, et le Musée de Cluny, que nous avons trouvé très, très intéressant. C'est celui où se trouvent toutes sortes d'objets historiques du moyen âge. Après cela nous nous sommes assis devant un café sur le Boulevard Saint-Michel, que les étudiants appellent dans leur argot Boul-Mich [bul miʃ]. Partout à Paris on trouve des tables et des chaises sur les trottoirs, et on voit des Parisiens et des Parisiennes qui commandent du café, du thé, du vin, ou quelque chose à manger. On se repose, on parle, et l'on[1] passe très agréablement une heure en regardant passer le monde.

J'espère que le beau temps va continuer; mais s'il pleut demain nous emploierons la journée à faire des emplettes; nous irons dans les grands magasins, nous achèterons toutes sortes de choses, et plus tard nous les enverrons en Amérique. Mais qui les paiera? Je n'ai pas d'argent, moi.

B. 1. He buys. 2. We buy. 3. I was beginning. 4. Let's eat. 5. They will lead. 6. We should hope. 7. We hope. 8. They hope. 9. They use. 10. They will use. 11. You use. 12. They used to eat. 13. He ate (*past definite*). 14. They ate (*past definite*). 15. We call. 16. They call. 17. Although he calls. 18. We shall call. 19. I send. 20. I shall send. 21. I have sent. 22. I was sending. 23. Although I am sending. 24. He would send. 25. He sends. 26. Let's send. 27. He pays. 28. He takes a walk. 29. We shall take a walk. 30. We take a walk.

---

[1] The "euphonic" **l'** may be inserted before the indefinite pronoun **on** when **on** is preceded by a conjunction (or a relative pronoun) which ends in a pronounced vowel or in a consonant that cannot be linked; however, the **l'** is not used if a closely following word begins with **l**. Instead of eliding the **e** of **que** before **on**, the **l'** is generally inserted if a closely following word begins with a **k**-sound:

La maison où l'on passera la nuit . . .
But: La maison où on les trouvera . . .
Et l'on pourra recommencer.
But: Quand on [kɑ̃t‿ɔ̃] pourra recommencer . . .
Les livres qu'on regardait . . .
But: Les livres que l'on comptait . . .

C. 1. He was announcing that there wouldn't be any classes today. 2. I did notice this: Parisians often take their children to the parks when the weather is fine. 3. I hope that you will make some purchases this morning so that the merchant may send what you buy before this evening. 4. In their office they employ six girls and ten young men. 5. Traffic is sometimes very difficult in Paris because there are so many taxicabs; they cost much less (dearly) than in New York. 6. Everywhere I saw many people (who were) eating at small tables on the sidewalks. 7. In (**à**) the Middle Ages, Paris was already a rather large city. 8. In the Latin Quarter one hears much slang: it is the students' quarter, a very old part of the city. 9. He will not write any letters this evening: he has been so busy for some days that he is too tired. 10. There is always something to (**à**) do in Paris; when the weather is too bad to (**pour**) go out, we go to the museums. 11. We must hurry if we want to get (take) tickets for that interesting play. 12. Isn't that stick the one that they use to announce that the play is going to begin? 13. I gave him what he asked for; but he wasn't satisfied. 14. Between him and me there were four old ladies who were beginning to (**à**) be afraid. 15. Let the cook take him to the kitchen and give him something to (**à**) eat.

D. 1. Est-ce que vous commencez à connaître Paris? 2. Qu'est-ce que votre père fait pour vous presque tous les jours? 3. Est-ce qu'on va facilement d'une partie de la ville à l'autre? 4. Quels moyens de circulation y a-t-il? 5. Trouvez-vous le Métro confortable? 6. Qu'est-ce que vous envoyez à vos amis? 7. Où êtes-vous allés hier? 8. Est-ce un quartier intéressant? 9. Qu'est-ce qu'il y a à voir au musée de Cluny? 10. Est-ce que les étudiants de Paris parlent argot? 11. Où est-ce que vous vous êtes reposés? 12. Y a-t-il beaucoup de cafés à Paris?

LESSON XXIX

78. Possessive Pronouns. The student must be careful to distinguish between a possessive adjective and a possessive pronoun. If the possessive modifies a noun, it is an adjective, the forms of which are given in Lesson V.; but if the possessive stands for a noun, it is a pronoun. Thus, in *Where is your hat? Mine is on the chair.*, **your** modifies **hat:** it is an adjective; **mine** stands for **my hat:** it is a pronoun.

79. Forms:

Singular	Plural	
le mien [mjɛ̃] m.	les miens [mjɛ̃] m.	*mine*
la mienne [mjɛn] f.	les miennes [mjɛn] f.	
le tien [tjɛ̃] m.	les tiens [tjɛ̃] m.	*thine*
la tienne [tjɛn] f.	les tiennes [tjɛn] f.	
le sien [sjɛ̃] m.	les siens [sjɛ̃] m.	*his, hers, its*
la sienne [sjɛn] f.	les siennes [sjɛn] f.	
le *or* la nôtre [noːtr]	les nôtres [noːtr]	*ours*
le *or* la vôtre [voːtr]	les vôtres [voːtr]	*yours*
le *or* la leur [lœːr]	les leurs [lœːr]	*theirs*

80. Uses. A possessive pronoun agrees in gender and number with its antecedent. Note especially that the form for *his*, *hers*, or *its*, is determined by the gender and number of the noun for which it stands, not by the gender of the possessor.

Following **de** or **à,** the definite article of the possessive contracts with the preposition in the usual places.

Sa plume et la mienne sont sur la table. *His* (or *her*) *pen and mine are on the table.*

Où sont nos livres? Les vôtres sont ici; je n'ai pas encore trouvé les miens. *Where are our books? Yours are here; I haven't yet found mine.*

Les parents de son père et du mien sont arrivés. *The relatives of his* (or *her*) *father and of mine have arrived.*

Voici mon crayon et le sien. *Here are my pencil and his* (or *hers*).

LESSON XXIX

81. Possession Expressed in the Predicate. In the predicate, possession is generally expressed by **à** and a noun or pronoun. The possessive pronoun used in the predicate is emphatic.

> Ce livre est à son père. *This book is his father's.*
> Ce livre est à moi. *This book is mine.*
> But: Ce livre est le mien. *This book is* **mine** (not *yours* or *his*).

82. pouvoir (*to be able*)   pouvant[1]   pu   je peux[2]   je pus
 Fut. Stem: *3rd plu. pres. ind.*
 pourr-   ils peuvent
        Pres. subj. stem:
        puiss- [3]

[1] No imperatives.

[2] An alternative form, **je puis,** must be used in the inverted order: **puis-je.** In other cases, **je puis** or **je peux** may be used indifferently. The other two singulars of the present indicative are derived from **je peux.**

[3] This irregular stem is used throughout the present subjunctive tense.

EXERCISE XXIX

actuel, -le [aktɥɛl] *present* (adj.)
aimable [ɛmabl] *lovable, kind*
air [ɛːr] m. *air; appearance*
amuser [amyze] *to amuse*
 s'amuser *to have a good time*
s'appeler *to be called*
après-midi [aprɛmidi] m. *or* f. *afternoon*
autrefois [otrəfwa] *formerly*
camarade [kamarad] m. *or* f. *comrade, mate*
changer [ʃɑ̃ʒe] *to change*
Chine [ʃin] f. *China*
chinois [ʃinwa] *Chinese*
cœur [kœːr] m. *heart*
compagnon [kɔ̃paɲɔ̃] m. *companion*
comprendre [kɔ̃prɑ̃ːdr] *to understand*
concierge [kɔ̃sjɛrʒ] m. *or* f. *porter*

corps [kɔːr] m. *body*
dedans [dədɑ̃] *within, in it, in them*
distinguer [distɛ̃ge] *to distinguish*
employé, -e [ɑ̃plwaje] m., f. *employé*
épaule [epoːl] f. *shoulder*
fâché [faʃe] *angry,* ——**(de)** *sorry*
fier, fière [fjɛːr] *proud*
fond [fɔ̃] m. *bottom, back, farther end*
franc [frɑ̃] m. *franc (French coin)*
 normally about twenty cents
géant [ʒeɑ̃] m. *giant*
gentil, —le [ʒɑ̃ti, ʒɑ̃tiːj] *nice*
habiter [abite] *to live in, inhabit*
haut [o] *high; aloud*
louer [lwe] *to rent; to praise*
lumière [lymjɛːr] f. *light*
même [mɛːm] *same; very;* (adj.); *even* (adv.)

numéro [nymero] m. *number*
or [ɔːr] m. *gold*
pouvoir [puvwaːr] *to be able*
président [prezidɑ̃] m. *president*

quart [kaːr] m. *quarter (one-fourth)*
(se) rappeler [raple] *to remember*
renvoyer [rɑ̃vwaje] *to send back (or away)*

aller (venir, etc) **à la rencontre** ([rɑ̃kɔ̃ːtr] f.) **de** ⎱ *to go (come,* etc.)
aller (venir, etc.) **au-devant de** ⎰   *to meet*
avoir l'air *to seem*
C'est dommage! [dɔmaːʒ] m. *It's a pity!*
en retard [r(ə)taːr] m. *late*
Comment vous appelez-vous? *What's your name?*
Je m'appelle Charles. *My name is Charles.*
tous les deux *both*

A. Cet après-midi un de mes amis est arrivé d'Amérique. C'est un de mes anciens camarades de classe. Sa mère et la mienne habitaient autrefois le même petit village quand elles étaient jeunes filles. Ma mère et moi sommes allés à
5 la gare à sa rencontre. Le train était un peu en retard, mais enfin il est arrivé. Mon ami a eu pour compagnon de voyage un jeune Chinois, fils du président actuel de la Chine. Quel gentil garçon!

Nous leur avons dit qu'ils pourraient peut-être avoir des
10 chambres dans la pension où nous demeurons, et nous les y avons menés tous les deux. Il y avait encore deux petites chambres libres au fond de la maison sur la cour où il y a beaucoup d'air et de lumière; ils les ont louées huit francs par jour. Quand le concierge a monté la malle à la chambre
15 de mon ami, celui-ci s'est écrié: «Mais cette malle-là n'est pas à moi; la mienne est plus longue et moins haute.» Le concierge l'a donc descendue et on l'a renvoyée à la gare. On a trouvé qu'un employé du chemin de fer avait changé les numéros des malles. Après un quart d'heure, mon ami
20 a pu trouver la sienne, et il n'en était pas fâché, je vous assure, parce qu'il avait besoin des vêtements qui se trouvaient dedans. Ç'aurait été dommage s'il l'avait perdue. Je ne puis pas comprendre comment cela est arrivé.

LESSON XXIX

Pour celui qui ne le connaît pas bien, mon ami a l'air un peu fier; mais il est très aimable. Il est grand et fort, large d'épaules—il a le corps d'un géant et le cœur d'or d'un enfant. Il s'appelle Philippe, comme mon frère. Je me rappelle que quand nous étions petits, nous l'appelions «le grand Philippe» pour le distinguer de mon frère, que tout le monde appelle toujours «le petit Philippe». Que nous allons nous amuser ensemble!

B. 1. His hat and mine. 2. Your purchases and mine. 3. My tickets and yours. 4. Their friends and ours. 5. Your voice and hers. 6. Her mother and his. 7. This cup is ours. 8. These cups are ours. 9. This knife is my brother's. 10. Of her friend and mine. 11. To their friends and his. 12. I am able. 13. Can I? 14. We should be able. 15. They will be able. 16. He can. 17. We have been able. 18. I used to be able. 19. Although he can. 20. Although we can. 21. They could (*past definite*). 22. Although they could. 23. They can. 24. We can. 25. I should have been able. 26. He remembers. 27. His name is John. 28. We change. 29. He used to change. 30. He doesn't understand.

C. 1. Our present teacher is not so tall as the one we had last year. 2. The latter could not stay because he always had a headache. 3. He is going to his father's, where he will be able to rest for several months. 4. I cannot tell you what my teacher's name is: he hasn't told (it to) us yet. 5. Do you remember what a good time we had (how we amused ourselves) at his house one afternoon last week? 6. But I am sorry to say that it was that same day that Charles broke his arm. 7. There is a former classmate of my cousin Philip. Isn't he nice? He now lives in this city: number nineteen, University Street. 8. If he were still living in England, he couldn't come to see us so often. 9. Aren't you glad that our room is at the back of the house? 10. Of course, we can't see people pass in the street; but I shouldn't like to hear the autobuses pass at all hours (*singular*) of the night. 11. If they ask more than fifteen francs for (**pour**) that little statue, I shall send it back to the store. 12. Can you tell me if he will understand me if I speak Chinese to him? 13. Formerly he used to rent that room at five francs a (the) day; now he pays nine francs [for] it. 14. I cannot stay long in this room; it hasn't enough light and air. 15. Your hat and mine are on the table; that one on the chair is my father's.

D. 1. Qui est arrivé hier? 2. Qui est allé au-devant de lui? 3. Le train était-il en retard? 4. Qui a accompagné votre ami? 5. Où les avez-vous menés? 6. Est-ce qu'ils ont loué des chambres dans votre pension? 7. Où sont ces chambres? 8. Combien les paient-ils? 9. Est-ce que votre ami a eu de la difficulté à trouver sa malle? 10. Comment est-ce que cela est arrivé? 11. Votre ami est-il petit? 12. Comment s'appelle-t-il?

E. 1. Note that the **u** in **distinguer,** although it occurs in all of the forms of the verb, is always silent. 2. Note that in **franc,** the final **c** is silent after the nasal. 3. Note that the final **l** in **gentil** is silent.

LESSON XXX

REVIEW

A. 1. What are the five principal parts of a French verb? 2. What forms are derived from each of the principal parts? 3. How is the future tense formed in regular verbs? In irregular verbs what part of the future may be irregular? 4. Having the future of any verb, how can we form the conditional? 5. How are the plurals of the present indicative formed? Which of these forms is often irregular? 6. Having the first and second persons plural of the present indicative, how do we form the plural imperatives? Are there many exceptions? 7. How is the imperfect indicative formed? Give two exceptions. 8. When the stem of the present subjunctive is irregular, in which of the forms of the tense does the irregularity occur? What is the stem of the other forms? In which verbs is the irregularity found throughout the tense? 9. Explain the two difficulties in connection with the formation of compound tenses: the use of the auxiliary and the agreement of the past participle. 10. What sequences are found in the endings of the singulars of the present indicative of regular verbs? What additional sequence may be found in irregular verbs? 11. How is the singular imperative formed? 12. Give the possible sequences in the endings of the past definite. Are there any variations within the tense? 13. How is the imperfect subjunctive formed? 14. Explain the uses of the imperfect indicative, the past indefinite, and the past definite. 15. Review all the verbs studied thus far.

B. 1. I am going. 2. If they had. 3. They would be. 4. They made (*p. def.*). 5. Seeing. 6. They have departed. 7. They have slept. 8. You would send. 9. He can. 10. He goes. 11. They will have. 12. Let us be. 13. I have made. 14. They see. 15. Although you can. 16. He leads. 17. They go. 18. Have (*polite imperative*). 19. He used to be. 20. You will see. 21. We should call. 22. You would buy. 23. Let's go. 24. He would have. 25. You have been. 26. He employs. 27. I shall make. 28. Although he goes. 29. He was (*p. def.*). 30. We used to see. 31. He is leaving. 32. They could (*p. def.*). 33. He was eating. 34. We shall go. 35. They have had. 36. Although we make. 37. I was leaving. 38. I can (*two ways*). 39. Let's begin. 40. They have gone. 41. Although he had. 42. We were making. 43. They will go out. 44. He had seen. 45. They can. 46. I hope. 47. They went (*p. def.*). 48. You are making. 49. We shall be able. 50. He sends. 51. I saw mine and my father's (*pens*). 52. It is I. 53. It is they. 54. I heard what he said. 55. He told me what has happened. 56. What have you? 57. What book have you? 58. Who is it? 59. Give me that. 60. I don't want this. 61. This one (*knife*). 62. That one (*fork*). 63. The one (*pencil*) on the table. 64. Those (*men*) to whom I was speaking. 65. He has all he wants. 66. Yours and hers (*mother*). 67. Theirs and ours (*friends*). 68. This ink is mine. 69. Those shoes are my brother's. 70. To his (*father*) from mine.

C. 1. Do you like this actor better than the ones we saw yesterday at the Théâtre-Français? 2. He is more handsome than they, but his voice is not so good as that of the man we heard last night. 3. We stood in line for (during) more than two hours because we hadn't any reserved seats. 4. He takes me everywhere when he isn't too busy. 5. Can they understand the play if they haven't read (**lu**) it? 6. If he had listened to you, he would have heard what you said. 7. His mother and mine will be able to spend the day there very agreeably. 8. What is your brother's name? How old is he? 9. Did they sit down in front of the office to wait for their tickets and ours? 10. The next (*precedes noun*) time I see (*future*) him I shall tell him that she has left. 11. From time to time we sent the maid to the porter's to ask whether (if) you had returned home. 12. Would you be glad if I could go to meet them? 13. Your American friend is always a little late, isn't she? What a pity! 14. If you do not find her at the back of the house, look for her in the yard. 15. He knocked three times and then he waited a long time.

LESSON XXXI

83. Negatives. 1. *Not* is generally expressed by **ne - pas.** A more emphatic *not* is **ne - point** [pwɛ̃]:

Il n'y ira pas. *He isn't going.*
Il n'y ira point. *He is **not** going.*

2. **Ne - plus** [ply] means *no more, no longer*:
Je ne le vois plus. *I no longer see him.*
Je n'ai plus de pain. *I have no more bread.*

3. **Ne - jamais** [ʒamɛ] means *never*:
Je ne l'ai jamais vu. *I have never seen him.*

4. **Ne - rien** [rjɛ̃] means *nothing*; **ne - personne** [pɛrsɔn] means *nobody*. Notice that the position of **rien** or **personne** depends upon its function in the sentence: as subject, object, etc. **Personne,** used in the predicate with a compound tense, follows the past participle; **rien** similarly used takes the position of **pas** (after the auxiliary):

Rien[1] n'est arrivé. *Nothing happened.*
Il ne pensait à rien. *He wasn't thinking of anything.*
Je n'ai rien vu. *I didn't see anything.*
Personne[1] n'est arrivé. *Nobody has come.*
Il ne pensait à personne. *He wasn't thinking of anybody.*
Je n'ai vu personne. *I didn't see anybody.*

5. **Ne - que** means *only, nothing but*. **Que** occupies the same position as *only* in English, but cannot be used with a subject:

Je ne vois que son frère. *I see only his brother.*
Il n'en a acheté que trois. *He bought only three.*
But: Lui seul peut le faire. *Only he can do it.*

Notice that **ne - que** is negative only in form; therefore it does not affect a partitive construction:

Il a acheté des livres. *He bought books.*
Il n'a acheté que des livres. *He bought nothing but books.*
But notice: Il n'a acheté de livres que ceux que je désire. *He bought no books except those that I want.*

[1] Note that these forms are neuter and cause no agreement.

A personal pronoun which is the object of a verb with **ne - que** is disjunctive:

Je n'ai vu que lui. *I saw only him.*

6. (a) **Ne - ni - ni** ordinarily means *neither - nor*, but is not limited to two terms as in English. **Ne** precedes the verb; **ni** precedes the words with which *neither* or *nor* is used in English:

Il ne veut ni lire ni jouer. *He wants neither to read nor to play.*
Il n'a ni lu ni joué. *He has neither read nor played.*
Ni lui ni son ami ne viendront.[1] *Neither he nor his friend will come.*
Je n'ai vu ni lui ni elle ni leur père. *I didn't see him or her or their father.*

(b) When used with two simple finite tenses, *neither - nor* is expressed by **ne - ni - ne:**

Il ne chante ni ne joue. *He neither sings nor plays.*

(c) Notice that after **ni - ni,** the sign of the partitive is omitted:

Ce ne sont pas des chevaux. *Those aren't horses.*
But: Ce ne sont ni chevaux ni chameaux. *Those are neither horses nor camels.*
Il n'a pas de frères. *He hasn't any brothers.*
But: Il n'a ni frères ni sœurs. *He has neither brothers nor sisters.*

7. Each of the above negatives may be used out of construction, but then **ne** is omitted:

Qui a fait cela? Pas moi. *Who did that? Not I.*
Allez! Point! *Go! (I will) not!*
Plus de pain. *No more bread.*
Irez-vous là-bas? Jamais! *Will you go? Never!*
Qu'avez-vous? Rien. *What ails you? Nothing.*
Qui avez-vous vu? Personne. *Whom did you see? Nobody.*
Il a commandé du pain. Que cela? *He ordered bread. Only (nothing but) that?*
Qui le veut? Ni lui ni moi. *Who wants it? Neither he nor I.*

---

[1] The verb is plural unless the sense is alternative: **Ni lui ni son fils ne sera roi.**

For further remarks on the negative, see the Appendix (p. 218).

84. vouloir (*to want*) voulant voulu je veux je voulus
   Fut. stem: *3rd plu. pres. ind.:*
    voudr-   veulent
                  Pres. subj. stem:
                  veuill-[a]

[a] The imperative form **veuillez** means *Please* or *Be so kind as to . . .*; it is followed by an infinitive.

falloir[b] (*to be necessary*) .... fallu ....

Future	Imperf. Ind.	Pres. Ind.	Past Def.
il faudra	il fallait	il faut	il fallut
Conditional	*Pres. Subj.*		*Imperf. Subj.*
il faudrait	il faille		il fallût

[b] This verb is impersonal: it may be used in any tense but only in the third person singular with the subject **il**. It has no forms except those given above; the past participle may be used with any tense of **avoir** (in the third person singular) to form the compound tenses: **il a fallu, il avait fallu,** etc.

EXERCISE XXXI

aussitôt que [osito kə] *as soon as*
banque [bɑ̃:k] f. *bank*
complet, complète [kɔ̃plɛ, kɔ̃plɛt] *complete, full*
fontaine [fɔ̃tɛn] f. *fountain*
garder [garde] *to keep, guard*
jamais [ʒamɛ] *ever*
kodak [kɔdak] m. *kodak*
loin [lwɛ̃] *far*
malheureusement [malœrøzmɑ̃] *unhappily, unfortunately*
manquer [mɑ̃ke] *to miss, fail, lack*
mois [mwa] m. *month*
monnaie [mɔnɛ] f. *coin, change*
se montrer [mɔ̃tre] *to appear*
nuage [nɥɑ:ʒ] m. *cloud*
oublier [ublie] *to forget*
palais [palɛ] m. *palace*
phrase [frɑ:z] f. *sentence*
plaisir [plɛzi:r] m. *pleasure*
prendre [prɑ̃:dr] p.p. **pris** [pri] *to take*
présenter [prezɑ̃te] *to present*
receveur [rə vœ:r] m. *conductor, ticket collector*
sans [sɑ̃] *without*
soleil [sɔlɛ:j] m. *sun*

sou [su] m. *sou (one cent)*　　　　　**vouloir** [vulwaːr] *to wish, to want*
surtout [syrtu] *above all, especially*
　　ni moi (**lui,** etc.) **non plus** *nor I* (*he,* etc.) *either*
　　du reste or **au reste** [rɛst] *moreover, besides; however*
　　vouloir bien *to be willing*
　　vouloir dire *to mean*
　　en vouloir à quelqu'un de quelque chose *to bear someone a grudge for something*

A. —Philippe, avez-vous jamais vu le palais de Versailles [vɛrsɑːj]?

—Non, je n'y ai jamais été.

—Ni moi non plus. Voudriez-vous y aller aujourd'hui?

—Oui, je veux bien. Est-ce loin?

—Pas trop. Il faut une heure en tramway, moins en chemin de fer. Est-ce que madame votre mère nous en voudra de la laisser seule?

—Mais non! Peut-on y arriver sans difficulté?

—Rien n'est plus facile. Nous n'aurons qu'à traverser ce pont et à prendre le tramway qui passe de l'autre côté du fleuve. Le tram nous mènera jusqu'au palais. N'oubliez pas votre kodak. En ce moment il y a des nuages, mais le soleil se montrera bientôt.

—Nous voilà à la Place de l'Alma. Malheureusement nous avons manqué le tram. Le voilà qui part. Du reste, il est complet.

—Que veut dire cette phrase-là? Je l'ai déjà entendue, mais je ne comprends pas.

—Cela veut dire que toutes les places sont prises. Quand il n'y a plus de places, personne ne peut entrer. Voici un autre tram. Montons. Aussitôt que le receveur se présentera je lui donnerai l'argent. Il nous donnera des billets, qu'il faut toujours garder. Avez-vous de la monnaie? Je n'ai que des billets de banque, qu'il faudra faire changer.

—J'ai trois ou quatre pièces de deux francs. Les voici. Il y a beaucoup de monde dans le tram.

—C'est surtout le premier dimanche de chaque mois d'été qu'on va à Versailles voir jouer les «grandes eaux»—c'est comme cela qu'on appelle les fontaines. C'est un des plaisirs des gens qui travaillent toute la semaine.

B. 1. He has no more matches. 2. I have only three. 3. We didn't keep anything. 4. I can't live there any longer. 5. They will want only paper and pencils. 6. He never buys butter. 7. He wasn't talking to anybody. 8. He was neither talking nor studying. 9. He has neither bought nor sold. 10. He can neither speak nor hear. 11. They have neither father nor mother. 12. Neither they nor their friends will go. 13. They will neither buy nor sell. 14. He wants. 15. They would want. 16. They want. 17. Although we want. 18. Although he wants. 19. If they wanted. 20. You want. 21. He would want. 22. We have wanted. 23. They wanted (*p. def.*) 24. Although he wanted. 25. It is necessary. 26. It used to be necessary. 27. It has been necessary. 28. It will be necessary. 29. It would be necessary. 30. It would have been necessary.

C. 1. You will wait for him here. I will *not* wait for him. 2. They will never be able to rest if you continue to (**à** *or* **de**) talk. 3. There were only two chairs and a table on the stage when the curtain rose. 4. Neither they nor their sons will ever hear anything of all that. 5. He looked everywhere, but he found nothing. 6. He no longer takes them to the theater in the evening. 7. Besides, the present maid has been here only a week. 8. Nobody spoke aloud; everybody was afraid. 9. What he said doesn't mean anything. 10. Who did that? Not I. Nor my brother either. 11. He wouldn't (=didn't want to) take the money and he wouldn't keep the books, either. 12. Have you ever lived abroad? Who? I? Never. 13. What did you ask him when you met him? Nothing at all. 14. Would you bear him a grudge if he didn't send you what you ordered? 15. I am willing to go with you, but I can't stay long. 16. I still have some money, but I no longer have any small change. 17. You will never be able to go out without your overcoat; you will be too cold. 18. He rang several times, but nobody appeared. 19. As soon as he arrives, I shall send him to his aunt's to get your kodak. 20. If we miss this train, it will be necessary to wait until tomorrow morning.

D. 1. Quel palais allez-vous visiter? 2. Est-ce que Versailles est loin de Paris? 3. Combien de temps faut-il pour y arriver en tramway? 4. Peut-on y aller en chemin de fer aussi? 5. Avez-vous déjà visité cette ville? 6. Est-ce qu'il faisait beau quand vous êtes partis? 7. On dit qu'un tram est complet. Qu'est-ce que cela veut dire? 8. À qui paie-t-on les places dans le tram? 9. Qu'est-ce qu'il vous donne? 10. Faut-il garder ces billets? 11. Quel jour surtout est-ce que beaucoup de gens vont à Versailles? 12. Pourquoi?

LESSON XXXII

85. Relative Pronouns. Forms.

Invariable:
  qui [ki]
  que [kə]
  dont [dɔ̃]
  où [u]
  quoi [kwa]

Variable:
  lequel [ləkɛl] *m. s.*
  laquelle [lakɛl] *f. s.*
  lesquels [lekɛl] *m. p.*
  lesquelles [lekɛl] *f. p.*

86. Uses of Relative Pronouns.
1. For the uses of **qui** and **que**, see Lesson VIII, §24.

2. **Dont** is equivalent to **de** and a relative:

  Voilà l'homme dont je parlais. *There is the man of whom I was speaking.*
  C'est la ville dont il est venu. *That's the city from which he came.*

Dont often translates the English relative adjective *whose*; but if the student will always bear in mind that it is really equivalent to **de** and a relative, he will have less difficulty with his French sentence order:

> Voilà l'homme dont le fils est arrivé. *There is the man whose son (of whom the son) has arrived.*
> Voilà l'homme dont j'ai vu le fils. *There is the man whose son I saw (of whom I saw the son).*

Dont cannot be used to modify a noun which is the object of a preposition:

> Voilà l'homme au fils de qui (duquel) je parlais. *There is the man to whose son I was speaking.*

3. **Où** is equivalent to a preposition expressing position and a relative:

> La maison où il demeure. *The house in which he lives.*
> Le jour où il est arrivé. *The day on which he arrived.*

4. **Quoi** has no noun or pronoun as a definite antecedent, but refers to a phrase, a clause, or an idea. It is generally the object of a preposition.

> Il m'a dit qu'il vous cherchait, sur quoi je l'ai envoyé chez vous. *He told me that he was looking for you, whereupon I sent him to your house.*

5. The variable forms may be used to replace any other relative except **quoi**; but it is desirable to use **qui, que, dont,** or **où** unless an ambiguity arises:

> L'homme et ses filles qui sont ici . . . *The man and his daughters who (daughters? man and daughters?) are here . . .*
> L'homme et ses filles lesquelles (*daughters*) . . .
> L'homme et ses filles lesquels (*man and daughters*) . . .

Lequel (or a variant) must be used when the relative is the object of a preposition and does not refer to persons. After the prepositions **à** and **de** the usual contractions take place:

C'est le train par lequel il est arrivé. . . .*by which* . . .
L'homme duquel (auquel) . . . Les hommes desquels (auxquels) . . .

For a table of relatives and interrogatives, see the Appendix, p. 216.

87. écrire (*to write*) écrivant écrit j'écris j'écrivis
connaître (*to know*) connaissant connu je connais je connus
3rd sing. pres. ind.
il connaît

EXERCISE XXXII

admirer [admire] *to admire*
allemand [almɑ̃] *German*
appartement [apartəmɑ̃] m. *apartment*
appétit [apeti] m. *appetite*
autour (de) [otuːr] *around*
danser [dɑ̃se] *to dance*
doute [dut] m. *doubt*
endroit [ɑ̃drwɑ] m. *place, location*
escalier [ɛskalje] m. *stairway*
fermer [fɛrme] *to close, shut*
feuille [fœːj] f. *leaf,* sheet (of paper)
fin [fɛ̃] f. *end*
galerie [galri] f. *gallery*
gâteau [gɑto] m. *cake*
honneur [ɔnœːr] m. *honor*
jeter [ʒəte] *to throw, cast*

montre [mɔ̃ːtr] f. *watch*
ombre [ɔ̃ːbr] f. *shade, shadow*
paix [pɛ] f. *peace*
paver [pave] *to pave*
peinture [pɛ̃tyːr] f. *painting*
pierre [pjɛːr] f. *stone*
possible [pɔsibl] *possible*
propre [prɔpr] *clean; own*
reine [rɛːn] f. *queen*
roi [rwɑ] m. *king*
sale [sal] *dirty*
serviette [sɛrvjɛt] f. *napkin, towel*
servir [sɛrviːr] *to serve*
signer [siɲe] *to sign*
sous [su] *under*
tour [tuːr] m. *tour, turn; trick*
vide [vid] *empty*

faire le tour (de) *to go around*

A. Devant le palais de Versailles il y a une grande cour pavée en pierres. C'est ce qu'on appelle « la cour d'honneur ». Nous sommes tout de suite entrés dans le palais et nous avons monté l'escalier au premier; le rez-de-chaussée était
5 fermé. Nous avons fait le tour des appartements où demeuraient autrefois le roi et la reine de France. La plupart en sont maintenant presque vides. Il y a des objets historiques et beaucoup de belles peintures. Nous avons surtout admiré

la galerie des glaces, dans laquelle, vous vous rappellerez, les Allemands ont signé la paix. Quelle jolie salle pour danser! J'ai visité beaucoup d'endroits, mais je n'ai jamais vu de palais plus magnifique. Et puis, il est très grand; toute la cour y demeurait.

Autour du palais il y a des jardins, dont vous avez sans doute entendu parler. Vers la fin de l'après-midi nous nous y sommes promenés, après quoi nous avons cherché un café dans la ville. Il était cinq heures à ma montre, et nous avions tous les deux très faim. Quand le garçon est venu avec sa serviette sur le bras, nous lui avons demandé s'il ne pourrait pas nous servir sous les arbres, dont les feuilles vertes jetaient une ombre si agréable; il faisait si chaud pour la saison. Il a répondu que c'était possible. Nous avons donc commandé du thé et des gâteaux. Comme les assiettes et les tasses étaient propres et les gâteaux très bons, nous avons mangé de bon appétit. Alors nous nous sommes dépêchés pour rentrer à Paris avant le dîner.

B. 1. I am writing. 2. He was writing. 3. We shall write. 4. You are writing. 5. They write. 6. Although he writes. 7. They used to write. 8. Let's write. 9. We have written. 10. They wrote (*p. def.*). 11. The man who came. 12. The women who left. 13. The pen that I bought. 14. The pencils which I sent. 15. The girls whom I met. 16. The hat which is on the chair. 17. The books which were on the table. 18. The man of whom he speaks. 19. The children whose teacher is here. 20. The boy whose father I saw. 21. The woman to whose husband I sent you. 22. The city in which he is now. 23. The room around which we walked. 24. The store around which they ran. 25. He ate, after which he went out. 26. He used to know. 27. He knows. 28. We know. 29. They have known. 30. They will know.

C. 1. He always used to eat his dinner with a good appetite. 2. The collars which we put on this morning are already dirty. 3. I want him to write the sentence which is on the blackboard. 4. The sheet of paper which I gave him was clean. 5. The napkins which we need (of which we have need) are on the small table over there. 6. We visited the hall in which (*two ways*) peace was signed. 7. There is the window through (**par**) which he throws stones. 8. Do you like cakes? There are some which were sent to us this morning. 9. Please close the door which opens on the street. 10. In the dining-room there was a large table around which the six men were seated. 11. We mounted the stairway which leads to his apartment. 12. There are good kings and there are some that are bad. 13. In the yard there are some large trees which give shade in summer. 14. At the end of the month he will send me the money that I shall need. 15. The man at whose house (*use* **chez**) I live, is my uncle.

D. 1. Qu'est-ce qu'il y a devant le palais de Versailles? 2. Est-ce que le palais est grand? 3. Quel étage avez-vous visité? 4. Pourquoi n'avez-vous pas visité le rez-de-chaussée? 5. Qu'est-ce qu'il y a dans les salles du palais? 6. Où sont les jardins? 7. Est-ce que vous vous y êtes promenés? 8. Où êtes-vous allés après? 9. Quelle heure était-il à votre montre? 10. Pourquoi avez-vous cherché un café? 11. Qu'avez-vous demandé au garçon? 12. Qu'est-ce qu'il vous a servi? 13. Avez-vous mangé de bon appétit? 14. Pourquoi vous êtes-vous dépêchés après?

LESSON XXXIII

88. Interrogative Pronouns. Forms.

Invariable:	Variable:
qui	lequel
que	laquelle
quoi	lesquels
qu'est-ce qui [kɛs ki]	lesquelles

LESSON XXXIII

89. Uses of Interrogative Pronouns. 1. For the uses of **qui** and **que**, see Lesson VIII, §25.

2. **Quoi,** meaning *what?*, is used as the object of a preposition or absolutely (out of construction):

> Sur quoi a-t-il mis le livre? *On what did he place the book?*
> De quoi parle-t-il? *Of what is he speaking?*
> J'ai vu quelque chose. Quoi? *I saw something? What?*

3. **Qu'est-ce qui,** meaning *what?*, is used as the subject of a verb:

> Qu'est-ce qui est arrivé? *What has happened?*

4. The variable forms mean *Which one?* or *Which ones?* They may refer to persons or things. The form agrees in gender and number with the antecedent. The usual contractions take place.

> Lequel (lesquels) de ces livres désirez-vous? *Which (one or ones) of these books do you want?*
> Donnez-lui deux pommes. Lesquelles? *Give him two apples. Which ones?*
> Auxquelles de ces dames avez-vous parlé? *To which (ones) of those ladies did you speak?*

5. Care must be taken to distinguish between *What?* as an adjective and *What?* as a pronoun.

> Qu'avez-vous à la main? *What (pronoun) have you in your hand?*
> Quel livre avez-vous à la main? *What (adjective) book have you in your hand?*
> Quel est ce livre que vous avez à la main? *What (=what book: adjective) is that book that you have in your hand?*

For a table of relatives and interrogatives, see Appendix, p. 216.

90. lire (*to read*) lisant   lu   je lis   je lus
    dire (*to say*) disant   dit   je dis   je dis
                 2nd plu. pres. ind.:
                 dites
                 2nd plu. imperative:
                 dites

EXERCISE XXXIII

adopter [adɔpte] *to adopt*
adversaire [advɛrsɛːr] m., f. *adversary, opponent*
agiter [aʒite] *to excite, agitate*
amateur [amatœːr] m. *lover, fancier, "fan"*
assistant [asistɑ̃] m. *one present, witness*
avancer [avɑ̃se] *to advance*
ballon [balɔ̃] m. *ball*
bas [bɑ] m. *stocking*
battre [batr] *to beat*
but [by(t)] m. *goal, end, aim, score*
camp [kɑ̃] m. *camp, field, territory*
contre [kɔ̃:tr] *against*
coup [ku] m. *stroke, blow*
croix [krwɑ] f. *cross*
culotte [kylɔt] f. *breeches*
différent [diferɑ̃] *different*
équipe [ekip] f. *team*
étonner [etɔne] *to astonish*
filet [filɛ] m. *net*
football [futbal] m. *football*
ground[1] [grɑund] m. *grounds, field*
intéresser [ɛ̃terɛse] *to interest*
jersey [ʒɛrsɛ] m. *jersey*
jeu [ʒø] m. *play, game*
joueur [ʒwœːr] m. *player*
lentement [lɑ̃tmɑ̃] *slowly*
lieu [ljø] m. *place, stead*
match [matʃ] m. *game*
mot [mo] m. *word*
nombre [nɔ̃:br] m. *number*
nul, -le [nyl] *no, none, not any, null*
opposition [ɔpozisjɔ̃] f. *opposition, resistance*
poteau [pɔto] m. *post*
récemment [resamɑ̃] *recently*
règle [rɛ:gl] f. *rule*
sport [spɔːr] m. *sport, athletics*
sportif [spɔrtif] *sporting, athletic*
stade [stad] m. *stadium*
Suisse [sɥis] f. *Switzerland*
suisse [sɥis] *Swiss*
victoire [viktwaːr] f. *victory*
vie [vi] f. *life*

au lieu de *instead of*
coup de pied *kick*
match nul *tie game*

—Madame Lenoir m'a dit qu'elle a lu dans le journal quelque chose qui nous intéresserait sans doute.

—Quoi? Dites-moi donc ce qu'elle a lu.

—C'est le match de football au Stade Pershing entre la France et la Suisse. Je lui ai demandé lequel des trams nous mènerait le plus près du stade, et elle m'a dit qu'on prend le numéro vingt. Après il faut monter en autobus. Comme vous avez dit que vos amis jouaient au football quand ils étaient au collège, j'ai pensé que nous pourrions tous y aller.

—Je veux bien.

[1] The genuine French word is *terrain* [tɛrɛ̃] m.

LESSON XXXIII

Eh bien! Nous avons vu le match. Les deux équipes étaient très fortes. Les Français portaient des jerseys bleus, des culottes blanches et des bas rouges; les Suisses, des jerseys rouges à la croix blanche et des culottes et des bas blancs. Mais le jeu m'a étonné; je m'attendais à voir quelque chose comme notre football, mais c'était tout à fait différent. Au lieu de porter le ballon assez lentement contre l'opposition des adversaires comme on le fait chez nous, on l'a envoyé par tout le ground à coups de pied. On avançait très vite vers le but, mais après deux minutes on était près de l'autre but. Qu'est-ce qui donne donc la victoire? C'est le nombre des buts. Quelles sont les règles du jeu? Oh, cela, je ne pourrais vous le dire. Il y a onze joueurs par équipe, dont l'un reste toujours près du but pour garder son camp. Jeter le ballon dans le filet entre les deux poteaux ce n'est donc pas chose facile, surtout parce qu'il faut le jeter assez bas.

Vous allez me demander laquelle des deux équipes a été battue. Ni l'une ni l'autre. D'abord les Suisses ont fait deux buts, puis les Français en ont fait un. Les assistants étaient bien agités. Enfin les Français ont fait encore un but, et le jeu a fini match nul.

Vous remarquerez qu'on emploie dans le sport beaucoup de mots anglais. C'est parce qu'on a très récemment adopté la vie sportive des Anglais. Autrefois les Français avaient très peu des jeux qu'on connaît maintenant; mais ils en sont très vite devenus amateurs.

B. 1. He reads. 2. Although he reads. 3. He was reading. 4. He will read. 5. He would read. 6. If he should read. 7. Read. 8. I have read. 9. They read (*present*). 10. They read (*p. def.*). 11. Tell (it to) him. 12. I was saying. 13. They will say. 14. They say. 15. Although we say. 16. We used to say. 17. They said (*p. def.*). 18. Although they said.

19. Who said that? 20. To whom did he give this? 21. Whom do you want? 22. Who is it? 23. I see a man. Whom? 24. They are leaving. Who? 25. What is it? 26. What ails you? 27. On what is he sitting? 28. I shall buy something. What? 29. What is interesting? 30. Which of these books is yours? 31. Which ones are your sister's? 32. What does he want? 33. Do you see what he wants? 34. What is that game you gave him? 35. To which of his friends did he give watches?

C. 1. Who was playing football (*see* A) at the Pershing Stadium? 2. Who told you which tram would take you there? 3. Which of the teams made the first goal? 4. Can you tell me what are the rules of the game? 5. Of what were you speaking when I came in? 6. Tell me what happened at the theater yesterday. 7. What is the most interesting game? 8. Something has greatly excited them. What? 9. Which of these two girls is going to accompany your mother? 10. What happened when you were leaving the hotel? 11. Instead of shirts they wore blue jerseys, didn't they? 12. Whom do you bear a grudge? I don't bear anybody a grudge. 13. Which of the teams played best? 14. Did those present find the game interesting? 15. I have often read that the English are lovers of sport. 16. I was told that the Swiss were expecting to beat the French. 17. Her own brother (**propre** *precedes noun*) would not have told you that. 18. Who gave the ball a kick?

D. 1. Qu'est-ce que Madame Lenoir a lu dans le journal? 2. Est-ce que cela vous a intéressés? 3. Comment est-ce qu'on peut aller au Stade Pershing? 4. Est-ce que le match vous a amusés? 5. Les équipes étaient-elles fortes? 6. Est-ce que le jeu est comme le nôtre? 7. Qu'est-ce qu'on fait au ballon? 8. Avez-vous compris les règles du jeu? 9. Combien de joueurs y a-t-il par équipe? 10. Qui a fait le premier but? 11. Laquelle des équipes a été battue? 12. Pourquoi est-ce qu'on emploie tant de mots anglais en parlant des sports?

LESSON XXXIV

91. Infinitive Complementary to a Verb. An infinitive is often dependent upon another verb. Sometimes the infinitive is the object of the verb upon which it depends: *He wants a book* (object). *He wants to read* (object). Sometimes a verb is in auxiliary relation to an infinitive: *He is going to read*.

When an infinitive depends upon another verb, the verb upon which the infinitive depends (never the infinitive itself) determines whether the infinitive is direct (i. e. has no sign), or is preceded by **à** or **de**. In most cases of this kind, it is necessary to know the usage in connection with a certain verb. See the lists in the Appendix, pages 225-227.

Il veut lire. *He wants to read.*
Il aime à lire. *He likes to read.*
Il cesse de lire. *He stops reading (ceases to read).*
Nous allons partir. *We are going to leave.*
Ils se sont décidés à partir. *They decided to leave.*
Je vous défends de partir. *I forbid you to leave.*

Sometimes the same verb may be followed by the infinitive with different signs:

Il commence à parler. Il commence de parler. *He begins to speak.*

Sometimes the meaning changes as the sign of the infinitive changes:

Il vient me voir. *He comes to see me.*
Il vient à me voir. *He happens to see me.*
Il vient de me voir. *He has just seen me.*

The sign of an infinitive may have a literal prepositional value:

> Il passe la soirée à lire. *He spends the evening* **in** *reading.*
> On l'a accusé de voler. *He was accused* **of** *stealing.*

Several infinitives may be used in succession, in which case each one determines the sign of the following one:

> Il va cesser d'essayer de (*or* à) les[1] décider à promettre de venir. *He is going to stop trying to induce them to promise to come.*

92. Infinitive Complementary to a Noun or an Adjective.
1. When an infinitive completes or explains the meaning of a noun or an adjective, the sign of the infinitive is generally **de**:

> J'ai l'intention de venir. *I intend to come.* (Literally: *I have the intention —What intention?—the intention to come*).
> Il est heureux de vous voir. *He is glad to see you.* (*What is the cause of his happiness? Why is he happy? To see you.*)

2. However, if the infinitive complementary to a noun or an adjective shows purpose, fitness, or tendency, the sign is **à**:

> Une chambre à coucher. *A sleeping room.* (*For that purpose.*)
> Une bonne à tout faire. *A maid of all work.* (*Purpose.*)
> Il est prêt à vous voir. *He is ready to see you.* (*Purpose of his readiness.*)
> Cette pomme est-elle bonne à manger? *Is this apple good to eat?* (*Fitness. Good for what purpose?*)

93. Infinitive as Logical Subject. An infinitive has the sign **de** when it is used as the logical (but not the grammatical) subject, and follows the verb:

> Il sera facile d'écrire cette lettre. *It will be easy to write this letter.*
> C'est un plaisir d'écrire cette lettre. *It is a pleasure to write this letter.*
> Cela m'amusera d'écrire cette lettre. *It will amuse me to write this letter.*
> But: Voir c'est croire.

---

[1] Notice that a personal pronoun object precedes an infinitive of which it is an object, and follows the sign if there be one.

In each of the first three sentences above, it will be noticed that the subject is meaningless: *To write this letter will be easy. To write this letter is a pleasure. To write this letter will amuse me.* In each case the infinitive, while it is not the grammatical subject, is the logical subject and follows the finite verb; it therefore has the sign **de.**

94. Infinitive Governed by a Preposition. In English a preposition generally governs a verb-form in **-ing.** In French the corresponding form in **-ant** is governed by only one preposition: **en.** Other prepositions, when they govern a verb-form, govern the infinitive:

En entrant il a ôté son chapeau. *On entering he took off his hat.*
Je l'ai regardé en passant. *In (while) passing I looked at him.*
But: Il est parti sans me parler. *He left without speaking to me.*

The preposition **après** (*after*) is followed by the perfect infinitive:

Après avoir fini mon ouvrage, je suis parti. *After finishing (having finished) my work, I left.*

The preposition **par** governs an infinitive only after **commencer** and **finir**:

Il a commencé par me dire tout ce qu'il avait fait. *He began by telling me all he had done.*
Il a fini par s'en aller. *He finally went away.*

The preposition **pour** with an infinitive generally expresse purpose. It is generally omitted, however, after verbs expressing *going* or *coming*:

Il faut étudier pour apprendre. *One must study in order to learn.*
Elle est allée au marché (pour) acheter des légumes. *She went to market in order to buy some vegetables.*

95. savoir (*to know*)   sachant   su   je sais   je sus
    Fut. stem: *Plu. pres. ind.:*   *Sing. imperative:*
    saur-   savons   sache
                      savez
                      savent   (Over)

Plu. imperatives:
sachons
sachez
Imperf. ind.:
savais, etc.

EXERCISE XXXIV

architecture [arʃitɛktyːr] f. *architecture*
assister (à) [asiste] *to witness, attend*
au-dehors (de) [o d(ə)ɔːr] *outside*
avis [avi] m. *mind, opinion*
bijou [biʒu] m. *jewel*
carré [kare] *square*
cathédrale [katedral] f. *cathedral*
cesser [sɛse] *to stop, cease*
chapelle [ʃapɛl] f. *chapel*
chimère [ʃimɛːr] f. *chimera*
cité [site] f. (old word for) *city*
drôle [droːl] *funny, strange*
s'élever [elve] *to rise (up)*
envie [ɑ̃vi] f. *wish, desire, longing*
épais, -se [epɛ, epɛs] *thick*
façade [fasad] f. *façade, front*
fonder [fɔ̃de] *to found*
gargouille [garguːj] f. *gargoyle*
île [iːl] f. *island*

intention [ɛ̃tɑ̃sjɔ̃] f. *intention*
intérieur [ɛ̃terjœːr] m. *interior*
justice [ʒystis] f. *justice, law*
lasser [lɑse] *to weary, tire*
se lasser *to grow weary*
merveilleux [mɛrvɛjø] *marvelous*
messe [mɛs] f. *mass* (church service)
milieu [miljø] m. *middle*
saint, -e [sɛ̃, sɛ̃ːt] *holy, sacred;* m. f. *saint*
savoir [savwaːr] *to know (how), be able*
sculpture [skyltyːr] f. *sculpture, carving*
somme [sɔm] f. *sum*
tour [tuːr] f. *tower*
trésor [trezɔːr] m. *treasure, treasury*
vitrail, pl. vitraux [vitraːj, vitro] m. *stained glass window*

avoir l'intention (de) *to intend*
en face [fas] f. (de) *opposite*
Île de la Cité *island in the Seine, the original city of Paris*
le long de *along*
Palais de Justice *Palace of Justice (court house, law courts)*

A. L'autre jour nos jeunes Américains ont visité la cathédrale de Notre-Dame de Paris. Ils s'étaient levés tard ce jour-là, et ils avaient passé la matinée à lire dans leurs chambres à coucher. Mais tout de suite après le déjeuner
5 ils étaient prêts à sortir. Il n'est pas difficile de trouver quelque chose à faire à Paris; on n'a qu'à choisir entre beau-

Une Aile du Palais de Versailles

La Cathédrale de Notre-Dame de Paris

LESSON XXXIV

coup de choses. En sortant ils avaient l'intention d'aller se promener au Bois de Boulogne, grand parc au-dehors des portes de la ville; mais quand Charles a dit qu'il avait envie de voir la grande cathédrale, tout le monde était content de l'y accompagner. Je trouve que c'est une bonne idée de changer d'avis quelquefois; cela m'amuse toujours de faire ce que je ne m'attendais pas à faire.

Notre-Dame est dans l'Île de la Cité, la partie la plus ancienne de Paris, qui a été fondé dans cette île: c'était autrefois tout ce qu'il y avait de la ville. On y voit encore l'ancien palais des rois, qui est maintenant le Palais de Justice. Au milieu du palais se trouve la Sainte-Chapelle, où le roi et la cour assistaient à la messe. C'est un bijou d'architecture, et les vitraux, très épais, sont parmi les plus beaux du monde. En face du palais s'élèvent les deux tours carrées de Notre-Dame.

Après avoir admiré la belle façade avec ses sculptures merveilleuses, nos jeunes gens ont visité l'intérieur de l'église. En payant une petite somme ils ont pu voir aussi le trésor. Ils ont fini par monter dans les tours, d'où l'on[1] a une vue magnifique sur Paris. Ils étaient étonnés de voir toutes ces drôles de figures de pierre, qu'on appelle des gargouilles et des chimères. Ils ne pouvaient pas se lasser de regarder; mais comme l'heure avançait, il a fallu descendre. Ils sont revenus à pied; et tout le long du chemin ils n'ont cessé de parler de ce qu'ils avaient vu. Je ne saurais vous dire combien cela les a intéressés.

B. 1. I know. 2. You know. 3. Know. 4. He will know. 5. They know. 6. Although he knows. 7. They would know. 8. He used to know. 9. They have known. 10. He knew (*p. def.*). 11. I like to read. 12. He knows how to read. 13. It's a pleasure to read. 14. Without reading. 15. After

[1] See note to Ex. XXVIII, A.

reading. 16. While (in) reading. 17. In order to read. 18. I'm glad to read. 19. He begins to read. 20. He wants to read. 21. He can read. 22. He is going to read. 23. He stopped reading. 24. He grows tired of reading. 25. He intends to read. 26. This book is good to read. 27. I am ready to read. 28. It amuses me to read. 29. He began by reading. 30. He is astonished to read that.

C. 1. I was watching them play, when I saw him fall. 2. I remember having seen him when he was only eight years old. 3. I am willing to stay here if it (**cela**) gives you pleasure to keep me with (near to) you. 4. He sought to make us leave, but he couldn't do it. 5. He takes pleasure in speaking to them. 6. They stopped talking and began to study. 7. He forgot to buy gloves. 8. They continued to dance, which never failed to weary them. 9. Is that water good to drink? 10. It will not be easy to find them this evening. 11. It won't be necessary to go to meet them. 12. While reading his paper this evening he rested; now he is ready to go out again. 13. They left without saying a word. 14. After finishing his book, he began to play. 15. She tells me to study (during) two hours in order that I may know my lessons. 16. If he asked for a hat, I shouldn't know which is his. 17. He knew how to read and write three years ago. 18. He has been wanting to go there for more than three weeks.

D. 1. Comment est-ce que les jeunes Américains ont passé la matinée? 2. Est-ce qu'il est facile de s'amuser à Paris? 3. Qu'est-ce qu'ils avaient l'intention de faire en sortant? 4. Qu'est-ce que Charles avait envie de faire? 5. Est-ce que les autres voulaient bien l'accompagner? 6. Où est Notre-Dame? 7. Quel autre grand monument se trouve dans l'île? 8. Qu'est-ce que c'est que la Sainte-Chapelle? 9. Est-ce que cette partie de Paris est moderne?

10. Peut-on voir le trésor de la cathédrale? 11. Est-ce que les jeunes gens sont montés dans les tours? 12. Qu'est-ce qu'ils ont vu du haut de Notre-Dame? 13. Pourquoi est-ce qu'il leur a fallu descendre? 14. Comment sont-ils revenus à la pension? 15. De quoi parlaient-ils le long du chemin?

LESSON XXXV

96. Infinitive with Change of Subject. 1. Ordinarily, when there is a change of subject, an infinitive cannot be used in French, but a clause construction is required.[1] Thus in *I want him to come*, *I* is the subject of *want*, and *him* is the subject of *come*. The French must then substitute a clause for the English infinitive: *I wish that he come*. But if the subject does not change, the infinitive is used: *I want to come*.

Je désire venir.   Je désire qu'il vienne.

2. However, after verbs of causing, permitting or perceiving (also verbs of commanding, inviting, preventing, forbidding), an infinitive is possible even when there is a change of subject:

Je l'ai fait venir. *I had him come.*
Je lui ai dit de venir. *I told him to come.*
Je l'ai empêché de venir. *I prevented his coming.*
Je vous défends de venir. *I forbid you to come.*
Il m'a laissé partir. *He let me go.*
Nous l'avons entendu chanter. *We heard him sing.*

Note—When the finite verb and the infinitive both have objects, the object of the finite verb is generally expressed in the dative:

Je l'ai fait écrire. *I had him write.*
But: Je lui ai fait écrire cette phrase. *I had him write that sentence.*
Je ferai écrire l'enfant. *I shall have the child write.*
But: Je ferai écrire cette phrase à l'enfant. *I shall have the child write that sentence.*

---

[1] An impersonal pronoun being meaningless, there is no difficulty involved in the use of an infinitive after an impersonal expression: Est-ce qu'il vous conviendra de l'attendre? *Will it suit you to wait for him?*

97. Present Participle. 1. The present participle, used as a modifier, generally modifies the subject of the clause in which it occurs:

> Voyant qu'il ne comprenait pas, je lui ai montré votre lettre. *Seeing that he didn't understand, I showed him your letter.*

2. The present participle agrees with a noun or pronoun modified only when it has lost all verb value and is purely an adjective:

> Il a rencontré une jeune fille charmante. *He met a charming girl.*
> Il a lu une histoire intéressante. *He read an interesting story.*
> But: Ayant peur, la jeune fille est restée à la maison. *Being afraid, the girl remained at home.* (**Ayant** is a verb: it governs the object **peur**; therefore it does not agree.)

3. The present participle with **en** generally has adverbial value:

> En marchant il est tombé. *While (he was) walking he fell.*

4. The English present participle is often replaced in French by an infinitive or a clause construction:

> Je m'amuse à lire. *I amuse myself by reading.*
> Il parle sans réfléchir. *He speaks without thinking.*
> Je le vois venir. *I see him coming.*
> Je l'ai entendu qui m'appelait. *I heard him (who was) calling me.*

98. devoir (*to owe*)   devant   dû[1] je dois je dus
Fut. stem: *3rd plu. pres. ind.:*
  devr-   doivent
          Pres. subj. stem:
            doiv-

recevoir [2] (*to receive*) recevant   reçu je reçois je reçus
Fut. stem: *3rd plu. pres. ind.:*
  recevr-   reçoivent
          Pres. subj. stem:
            reçoiv-

---

[1] The accent is omitted when there is an agreement of the past participle.

[2] These two verbs are exactly alike in conjugation except for the orthographic signs.

EXERCISE XXXV

adieu [adjø] m. *good-bye*
agréable [agreabl] *agreeable*
appareil [aparɛ:j] m. *outfit, set*
batelier [batəlje] m. *boatman*
chanter [ʃāte] *to sing*
chat [ʃa] m. *cat*
chien [ʃjɛ̃] m. *dog*
clair [klɛ:r] *clear, bright;* m. *light*
commerce [kɔmɛrs] m. *trade*
copie [kɔpi] f. *copy*
corde [kɔrd] f. *rope, cord*
dangereux [dā·ʒrø] *dangerous*
devoir [dəvwa:r] *to owe*
dur [dy:r] *hard*
écriteau [ekrito] m. *sign*
s'ennuyer [ānɥije] *to be bored*
est [ɛst] m. *east*
étendre [etā:dr] *to extend, spread*
faubourg [fobu:r] m. *suburb*
fil [fil] m. *thread, wire*
s'imaginer [imaʒine] *to imagine*
jetée [ʒəte] f. *pier, mole*
linge [lɛ̃:ʒ] m. *linen, laundry*
lune [lyn] f. *moon*
nord [nɔ:r] m. *north*
ouest [wɛst] m. *west*

particulier, particulière [partikylje partikyljɛ:r] *private; peculiar*
paysage [pɛiza:ʒ] m. *landscape*
pendant que [pādā kə] *while*
pénétrer [penetre] *to penetrate, enter*
permettre [pɛrmɛtr] p.p. **permis** [pɛrmi] *to permit*
peuple [pœpl] m. (a) *people, race; lower classes*
point [pwɛ̃] m. *point*
propriété [prɔpriete] f. *property, estate*
province [prɔvɛ̃:s] f. *province*
radioconcert [radjokɔ̃sɛ:r] m. *wireless concert*
recevoir [rəsvwa:r] *to receive*
repas [rəpa] m. *meal*
restaurant [rɛstɔrā] m. *restaurant*
sécher [seʃe] *to dry*
service [sɛrvis] m. *service*
téléphonie [telefɔni] f. *telephone (system of communication—not the instrument)*
terrasse [tɛras] f. *terrace*
tôt [to] *early, (too) soon*
vivre [vi:vr] *to live*
vrai [vrɛ] *true*

tout de même *just the same*

1. **Il me doit trois francs.** *He owes me three francs.*
   Vous ne devriez pas faire cela. *You ought not to do that.*
   J'aurais dû partir. *I ought to have left.*
   Il a dû partir. *He had to leave*
2. **Il doit chanter ce soir.** *He is to sing this evening.*
   Il devait arriver hier. *He was to arrive yesterday.*
3. **Il doit avoir vingt ans.** *He must be twenty years old.*
   J'ai dit qu'il devait être malade. *I said he must be sick.*
   Vous avez dû la connaître. *You must have known her.*

Note—In the first group **devoir** expresses obligation; in the second, prophecy; in the third, that which is necessarily true.

A. On entend dire quelquefois que Paris c'est la France, mais ce n'est pas vrai. Pour bien comprendre un peuple il faut connaître la vie des petites villes et de la campagne. Nous avons donc l'intention de voyager pendant quelques
5 semaines "en province," comme on dit, parce que tout ce qui n'est pas Paris est province. Nous devons partir dans trois jours. Mais avant de dire adieu à Paris, nous voulions nous promener en bateau sur la Seine. Il y a de petits bateaux qui font le service de Maisons-Alfort au sud-est de la
10 ville jusqu'à Suresnes au nord-ouest. Nous avons donc pris le bateau au pont de l'Alma et nous avons descendu le fleuve jusqu'à Saint-Cloud. Tout le long de la route nous avons vu des choses intéressantes.

Il y a beaucoup de bateaux de commerce sur la Seine.
15 Très souvent les familles des bateliers vivent sur ces bateaux. Nous avons vu, par exemple, une femme qui lavait le linge et l'étendait sur des cordes pour le faire sécher. Pendant qu'elle travaillait, ses enfants jouaient avec un chat et un chien. La mère n'avait pas besoin de chercher ses petits;
20 elle savait qu'ils ne pouvaient pas être loin. Bien entendu, un enfant tombe à l'eau de temps en temps. Naturellement ce sont les gens du bas peuple qui vivent comme cela; c'est une vie dure, mais on ne s'ennuie pas! Tout de même ce ne peut pas être agréable par le mauvais temps et surtout
25 quand on est malade.

On a une très belle vue du bateau; des deux côtés du fleuve on voit de très jolis paysages. À un endroit près d'Auteuil, faubourg de Paris, il y a sur une jetée dans la Seine une statue de la Liberté, copie de celle à New-York mais moins
30 grande. Vous vous rappellerez que cette dernière a été donnée aux États-Unis par la nation française.

Tout d'un coup j'ai entendu chanter, mais je ne savais pas où. Alors j'ai remarqué qu'il y avait à bord un appareil de téléphonie sans fil et je me suis dit que ce devait être un radioconcert de la Tour Eiffel que nous entendions. Imaginez-vous cela sur un petit bateau de la Seine!

Nous sommes arrivés trop tôt à Saint-Cloud; nous aurions voulu rester plus longtemps sur le fleuve. Nous sommes montés sur la terrasse et nous nous sommes promenés à pied. Mon père ne nous a pas permis de pénétrer dans les propriétés particulières; du reste, à presque toutes les portes de jardin on voyait cet écriteau: Chien dangereux! Après un très bon repas dans un petit restaurant, nous sommes revenus au clair de lune. Quelle bonne journée!

B. 1. He owes. 2. We owe. 3. They owe. 4. You will owe. 5. They have owed. 6. I used to owe. 7. Although he owes. 8. They receive. 9. We receive. 10. They received (*p. def.*). 11. I want to go. 12. I want him to go. 13. I saw him leave. 14. I heard him go out. 15. I have let him enter. 16. I had him sing. 17. I had him write his lesson. 18. Having finished his work, he left. 19. While going down the stairway, he fell. 20. They can't live without eating.

C. 1. They went to the city to have some clothes made. 2. I told her to (**de**) send him to market to get some vegetables. 3. I want to go, but I don't want him to go. 4. As I was going home, I heard him singing. 5. Hearing voices (which were) calling them, they raised their eyes. 6. It will be difficult to watch him do that. 7. I shall be glad to see them leave. 8. I am not afraid that he will make them leave. 9. Did you see that woman washing her linen? 10. If he has not told them to go with her, it (**ce**) must be because he has forgotten. 11. We were to leave yesterday; but as my brother fell ill, we shall have to wait until tomorrow. 12. He must be very poor; he has owed me ten francs for three months. 13. You should have told him that you will pay him for those books as soon as you have (*future*) the money. 14. It is your duty to make him work; he has never learned anything, he doesn't even know how to read. 15. They must have been very happy.

D. 1. Que faut-il faire pour bien comprendre un peuple? 2. Qu'avez-vous l'intention de faire dans trois jours? 3. Comment appelle-t-on toute la France qui n'est pas Paris? 4. Où vouliez-vous aller avant de quitter Paris? 5. Où avez-vous pris le bateau? 6. Est-ce que les petits bateaux de la Seine marchent vite? 7. Quelle statue avez-vous vu en route? 8. Qu'est-ce que vous avez entendu à bord? 9. Qu'avez-vous vu sur un autre bateau? 10. Qu'est-ce que les enfants faisaient? 11. Qu'avez-vous fait après être arrivés à Saint-Cloud? 12. Quand êtes-vous revenus?

LESSON XXXVI
REVIEW

A. 1. Compare the uses of **qui** as a relative pronoun and **qui** as an interrogative pronoun. 2. Compare the uses of **que** as a relative pronoun and **que** as an interrogative pronoun. 3. When an infinitive is complementary to another verb, what determines the sign of the infinitive? 4. When an infinitive is complementary to a noun or an adjective, what is usually the sign? When is **à** the sign? 5. When an infinitive is the logical but not the grammatical subject and follows the verb, what is the sign? 6. In XXXIII, A, l. 25, notice that although **ce** is the grammatical subject and **jeter** the logical subject, the infinitive has no sign since it precedes the verb of which it is the subject. 7. What part of the verb does a preposition usually govern? Which preposition governs the form in **-ant**? Which preposition always governs a perfect infinitive? 8. When the subject of an English infinitive is not the same as the subject of the finite verb, what construction is generally used in French? With what verbs may the infinitive be used even when there is a

LESSON XXXVI

change of subject? 9. When does a present participle agree with a noun or pronoun modified? 10. In XXXIV, A, account for all infinitive constructions. 11. Account for all partitives in XXXI, A. 12. In XXXIII, A, l. 8, notice that *to play a game* is **jouer à un jeu.** *To play a musical instrument* is **jouer de: Il joue du piano.** 13. In XXXIV, A, l. 15, What is the antecedent of **qui**? How do you know?

B. 1. He isn't going there. 2. He is *not* going there. 3. He doesn't sell them any more. 4. He never enters it. 5. He doesn't buy anything there. 6. He won't send anybody there. 7. He found only three bank notes. 8. He speaks neither to him nor to her. 9. Nothing is going to happen. 10. Nobody will know. 11. Neither he nor she will write. 12. He will neither read nor write. 13. I saw nobody but my brother. 14. The man who sings. 15. Who accompanied him? Who? 16. The man whom I saw. 17. Whom did you see? Whom? 18. The handsome man that he is. 19. Who is it? 20. The man to whom I spoke. 21. To whom did you speak? 22. The man of whom I spoke. 23. Of whom did you speak? 24. The book which I showed him. 25. Which books did you buy? Which ones? 26. What did you buy? 27. What is it? 28. Of what were you speaking? 29. What will happen? What? 30. The house in which he lives. 31. In which house does he live? 32. In which of those houses did she die? 33. The man whose son I saw. 34. The man to whose son I spoke. 35. The man whose son has gone. 36. Whose son is he? 37. Whose is that book? 38. My brother's wife who (*i. e. the wife*) has returned. 39. He stopped coming here. 40. He has a longing to go to the country. 41. He intends to go to the country. 42. He grows weary of reading. 43. He likes to play. 44. He knows how to explain it. 45. He wants to study. 46. He begins (*three ways*) to seek. 47. It was hard to leave them. 48. He will permit me to visit them. 49. He got up early to read the paper.

50. He forgot to do that. 51. He will have to go to bed.
52. It's a pleasure to remain here. 53. It amuses me to watch them. 54. I amuse myself by reading. 55. After breaking it.
56. While saying it. 57. He would be glad to take a walk.
58. He must be ready to travel. 59. These apples are good to eat. 60. I am interested in following it. 61. I have him work. 62. I told him to go on board. 63. I let him go out.
64. I hear him knocking. 65. He amuses himself without having any friends. 66. I want him to sing. 67. I begged him to play the piano. 68. He used to play football. 69. I have no time to waste. 70. I invited him to spend the evening here.

C. 1. Remember that the present church is not the one in which your relatives attended mass. 2. My traveling companion doesn't like to get up early, but I do not permit him to remain in bed late. 3. Although our teacher doesn't want us to be late, it is sometimes impossible to be at school at nine o'clock. 4. I should like to know the best way to travel without getting tired. 5. If I had change, I shouldn't have asked him for any. 6. As soon as he stops working, I shall tell him not to forget to (make to) dry his clothes.
7. Unfortunately we missed the train and we had to return to my brother's to spend another night (there). 8. He couldn't tell you that your face was not clean, since his own face was dirty. 9. I have not read the letter he wrote, but just the same I know what he means. 10. I am willing to close both the windows, but the door must remain open.
11. He bears me a grudge for having made him go around the garden three times. 12. Instead of attending his classes, he is to go to meet his brother and his mother. 13. He struck the big bell and made it ring. 14. As I was walking along the street, I noticed that your house is not so high as the one opposite. 15. It must be very pleasant to hear good music while one is taking a meal alone in a restaurant. 16. From

the square towers of the cathedral of Notre Dame, one ought to be able to see a good part of old Paris. 17. My little brother wants a wireless telephone set so that he can hear the first news of the football games. 18. He doesn't like to live at hotels; he is going to look for a room in a private house.

LESSON XXXVII

99. Compound Tenses. 1. Forming the compound tenses is a matter of conjugating **avoir** or **être,** adding the past participle, and applying the rules for the agreement of the past participle.

Perfect Infinitive:	avoir vu, *to have seen*
	être allé(e)(s), *to have gone*
Perfect Participle:	ayant vu, *having seen*
	étant allé(e)(s), *having gone*
Past Indefinite:	j'ai vu, etc., *I have seen, etc.*
	je suis allé(e), etc., *I have gone, etc.*
Pluperfect:	j'avais vu, etc., *I had seen, etc.*
	j'étais allé(e), etc., *I had gone, etc.*
Past Anterior:	j'eus vu, etc., *I had seen, etc.*
	je fus allé(e), etc., *I had gone, etc.*
Future Anterior:	j'aurai vu, etc., *I shall have seen, etc.*
	je serai allé(e), etc., *I shall have gone, etc.*
Conditional Anterior:	j'aurais vu, etc., *I should have seen, etc.*
	je serais allé(e), etc., *I should have gone, etc.*
Perfect Subjunctive:	quoique j'aie vu, etc., *altho I have seen, etc.*
	quoique je sois allé(e), etc., *altho I have gone, etc.*
Pluperfect Subjunctive:	quoique j'eusse vu, etc., *altho I had seen, etc.*
	quoique je fusse allé(e), etc., *altho I had gone, etc.*

100. Passive Voice. The past participle of the verb to be put into the passive voice is added to the proper form of **être,** which may itself be a compound tense. The past participle of the passive verb agrees in gender and number with the subject.

Passive Present Infinitive: être trouvé(e)(s), *to be found*

Passive Perfect Infinitive: avoir été trouvé(e)(s), *to have been found*

Passive Present Participle: étant trouvé(e)(s), *being found*

Passive Perfect Participle: ayant été trouvé(e)(s), *having been found*

Pres. Ind.: elle est trouvée, etc., *she is found, etc.*

Imperf. Ind.: elle était trouvée, etc., *she was found, etc.*

Past Def.: elle fut trouvée, etc., *she was found, etc.*

Future: elle sera trouvée, etc., *she will be found, etc.*

Conditional: elle serait trouvée, etc., *she would be found, etc.*

Pres. Subj.: quoiqu'elle soit trouvée, etc., *altho she be found, etc.*

Imperf. Subj.: quoiqu'elle fût trouvée, etc., *altho she were found, etc.*

Past Indef.: elle a été trouvée, etc., *she was (has been) found, etc.*

Pluperf.: elle avait été trouvée, etc., *she had been found, etc.*

Past Anterior: elle eut été trouvée, etc., *she had been found, etc.*

Fut. Ant.: elle aura été trouvée, etc., *she will have been found, etc.*

Cond. Ant.: elle aurait été trouvée, etc., *she would have been found, etc.*

Perfect Subj.: quoiqu'elle ait été trouvée, etc., *altho she has been found, etc.*

Pluperf. Subj.: quoiqu'elle eût été trouvée, etc., *altho she had been found, etc.*

Note 1. The student need not be dismayed by the formidable array of passives here given in outline: each form is a literal rendering of the English, the only additional difficulty being the agreement of the past participle with the subject.

Note 2. It is suggested that the student examine forms given in §99 and §100, and that he produce each tense in full. It will probably not be very profitable to dwell too long upon the compounds and the passives; they are given here to acquaint the student with their meanings. It will be remembered that the passive is avoided whenever possible (See Lesson XV, §42, 2).

101. Reciprocal Value of the Reflexive Form. The reflexive pronouns may have reciprocal value (Cf. §38). Thus, **Ils se sont vus** may mean *They saw themselves* or *They saw each other*; **Ils se sont parlé** may mean *They spoke to themselves* or *They spoke to each other*.

The reciprocal value may be made clear by the use of **l'un l'autre, les uns les autres, l'un à l'autre,** or **les uns aux autres:**

Ils se sont vus l'un l'autre (les uns les autres). *They saw each other.*
Ils se sont parlé l'un à l'autre (les uns aux autres). *They spoke to each other.*

102. venir (*to come*) venant   venu je viens je vins
   Fut. stem: *3rd plu. pres. ind.:*
    viendr-   viennent
               Pres. subj. stem:
               vienn-

  tenir (*to hold*) tenant   tenu je tiens je tins
   Fut. stem: *3rd plu. pres. ind:*
    tiendr-   tiennent
               Pres. subj. stem:
               tienn-

Note 1. These two verbs are conjugated alike, except that **être** is the auxiliary for **venir** and **avoir** for **tenir** (except when it is reflexive).

Note 2. **N** is inserted after **i** throughout the past definite and the imperfect subjunctive. The circumflex is written in the usual places: nous **vînmes** [vɛ̃ːm], vous **vîntes** [vɛ̃ːt]; **il vînt** [vɛ̃].

Note 3. In these two verbs **-ien-** (except where **n** is doubled) is pronounced [jɛ̃]: **je viens** [vjɛ̃]; **ils viendront** [vjɛ̃drɔ̃], etc. But: **ils viennent** [vjɛn]

EXERCISE XXXVII

arrivée [arive] f. *arrival*
brigand [brigɑ̃] m. *brigand*
dès [dɛ] *as early as, even at*
ignorer [iɲɔre] *not to know, to be ignorant of*
malgré [malgre] *in spite of*
paraître [parɛːtr] *to appear*
pardon [pardɔ̃] m. *pardon*
pluie [plɥi] f. *rain*

procurer [prɔkyre] *to procure*
promesse [prɔmɛs] f. *promise*
récompenser [rekɔ̃pɑ̃se] *to repay*
rendre [rɑ̃ːdr] *to return, give back*
retenir [rətniːr] *to detain*
signe [siɲ] m. *sign, signal*
tenir [təniːr] *to hold, keep*
voler [vɔle] *to steal, rob; fly*

à cause ([koːz] f.) **de** *because of*
s'agir [aʒiːr] **de** *to concern, to be a question of*
dès son arrivée *as soon as he (she) arrived*
tenir à *to insist upon, to want to, to be anxious to*
venir de *to have just (done)*
   Il vient d'arriver. *He has just arrived.*
   Nous venons de faire cela. *We have just done that.*
   Je venais de le voir. *I had just seen him.*
   Ils venaient de parler. *They had just spoken.*

A. Je vous demande pardon de ne pas avoir tenu la promesse que je vous ai faite de venir chez vous hier soir. Malgré la pluie je serais venu, si je n'avais pas été retenu par une visite. Je venais de rentrer à la maison quand j'ai
5 vu mon voisin qui me faisait signe de venir chez lui. J'ignorais ce qu'il voulait, mais je me suis dit qu'il devait avoir besoin de moi. Quand j'y suis arrivé, il m'a dit: «Je viens de rencontrer à l'hôtel un monsieur qui demande à vous être présenté. C'est un ancien ami de votre père. Je vais donc
10 l'accompagner chez vous.»

Je n'avais jamais entendu parler de ce monsieur, qui s'appelle André. Il paraît que, quand mon père voyageait en Chine, ils se sont rencontrés à Pékin. Monsieur André avait été volé par des brigands dès son arrivée. Mon père
15 avait pu lui procurer de l'argent. Monsieur André était resté en Chine pendant quelques années, mais mon père était revenu en France. Les affaires de M. André marchaient bien. Devenu riche, il voulait récompenser mon père; mais comme ils ne s'étaient jamais écrit, ils s'étaient perdus de
20 vue. Comme il ne s'agissait pas d'une grosse somme, mon père a dû l'oublier tout à fait. Mais M. André tient à me la rendre. C'est pourquoi il a voulu me connaître.

B. 1. I am coming. 2. They are coming. 3. We come. 4. He will come. 5. They would come. 6. Although he comes. 7. Although you come. 8. You used to come. 9. He has come. 10. She had come. 11. We shall have come. 12. You would have come. 13. Although he has come. 14. Although I have held. 15. Although she had come. 16. Although they had held. 17. They came (*p. def.*). 18. He held (*p. def.*).

C. 1. If my friend does not arrive this evening, I shall come to your house. 2. If he came early, I should accompany him. 3. If they have come, we shall be glad. 4. If they had not come, we should have accompanied you. 5. Although he is old, he insists upon walking fast. 6. Although he has come, I shall have to leave. 7. After having read the papers, they went out. 8. They met each other at my cousin's last year. 9. He and Mary have often written to each other 10. When we meet in the street, we stop and talk to each other. 11. My books have not yet been found, although my brother and his friend have been looking for them for an hour. 12. When they have been found, I shall prepare my lessons. 13. We have just read the papers which were brought by your brother. 14. It is not a question of procuring a large sum of money. 15. She had just appeared when he made me a sign to leave.

D. 1. De quoi est-ce que votre ami vous demande pardon? 2. Est-ce à cause de la pluie qu'il n'est pas venu? 3. Qui est-ce qui lui a fait signe de venir? 4. Savait-il ce que son voisin voulait? 5. Qu'est-ce qu'il s'est dit? 6. Qui est-ce que son voisin avait rencontré? 7. Que voulait ce monsieur? 8. Qu'est-ce qui lui était arrivé en Chine? 9. Qui lui avait procuré de l'argent? 10. Est-ce qu'il est resté pauvre? 11. Pourquoi est-ce qu'il n'a pas récompensé votre père? 12. Est-ce qu'il s'agissait d'une grosse somme?

LESSON XXXVIII

103. Cardinal Numerals.

1. un [œ̃], une [yn]
2. deux [dø]
3. trois [trwɑ]
4. quatre [katr]
5. cinq [sɛ̃ːk]
6. six [sis]
7. sept [sɛt]
8. huit [ɥit]
9. neuf [nœf]
10. dix [dis]
11. onze [ɔ̃ːz]
12. douze [duːz]
13. treize [trɛːz]
14. quatorze [katɔrz]
15. quinze [kɛ̃ːz]
16. seize [sɛːz]
17. dix-sept [dissɛt]
18. dix-huit [dizɥit]
19. dix-neuf [diznœf]
20. vingt [vɛ̃]
21. vingt et un [vɛ̃t‿e œ̃]
22. vingt-deux [vɛ̃ dø]
23. vingt-trois [vɛ̃t trwɑ]
24. vingt-quatre [vɛ̃t katr]
30. trente [trɑ̃ːt]
40. quarante [karɑ̃ːt]
50. cinquante [sɛ̃kɑ̃ːt]
60. soixante [swasɑ̃ːt]
70. soixante-dix[1] [swasɑ̃ːt dis]
71. soixante (et) onze [swasɑ̃ːt (e)ɔ̃ːz]
72. soixante-douze [swasɑ̃ːt duːz]
73. soixante-treize [swasɑ̃ːt trɛːz]
80. quatre-vingts [katrə vɛ̃]
81. quatre-vingt-un [katrə vɛ̃ œ̃]
90. quatre-vingt-dix[1] [katrə vɛ̃ dis]
91. quatre-vingt-onze [katrə vɛ̃ ɔ̃ːz]
100. cent [sɑ̃]
101. cent un [sɑ̃ œ̃]
200. deux cents [dø sɑ̃]
220. deux cent vingt [dø sɑ̃ vɛ̃]
1000. mille [mil]
1003. mille trois [mil trwɑ]
2000. deux mille [dø mil]
1000000. un million [œ̃ miljɔ̃]
2000000. deux millions [dø miljɔ̃]
1000000000. un milliard [œ̃ miljaːr]

104. Observations. 1. Only *one* has a masculine form and a feminine form. 2. **Quatre-vingt** and the multiples of **cent** are pluralized; however, **s.** is generally not written when a numeral follows: **quatre-vingts livres, j'en ai quatre-vingts; trois cents livres, j'en ai trois cents;** but **quatre-vingt(s)-neuf livres, trois cent(s) trois livres.** 3. *One hundred* is **cent** (without **un**); *one thousand* is **mille**. 4. **Million** and **milliard** are nouns of number. They may be preceded by **un**. In the plural they take **s** like other nouns. Before a noun they re-

---

[1] Note that the numerals from 70 to 79 and from 90 to 99 are made by adding the numerals from 10 to 19 to the numerals 60 and 80 respectively.

quire the preposition **de: un million de francs,** etc. 5. **Et** occurs in 21, 31, 41, 51, 61, and may be used in 71. The hyphen is used in compounds less than 100 unless **et** is used.

The final consonant of 5, 6, 7, 8, 9, 10, 17, 18, 19, is silent when the numeral modifies a noun with initial consonant or a noun preceded by an adjective with initial consonant: **cinq hommes** [sɛk‿ɔm], **cinq livres** [sɛ̃ liːvr], **cinq grands hommes** [sɛ̃ grɑ̃z‿ɔm]; but **le cinq janvier** [lə sɛɪk ʒɑ̃vje].

The final consonant of 1 (**un**), 2, 3, 5, 6, 7, 8, 9, 10, 17, 18, 19, 20, may be linked before a vowel (**s** and **x** link as [z], **f** as [v]): **six hommes** [siz‿ɔm], **neuf heures** [nœv‿œɪr]; but **le dix avril** [lə dis avril], **le deux août** [lə dø u].

The **h** of **huit** is aspirate, and **onze** is treated as if it had an initial aspirate **h;** therefore no linking or elision can occur before these numerals: **les huit hommes** [le ɥit‿ɔm], **le huit octobre** [lə ɥit ɔktɔbr], **les onze livres** [le ɔ̃z liːvr], **le onze avril** [lə ɔ̃ːz avril].

105. Ordinal Numerals. Notice **premier** [prəmje], *first*; **second** [səgɔ̃], or **deuxième** [døzjɛm], *second*; **cinquième** [sɛ̃kjɛm], *fifth*; **neuvième** [nœvjɛm], *ninth*. Other ordinal numerals are made by adding **-ième** to the cardinal numeral, except that a final **e** of the cardinal is dropped: **troisième** [trwɑzjɛm], **quatrième** [katriɛm], etc.

106. Fractions. Notice **la moitié** [mwatje] (noun) and **demi** [dəmi] (adjective), *half*; **un tiers** [tjɛɪr], *one-third*; **un quart** [kaɪr], *one-fourth*. Other fractions are expressed as in English: the numerator by a cardinal, the denominator by an ordinal: *five-eighths*, **cinq huitièmes.** Before a noun **demi** is invariable and is joined to the noun by the hyphen: **une demi-heure;** but after a noun it agrees in gender: **une heure et demie.**

107. Dates and Titles. Days of the month and numerical titles (except *first*) are expressed in French by the cardinal numerals: **Charles premier, Georges cinq; le premier mai, le deux mai.**

In dates from 1000 to 1099, **mil** is used; from 1100 upward, either **mil** or the hundreds: **en (l'an) mil quatre-vingt-dix; en (l'an) mil neuf cent vingt-quatre** or **en (l'an) dix-neuf cent vingt-quatre.**

108. ouvrir (*to open*)   ouvrant   ouvert   j'ouvre   j'ouvris

EXERCISE XXXVIII

Alain [alɛ̃] *Alan, Allen*
assassiner [asasine] *to assassinate*
assurance [asyrɑ̃ːs] f. *assurance*
Blois [blwɑ] city and castle on the Loire, southwest of Paris
cas [kɑ] m. *case*
célèbre [selɛbr] *celebrated, famous*
Chambord [ʃɑ̃bɔːr] castle near Blois
charmant, -e [ʃarmɑ̃, ʃarmɑ̃ːt] *charming*
château [ʃato] m. *castle*
Chinon [ʃinɔ̃] city and castle
comte [kɔ̃ːt] m. *count (noble)*
consentir [kɔ̃sɑ̃tiːr] *to consent*
disposition [dispozisjɔ̃] f. *arrangement*
drapeau [drapo] m. *flag*
duc [dyk] m. *duke*
entrée [ɑ̃tre] f. *entrance, entry*
environs [ɑ̃virɔ̃] m. pl. *vicinity*
excursion [ɛkskyrsjɔ̃] f. *excursion*
François [frɑ̃swɑ] *Francis*

Guise [giːz] noble French family of the XVIth and XVIIth centuries
imposer [ɛ̃poze] *to impose*
Jeanne d'Arc [ʒan d ark] *Joan of Arc*
Loire [lwaːr] f. river in France
préférer [prefere] *to prefer*
rampe [rɑ̃ːp] f. *flight of stairs*
refuser [rəfyze] *to refuse*
répéter [repete] *to repeat*
royal [rwajal] *royal*
ruine [rɥin] f. *ruin*
sentiment [sɑ̃timɑ̃] m. *sentiment, regard*
siècle [sjɛkl] m. *century, cycle*
spirale [spiral] f. *spiral*
tandis que [tɑ̃di(s) kə] *while*
Touraine [turɛːn] old French province
Tours [tuːr] city on the Loire
tricolore [trikɔlɔr] *tricolored*

Names of the months (all masculine): **janvier** [ʒɑ̃vje], **février** [fevrie], **mars** [mars], **avril** [avril], **mai** [mɛ], **juin** [ʒɥɛ̃], **juillet** [ʒyjɛ], **août** [u], **septembre** [sɛptɑ̃ːbr], **octobre** [ɔktɔbr], **novembre** [nɔvɑ̃ːbr], **décembre** [desɑ̃ːbr].

La Tour Eiffel, Paris

Le Grand Escalier, Château de Blois

LESSON XXXVIII

Tours, le 12 Juillet, 1923.

Mon cher Charles:—

Le premier juin j'ai quitté Paris pour aller en Touraine voir les châteaux. J'ai loué une chambre à Tours chez une charmante vieille dame française, et tous les jours je fais des excursions aux environs de la ville. En quinze jours j'ai vu douze châteaux. Il y en a qui sont très beaux, et tous sont intéressants. Il y a huit jours j'ai été à Chinon, où l'on voit les ruines du château où Jeanne d'Arc a été présentée à Charles VII le 8 mars 1429. Un des châteaux les plus intéressants est celui de Blois, dont tous les coins vous rappellent des noms célèbres dans l'histoire de la France au XVIe siècle. Louis XII et François Ier ont habité à Blois, et c'est dans ce château que le roi Henri III a fait assassiner le duc de Guise le 23 décembre 1588. À Chambord j'ai vu le grand escalier célèbre par la disposition de ses rampes en spirales, qui permet à deux personnes, dont l'une monte et l'autre descend, de ne pas se rencontrer. On y voit aussi les voitures qui devait servir à l'entrée royale du comte de Chambord à Paris en 1873 au cas où il aurait consenti à devenir Henri V. On dit qu'il a refusé parce qu'on voulait lui imposer le drapeau tricolore, tandis qu'il voulait le drapeau blanc des anciens rois de France. J'ai appris beaucoup de l'histoire de France en visitant ces grands monuments historiques. Personne ne peut bien connaître la France sans avoir visité les châteaux de la Loire.

Recevez l'assurance de mes meilleurs sentiments.

Alain.

B. 1. I have opened. 2. He opens. 3. They used to open. 4. We are opening. 5. Although you open. 6. They will open. 7. He would open. 8. They opened (*p. def.*). 9. We had opened. 10. You will have opened. 11. He would have opened. 12. Opening. 13. Five books. 14. Five men.

15. Six pens. 16. Six friends. 17. I have six. 18. 21 pens.
19. 31 pencils. 20. 8 girls. 21. I saw eight. 22. *Count from 1 to 20.* 23. *From 39 to 50.* 24. *From 69 to 80.* 25. *Continue:* sept fois un font sept, etc. 26. *Continue:* neuf fois un font neuf, etc. 27. *Give the following numerals in French:* 4, 14, 44, 400, 4441, 16, 17, 18, 19, 21, 75, 83, 93, 1294, 1492, 1553, 1607, 1776, 1789, 1812, 1923, 888, 1st, 2nd, 3rd, 4th, ½, ⅔, ¾, ⅘.

C. 1. The French kings had many beautiful castles. 2. Louis XIV, one of the greatest of the kings of France, was born (**né**) in 1638 and died in 1715. 3. Your brother and I are going to spend two weeks at Tours. 4. We arrived yesterday, the first of June, and we shall leave the fifteenth. 5. Since the year 1789 the tricolor has been the flag of France. 6. There are more than twenty castles in the vicinity of Tours. 7. We visited seven in ten days. 8. I shall be glad to see the little garden of Madam Deschamps; it must be quite charming. 9. Which of the castles did you find the most interesting? 10. It is possible to go up the stairs at Chambord without meeting a person who is coming down. 11. It is easier to study the history of France in France. 12. Why did the Count de Chambord refuse to become king of France?

D. 1. Quel jour du mois est-ce aujourd'hui? (*Answer:* C'est aujourd'hui . . . etc.) 2. Quel jour de la semaine était-ce hier? 3. Est-ce que ce sera demain le quatre juillet? 4. Combien de jours le mois de février a-t-il? 5. Répétez les noms des mois qui ont trente et un jours. 6. Dans quel mois est-ce que l'hiver commence? Le printemps? 7. Quel mois préférez-vous? Pourquoi? 8. Avez-vous vu les grands monuments historiques de Paris? 9. Qui est-ce que le roi Henri III a fait assassiner à Blois? 10. Où est-ce que Jeanne d'Arc a été présentée à Charles VII?

LESSON XXXIX

109. Indefinite Pronouns and Adjectives. 1. The uses of **on** have already been explained (§42).

2. Distinguish between **quelque(s)** [kɛlk(ə)], *some*, and the partitive: **quelque(s)** is limited in quantity, the partitive is quite indefinite:

> Il a quelques livres. *He has some (a few) books.*
> Il a des livres. *He has some books (any number).*

3. An adjective modifying **quelque chose** [kɛlkəʃoːz], *something*, or **rien,** *nothing*, is always uninflected and must be preceded by **de:**

> Il m'a dit quelque chose de nouveau. *He told me something new.*
> Je n'ai rien trouvé de bon. *I didn't find anything good.*

4. In the following, note the apostrophe (') in the singular, and the hyphen (-) in the plural:

> Avez-vous vu quelqu'un [kɛlkœ̃]? *Have you seen anybody?*
> Je voudrais quelqu'une [kɛlkyn] de ces plumes. *I should like (any) one of those pens.*
> A-t-il des livres? Il en a quelques-uns [kɛlkəz‿œ̃]. *Has he any books? He has a few.*
> Est-ce que quelques-unes [kɛlkəz‿yn] de ces dames désirent m'accompagner? *Do any of the ladies want to go with me?*

5. Note these forms and meanings of **tout** [tu]:

tout homme, *each* (or *every*) *man*
tout le temps, *all the time*
tout le livre, *the whole book*
toute [tut] femme, *each* (or *every*) *woman*
toute la journée, *the whole day*
tous [tu] les jours, *every day*
tous les deux jours, *every other day*
toutes [tut] les fois, *every time*

6. The adjective **chaque** [ʃak], *each*, has only one form; the pronoun **chacun** [ʃakœ̃] has a feminine **chacune** [ʃakyn]:

chaque homme, chaque femme, *each man, each woman*
chacun des hommes, *each of the men*
chacune des femmes, *each of the women*

7. Note the position of **tel**[1] [tɛl] after the indefinite article:

un tel homme, *such a man*
une telle femme, *such a woman*
Notice: Monsieur Un Tel, *Mr. So-and-So.*

8. The adjective **même** before a noun modified means *same*; after its noun it lends emphasis:

le même [mɛm] jour *the same day*
le jour même [mɛɪm] *that very day*

9. **Plusieurs** [plyzjœɪr], *several*, is an adjective with only one form. Note that it is not classed among expressions of quantity followed by the partitive construction:

plusieurs hommes, plusieurs femmes, *several men, several women.*

10. Distinguish between **un (une) autre,** *another, i. e. a different one,* and **encore un (une),** *another of the same kind:*

Je n'aime pas cette pomme; donnez-m'en une autre. *I don't like this apple; give me another one (a different one).*
Cette pomme est très bonne; donnez-m'en encore une. *This apple is very good, give me another one (like it).*

Notice also:

encore deux pommes, *two more apples*
encore des pommes, *some more apples*

110. prendre (*to take*)   prenant   pris   je prends   je pris
                    3rd plu. pres. ind.:
                    prennent
                  Pres. subj. stem:
                    prenn-

      boire (*to drink*)   buvant   bu   je bois   je bus
                    3rd plu. pres. ind.:
                    boivent
                  Pres. subj. stem:
                    boiv-

---

[1] (fem. **telle** - plurals regular)

EXERCISE XXXIX

abondance [abɔ̃dɑːs] f. *abundance*
amitié [amitje] f. *friendship, love*
anniversaire [anivɛrsɛːr] m. *anniversary*
Armand [armɑ̃] proper name
Avignon [aviɲɔ̃] city of Provence
boire [bwaːr] *to drink*
briller [brije] *to shine*
chacun, -e [ʃakœ̃, ʃakyn] *each one*
conte [kɔ̃ːt] m. *tale, short story*
convive [kɔ̃viːv] m. f. *guest, table companion*
cordial [kɔrdjal] *cordial*
coup [ku] m. *draught, "drop"*
courant [kurɑ̃] m. *current*
Daudet [dodɛ] French writer (1840-97)
exactement [ɛgzaktəmɑ̃] *exactly*
façon [fasɔ̃] f. *manner*
filleul, -e [fijœl] m.f. *godson (daughter)*
guerre [gɛːr] f. *war*
hospitalier [ɔspitalje] *hospitable*
hôte, hôtesse [oːt, otɛs] m. f. *host, hostess*

impression [ɛ̃prɛsjɔ̃] f. *impression*
littérature [literatyːr] f. *literature*
Midi [midi] m. *South (of France)*
mule [myl] f. *mule*
naissance [nɛsɑ̃ːs] f. *birth*
Nîmes [niːm] city of Provence
olivier [ɔlivje] m. *olive tree*
pape [pap] m. *pope*
postal [pɔstal] *postal*
précieux [presjø] *precious*
profiter [prɔfite] *to profit*
Provence [prɔvɑ̃ːs] f. old province
raconter [rakɔ̃te] *to tell, relate*
reste [rɛst] m. *remains*
Romain [rɔmɛ̃] m. *Roman*
roman [rɔmɑ̃] m. *novel*
santé [sɑ̃te] f. *health*
souvenir [suvniːr] m. *memory*
Tarascon [taraskɔ̃] city of Provence
Tartarin [tartarɛ̃] unique character created by Daudet
tel, -le [tɛl] *such*
touchant [tuʃɑ̃] *touching*

tenir au courant *to keep informed*
anniversaire de naissance *birthday anniversary*
aujourd'hui même *this very day*
rien de tel *nothing like it*

Alais, le 23 Juillet, 1923.

Mon cher Charles:—

Il ne faut pas vous attendre à recevoir de longues lettres; je profite du temps précieux dans ce joli pays pour voyager un peu partout, je ne peux pas passer toutes mes journées à écrire mes impressions. Je vous envoie de temps en temps des cartes postales, qui vous tiennent au courant de ce que je fais.

Cette fois-ci je suis content de vous dire que je suis en Provence, où le soleil brille et où tout le monde est gai. Il y a quelques jours j'ai quitté «le jardin de France», comme on appelle la Touraine et ses environs, pour venir dans le Midi. Ce n'est pas exactement le moment de visiter le Midi, c'est vrai; il fait très chaud depuis quelque temps. Mais je tenais à passer le 22 juillet chez mon filleul de guerre dont c'est l'anniversaire de naissance. La façon dont j'ai été reçu était quelque chose de touchant. Ces gens du Midi sont si cordiaux, si hospitaliers, si aimables!

Hier j'ai dîné chez mon petit ami, qui s'appelle Armand. Quelle abondance de bonnes choses! Chacun des convives a fait honneur à la cuisine française; mais notre hôtesse voulait que nous prenions encore quelque chose et que nous buvions encore un coup à la santé de son fils. Nous avons passé toute l'après-midi sous les oliviers, et le soir je suis rentré à mon hôtel. Je voudrais rester plus longtemps ici dans ce charmant coin de France; mais il faut que je parte aujourd'hui même; quelques-uns de nos compagnons à Paris sont prêts à partir pour l'Amérique, et je voudrais les voir encore une fois avant leur départ.

Une autre fois je vous raconterai ma visite à Nîmes, où il y a des restes du temps des Romains, et à Avignon, où l'on voit encore le palais des papes. Vous rappelez-vous le conte de Daudet, La Mule du Pape? J'ai passé par Tarascon, aussi. Vous savez que Daudet a écrit plusieurs romans sur Tartarin de Tarascon. Rien de tel dans la littérature française. Il faudra les lire un des ces jours.

Enfin, je suis bien content d'être venu dans le Midi; j'en garderai toujours un bon souvenir.

Toutes mes amitiés!

Alain.

LESSON XXXIX

B. 1. He takes. 2. They take. 3. You take. 4. They will take. 5. He was taking. 6. Although he takes. 7. Let us take. 8. We had taken. 9. They took (*p. def.*). 10. He drinks. 11. Although he drinks. 12. We drink. 13. They drink. 14. I shall drink. 15. We were drinking. 16. Although we drink. 17. He had drunk. 18. He drank. (*p. def.*). 19. Such a man. 20. Such women. 21. Something good. 22. Nothing new. 23. Every day. 24. The whole day. 25. All my books. 26. Each of the pens. 27. The same man. 28. That very man. 29. Some more stories. 30. Two more novels.

C. 1. Several of my friends and a few of yours will accompany us to the South. 2. I should not want to do such a thing. 3. That very day he told us the same story of the Romans. 4. As these apples are too green, I am going to buy others. 5. Each man raised his glass and drank to the health of our host. 6. One ought not to repeat such stories. 7. Another man has returned from the fields; there are only three who are still working. 8. He asked me for something to eat, but I hadn't anything to give him. 9. I am not surprised that he is sick; for some weeks he has been spending his days in working and his nights in studying. 10. I wasn't expecting to see so many people at their house. 11. If you haven't anything warm, give him some cold meat and some bread. 12. I shall keep you informed of all that happens. 13. He asked me if yesterday was my birthday; he must have forgotten that I was born on the 29th of February. 14. If he hadn't sent me postcards from time to time, I shouldn't have known where he was. 15. I have never seen anything like it.

D. 1. D'où est-ce que votre ami écrit cette fois? 2. Est-ce qu'il est content d'être dans le Midi? 3. Est-ce qu'il fait chaud à Alais au mois de juillet? 4. Pourquoi est-ce qu'il

y est allé en cette saison? 5. Comment s'appelle son filleul?
6. Est-ce que votre ami a été bien reçu? 7. Qu'est-ce qu'il a fait le 22 juillet? 8. Son hôtesse qu'est-ce qu'elle voulait?
9. Pourquoi est-ce qu'il reste si peu de temps dans le Midi?
10. Est-ce qu'il a visité d'autres villes?

LESSON XL

111. Omission of Article. 1. The preposition **en** is followed by the definite article in only five fixed expressions: **en l'absence** (**de**), *in the absence* (*of*); **en l'air**, *in the air*; **en l'an, en l'année**, *in the year*; **en l'honneur** (**de**), *in honor* (*of*). See §56.

Note the omission of the indefinite article in the following:

Nous retournerons en voiture. *We shall go back in a carriage.*
Elle était habillée en homme. *She was dressed as a man.*

2. There is no article with an unmodified noun in the predicate expressing rank, position, title, profession, religion, or nationality:

Il est président. *He is president.*
Son père est capitaine. *His father is a captain.*
Elle sera duchesse. *She will be a duchess.*
Mon ami est médecin. *My friend is a doctor.*
Est-ce que vous êtes catholique? *Are you a catholic?*
Je suis Américain. *I am an American.*
But: Son père est un général célèbre. *His father is a famous general.*
Mon ami est un bon catholique. *My friend is a good catholic.*

The article must be used if **ce** is the subject:

Qui est cet homme? C'est le président. C'est un général.

3. No article is used before a noun in apposition which simply adds information, but does not distinguish:

George V, roi d'Angleterre. *George V, king of England.*
Paris, ville de France. *Paris, a city in France.*
But: Mon frère, le médecin. *My brother, the doctor.*

112. Definite Article Used Distributively. 1. The French definite article generally takes the place of the English indefinite article in expressions of measure involving price:

> Il a payé ces bananes deux francs la douzaine. *He paid two francs a dozen for these bananas.*
> Combien ce ruban? Quinze sous le mètre. *How much for this ribbon? Fifteen cents a meter.*
> Des gants à deux dollars la paire. *Gloves at two dollars a pair.*

2. But in other expressions, especially expressions of time, **par** is used distributively:

> Cinq dollars par jour. *Five dollars a day.*
> Trois fois par semaine. *Three times a week.*

3. The definite article is sometimes used with names of days to express indefinite time:

> Elle reste chez elle le jeudi. *She is at home every Thursday.*
> Il vient le mercredi. *He comes on Wednesdays.*

But:

> Il est venu mercredi. *He came last Wednesday.*
> Il viendra mercredi. *He will come next Wednesday.*

113. Expressions of Time of Day. Observe the following time expressions, and notice that **il** always translates *it* in expressions of time of day:

> Quelle heure est-il? *What time is it?*
> Voulez-vous me dire l'heure? *Will you tell me what time it is?*
> Il m'a demandé l'heure. *He asked me what time it was.*
> Il est une heure—cinq heures. *It is one o'clock—five o'clock.*
> Il est cinq heures[1] et demie.[2] *It is half-past five.*
> Il est midi (minuit)[3] et demi.[4] *It is half-past twelve.*
> Six heures (et) un quart. *A quarter after six.*
> Quatre heures (et) dix (minutes). *Ten minutes after four.*
> Huit heures trois quarts. *Eight forty-five.*

[1] **Heure,** *o'clock,* cannot be omitted as in English.
[2] Note the feminine form. See §106.
[3] The French do not say *"twelve o'clock"*: always *"noon"* or *"midnight."*
[4] Note the masculine form, both **midi** and **minuit** being masculine.

Huit heures moins un quart. *A quarter to eight.*
Huit heures moins cinq (minutes). *Five minutes to eight.*
À deux heures précises. *At exactly two o'clock.*
À midi précis. *At exactly twelve o'clock (noon).*
Une heure sonne. *It is striking one.*
Sept heures viennent de sonner. *It has just struck seven.*
Vers (les) dix heures. *At about ten o'clock.*
Sur les deux heures. *At about two o'clock.*
Six heures du matin—du soir. *Six o'clock in the morning—evening.*
But: le matin—le soir. *in the morning—in the evening.*

Officially, the hours from noon to midnight are numbered thirteen to twenty-four; they appear thus in railway schedules, etc.: 20¾ h. = 8.45 P.M. In every-day life, however, French people still say: **huit heures du soir** and **huit heures du matin.**

114. mettre (*to put*)   mettant   mis   je mets   je mis

EXERCISE XL

aéroplane [aerɔplan] m. *airplane*
aise [ɛːz] f. *ease*
autocar [otɔkaːr] m. *autocar*
Bretagne [brətaɲ] f. *Brittany*
brûler [bryle] *to burn*
côte [koːt] f. *coast*
ensuite [ɑ̃sɥit] *then, next*
ingénieur [ɛ̃ʒenjœːr] m. *engineer*
kilomètre [kilɔmɛːtr] m. *kilometer*
Londres [lɔ̃ːdr] *London*

Mont-Saint-Michel [mɔ̃ (m.) sɛ̃ miʃɛl] island off the coast of Normandy
Normandie [nɔrmɑ̃di] f. old province
pittoresque [pitɔrɛsk] *picturesque*
repartir [rəpartiːr] *to set out again*
revoir [rəvwaːr] *to see again*
Rouen [rwɑ̃] city in Normandy
Saint-Malo [sɛ̃ malo] French seaport
salutation [salytɑsjɔ̃] f. *greeting*
surprendre [syrprɑ̃ːdr] *to surprise*

à son aise *at one's ease, comfortably*
où bon nous semblait *where we pleased*

Paris, le 20 Août, 1923.

Cher Ami:—

Ma dernière lettre de France! Depuis quelques semaines nous voyageons presque tout le temps. Je suis revenu du
5 Midi le 24 juillet. Deux jours plus tard je suis reparti. Avec un Français de mes amis, qui est ingénieur, j'ai quitté

La Maison Carrée (Reste Romain), Nîmes

Le Mont-Saint-Michel

Paris à sept heures trois quarts du matin pour aller à Rouen, jolie ville de Normandie. C'est là que les Anglais ont brûlé Jeanne d'Arc en 1431. Nous avons trouvé la vieille ville très intéressante—surtout les belles églises et les vieilles maisons. De Rouen nous sommes allés à Saint-Malo pour nous rendre au Mont-Saint-Michel. Ensuite nous avons pris une automobile pour faire le tour de la côte de Bretagne. Nous avons payé l'automobile deux francs le kilomètre, ce qui nous a permis d'aller où bon nous semblait. Je n'ai jamais rien vu de plus pittoresque que ce pays. Quand vous viendrez en France l'année prochaine vous ferez bien de le visiter. Il y a un autocar qui fait ce tour une fois par semaine; c'est un moyen de visiter la Bretagne à très bon marché et à son aise, mais on ne voit pas les plus jolis endroits.

Nous sommes de retour à Paris depuis samedi. Je n'aime pas trop à voyager en chemin de fer; c'est pourquoi je suis revenu la nuit en wagon-lit. Demain à midi je pars pour Londres, où je compte arriver vers trois heures de l'après-midi. Cela vous surprend qu'on puisse aller si vite de Paris à Londres? En aéroplane, mon cher! Je vais à Londres en aéroplane! Après trois ou quatre semaines en Angleterre je m'embarquerai à Liverpool pour retourner en Amérique. Il est dur de dire adieu à la France, mais je serai bien heureux de revoir mon propre pays.

Mes salutations à vous et à votre famille.

Alain.

B. 1. He puts. 2. They put (*pres.*). 3. We shall put. 4. Although he puts. 5. Put. 6. He would put. 7. I was putting. 8. We should put. 9. They put (*p. def.*). 10. Five francs an hour. 11. Thirteen francs a dozen. 12. He is a teacher. 13. His brother is a famous doctor. 14. He died in the year 1896. 15. It is six o'clock. 16. At half-past six. 17. At about a quarter past eight. 18. In the morning.

19. At ten minutes to nine in the morning. 20. At exactly eleven o'clock. 21. It is striking twelve. 22. What time is it? 23. He didn't know what time it was. 24. At half-past twelve.

C. 1. He set out for London last week, didn't he? 2. Is this the last letter he wrote you from France? 3. Rouen is an old city, which we found very interesting. 4. We have been travelling in Normandy since the fourteenth of July. 5. I was travelling with a young man who is a teacher. 6. I don't want him to pay more than ten francs a dozen for those apples. 7. If he doesn't start before six o'clock, he will not arrive before midnight. 8. She always comes to my house on Tuesday. 9. Last Tuesday she brought me some beautiful flowers and a few apples. 10. We went to bed at half-past eight in the evening and slept until six o'clock in the morning. 11. In the evening we are sometimes very tired. 12. If he asked me what time it is, I couldn't tell (it to) him: I have lost my watch. 13. Will it be easy for you to say good-bye to France? 14. This evening we are going to have a good dinner in honor of one of my father's friends. 15. Louis IX, king of France, is sometimes called Saint Louis.

D. 1. Quelle heure est-il à votre montre? 2. À quelle heure vous êtes-vous levé ce matin? 3. Avez-vous déjeuné avant de vous lever? 4. En quel an est-ce que Jeanne d'Arc a été mise à mort? 5. Qu'est-ce qu'on peut voir à Rouen? 6. Aimez-vous à voyager en chemin de fer? 7. Qu'est-ce que c'est que la Bretagne? 8. Est-ce que notre ami sera content de quitter la France? 9. Comment est-ce qu'il compte aller en Angleterre? 10. Combien de temps faut-il pour aller de Paris à Londres en aéroplane?

APPENDIX

SOME COMMON IRREGULAR FEMININES

I. Nouns.

Masculine		Feminine
acteur	*actor*	actrice
ambassadeur	*ambassador*	ambassadrice
baron	*baron*	baronne
compagnon	*companion*	compagne
comte	*count*	comtesse
danseur	*dancer*	danseuse
dieu	*god*	déesse
directeur	*director*	directrice
duc	*duke*	duchesse
empereur	*emperor*	impératrice
étranger	*stranger*	étrangère
héros	*hero*	héroïne
maître	*master*	maîtresse
nègre	*negro*	négresse
paysan	*peasant*	paysanne
prince	*prince*	princesse
serviteur	*servant*	servante
Suisse	*Swiss*	Suissesse
tsar	*czar*	tsarine

II. Adjectives.

Masculine		Feminine
actif	*active*	active
aigu	*acute*	aiguë
ancien	*ancient*	ancienne
bas	*low*	basse
beau (bel)	*beautiful*	belle
blanc	*white*	blanche
bon	*good*	bonne
ce (cet)	*this, that*	cette
cher	*dear*	chère
complet	*complete*	complète
cruel	*cruel*	cruelle
doux	*soft, sweet*	douce

II. Adjectives (continued).

Masculine		Feminine
épais	*thick*	épaisse
faux	*false*	fausse
favori	*favorite*	favorite
fou (fol)	*foolish*	folle
frais	*fresh*	fraîche
franc	*frank*	franche
gentil	*nice*	gentille
gros	*big*	grosse
heureux	*happy*	heureuse
inquiet	*anxious*	inquiète
léger	*light*	légère
long	*long*	longue
mou (mol)	*soft*	molle
muet	*mute*	muette
nouveau (nouvel)	*new*	nouvelle
public	*public*	publique
sec	*dry*	sèche
sot	*stupid*	sotte
turc	*Turkish*	turque
vieux (vieil)	*old*	vieille

THE GENDER OF NOUNS

The following paragraphs may be of some slight aid to the student in the learning of the gender of nouns. Rules for gender are likely to be so complicated or to have so many exceptions that they are of little value; in most cases the student must learn the gender of the noun as he learns the noun.

I. Gender by Meaning:

1. Names of male beings are generally masculine: **homme** (*man*), **monsieur** (*gentleman*), **père** (*father*), **fils** (*son*), **oncle** (*uncle*), **neveu** (*nephew*), **mari** (*husband*), etc.

2. Names of female beings are generally feminine: **femme** (*woman, wife*), **dame** (*lady*), **mère** (*mother*), **fille** (*daughter*), **tante** (*aunt*), **nièce** (*niece*), **sœur** (*sister*), etc.

3. Some nouns are masculine when applying to male beings and feminine when applying to female beings: **enfant** (*child*), **élève** (*pupil*), etc.

4. Some nouns have separate forms for the masculine and the feminine: **ami, amie** (*friend*); **lion** (*lion*), **lionne** (*lioness*); **nègre** (*negro*), **négresse** (*negress*); etc. (See p. 211)

5. Some nouns are masculine whether applying to males or females, especially nouns denoting profession: **docteur** (*doctor*), **médecin** (*physician*), **avocat** (*lawyer*), **écrivain** (*writer*), **auteur** (*author*), **éléphant** (*elephant*), etc. Note: **un écrivain femme, un éléphant femelle,** etc.

6. Some nouns are feminine whether applying to males or females: **connaissance** (*acquaintance*), **personne** (*person*), **sentinelle** (*sentinel*), **victime** (*victim*), **fourmis** (*ant*), **souris** (*mouse*), etc.

7. The following are masculine: names of directions, of seasons, of months, of days of the week, of words or phrases not nouns but used as such: **sud** (*south*), **hiver** (*winter*) [**automne** (*autumn*) is masculine or feminine], **mai** (*May*), **lundi** (*Monday*), **un que, le vrai** (=ce qui est vrai), **le mentir** (*lying*), **le devant** (*the front part*), etc.

8. Some nouns change gender as the meaning varies: **le livre** (*book*), **la livre** (*pound*); **le tour** (*tour, turn, trick*), **la tour** (*tower*); **le somme** (*nap*), **la somme** (*sum*); etc.

9. Some nouns are either masculine or feminine with the same meaning: **après-midi** (*afternoon*), **automne** (*autumn*), **automobile** (*automobile*), etc.

II. Gender by Derivation:

1. Nouns that were masculine or neuter in Latin are regularly masculine in French: **pied** (*foot*) from L. masc. **pes, pedem**; **péril** (*peril*) from L. neut. **periculum**; etc.

2. Nouns that were feminine in Latin are regularly feminine in French: **fille** (*daughter*) from L. **filia**; **église** (*church*) from L. **ecclesia**; etc.

3. There are many exceptions, notably nouns formed by false analogy from neuter plurals, which looked like feminine singulars: **feuille** [f.] (*leaf*) from L. neut. pl. **folia**; etc.

The above rules are, of course, of no use to the student who has not studied Latin.

III. Gender by Ending:

1. A noun ending in **-tion, -sion,** or **-aison** is feminine: **nation** (*nation*), **intention** (*intention*), **notion** (*notion*), **punition** (*punishment*), **pollution** (*defilement*), **occasion** (*occasion, opportunity*), **corrosion** (*corrosion*), **illusion** (*delusion*), **maison** (*house*), **conjugaison** (*conjugation*), etc.

Exception: **bastion** [m.] *bastion*.

2. A noun is feminine when it ends in a mute **e** preceded by a vowel or a double consonant: **vue** (*view*), **craie** (*chalk*), **journée** (*day*), **queue** (*tail*), **vie** (*life*), **avenue** (*avenue*), **boue** (*mud*), **joie** (*joy*), **classe** (*class*), **nappe** (*table cloth*), **fourchette** (*fork*), **pierre** (*stone*), **pomme** (*apple*), **salle** (*room*), **personne** (*person*), etc., etc.

Exceptions: **musée** (*museum*), **foie** (*liver*), **somme** (*nap*), **homme** (*man*), **tonnerre** (*thunder*), **verre** (*glass*), etc.

3. A noun ending in **-é** is generally masculine when concrete and feminine when abstract: Masculine: **café** (*coffee*), **côté** (*side*), **thé** (*tea*), **blé** (*wheat*); Feminine: **bonté** (*goodness*), **vérité** (*truth*), **santé** (*health*), **beauté** (*beauty*), **difficulté** (*difficulty*), **liberté** (*liberty*), **égalité** (*equality*), **fraternité** (*fraternity*), etc.

Exceptions: These are masculine: **gré** (*will*), **péché** (*sin*), etc.

4. A noun ending in **-eau** or **-age** is generally masculine: **morceau** (*piece*), **oiseau** (*bird*), **tableau** (*picture*), **tombeau** (*tomb*), **veau** (*calf*), **seau** (*pail*), **sceau** (*seal*), **voyage** (*journey*), **courage** (*courage*), etc.

Exceptions: These are feminine: **eau** (*water*), **peau** (*skin*), **image** (*picture*), **plage** (*beach*), etc.

5. A noun ending in **-ment** is generally masculine: **traitement** (*salary*), **règlement** (*regulation*), **grognement** (*growl*), **ébranlement** (*shaking*), etc.

Exception: **jument** (*mare*).

TABLE OF PERSONAL PRONOUNS

CONJUNCTIVE

	Subject	Direct Object	Indirect Object	DISJUNCTIVE
1.s.:	**je** *I*	**me** *me, myself*	**me** *(to, for) me, myself*	**moi** *I, we*
2.s.:	**tu** *thou*	**te** *thee, thyself*	**te** *(to, for) thee, thyself*	**toi** *thou, thee*
3.s.m.:	**il** *he, it*	**le** *him, it* **se** *himself, itself*	**lui*** *(to, for) him, it* **se** *(to, for) himself, itself*	**lui*** *he, him, it*
3.s.f.:	**elle** *she, it*	**la** *her, it* **se** *herself, itself*	**lui*** *(to, for) her, it* **se** *(to, for) herself, itself.*	**elle** *she, her, it*
1.pl.:	**nous** *we*	**nous** *us, ourselves*	**nous** *(to, for) us, ourselves*	**nous** *we, us*
2.pl.:	**vous** *you*	**vous** *you, yourself, yourselves*	**vous** *(to, for) you, yourself, yourselves*	**vous** *you*
3.pl.m.:	**ils** *they*	**les** *them* **se** *themselves*	**leur** *(to, for) them* **se** *(to, for) themselves*	**eux** *they, them*
3.pl.f.:	**elles** *they*	**les** *them* **se** *themselves*	**leur** *(to, for) them* **se** *(to, for) themselves*	**elles** *they, them*

* Note—As a conjunctive, **lui** is masculine or feminine:
    Je lui parle. *I am speaking to him.* or *I am speaking to her.*
As a disjunctive, **lui** is masculine only; **elle** is the feminine form:
    Je pense à lui. *I am thinking of him.*
    Je pense à elle. *I am thinking of her.*

TABLES OF RELATIVE AND INTERROGATIVE PRONOUNS[1]

RELATIVES

	Persons (*Whom*)	Persons or Things (*Who, whom, which, that*)	Things (*Which, that*)
Subject of a verb:		1. **qui** (*or* **lequel**)	
Object of a verb:		2. **que** (or **lequel**)	
Predicate nominative:		3. **que** (*or* **lequel**)	
Object of a preposition:	4. **qui**	5. **lequel** [2]	6. (**quoi**) [2]
de + a relative:	7. **de qui** [3]	8. **dont** (*or* **duquel**)	9. (**d'où**)
à (**en, dans, sur**) + a relative:	10. **à qui**, etc.	11. **auquel**, etc.	12. **où**

INTERROGATIVES

	Persons (*Who? Whom?*)	Persons or Things (*Which one(s)?*)	Things (*What?*)
Subject of a verb:	1. **qui?**[4]	2. **lequel?**	3. **qu'est-ce qui?**
Object of a verb:	4. **qui?**	5. **lequel?**	6. **que?**
Predicate nominative:	7. **qui?**	8. **lequel?**	9. **que?**
Object of a preposition:	10. **qui?**	11. **lequel?**	12. **quoi?**
Out of construction:	13. **qui?**	14. **lequel?**	15. **quoi?**

---

[1] Only **lequel** changes its form for gender and number; the variants are **lequel, laquelle, lesquels, lesquelles.** The usual contractions take place.

[2] This is the only case in which **lequel** (relative) is required: as the object of a preposition and referring definitely to a noun that names a thing—which **quoi** does not. In other cases **lequel** is desirable only when it clears up an ambiguity.

[3] Note: La famille **d'où** il sort . . .

[4] Or **qui est-ce qui.**

Examples—Relatives

1. Le monsieur (la dame) **qui** est ici . . .
   Les messieurs (les dames) **qui** sont ici . . .
   Le livre (la plume) **qui** est sur la table . . .
   Les livres (les plumes) **qui** sont sur la table . . .
   Le père de ma cousine **lequel** est ici . . .
   La mère de mon cousin **laquelle** est ici . . .
   Les sœurs de mon ami **lesquelles** sont ici . . .
   Les cousins de ma mère **lesquels** sont ici . . .
   Le chapeau de ma sœur **lequel** n'est pas ici . . . etc., etc.
2. Le monsieur (la dame, les messieurs, les dames, le livre, la plume, les livres, les plumes) **que** je cherche . . .
   Le père de ma cousine (le chapeau de ma sœur) **lequel** je cherche . . . etc.
3. Il l'a fait comme l'honnête homme **qu'**il est.
   Il m'a dit ce **que** c'est.
4. Le monsieur (les dames) devant **qui** je me trouvais . . . etc.
5. La dame (la maison) près de **laquelle** je me trouvais . . . etc.
6. Il a mangé, après **quoi** il s'est endormi.
7. L'ami (les cousines) de **qui** je parlais . . .
8. Ma sœur (mes livres) **dont** je parlais . . .
   La femme de mon frère (la plume de votre père) de **laquelle** je parlais . . .
9. La ville (le pays) **d'où** il vient . . .
10. Le monsieur (les dames) à **qui** je parlais . . .
11. Les dames (les pièces) **auxquelles** je pensais . . .
12. La ville **où** il arrivera demain . . .
    Le jour **où** il arrivera . . .
    La table **où** (=sur **laquelle**) il a mis le livre . . . etc., etc.

Examples—Interrogatives

1. **Qui** est arrivé?
2. **Laquelle** de vos sœurs (**laquelle** de vos plumes) est dans la maison?
3. **Qu'est-ce qui** est arrivé?
4. **Qui** avez-vous vu?
5. J'ai cinq frères (cinq livres). **Lesquels** avez-vous vus?
6. **Qu'**a-t-il?
7. **Qui** est-ce?
8. Il y a trois enfants (trois crayons). **Lequel** est-ce?
9. **Qu'**est-ce?
10. Avec **qui** parlait-il?

11. **Auquel** de vos amis (**auquel** de vos livres) pensez-vous?
12. Sur **quoi** a-t-il mis le livre?
13. Quelqu'un est arrivé. **Qui?**
    J'ai vu quelqu'un. **Qui?**
14. Un garçon est parti. **Lequel?**
    J'ai vu deux de ses sœurs. **Lesquelles?**
    Un livre est perdu. **Lequel?**
    J'ai trouvé trois de vos livres. **Lesquels?**
15. Quelque chose est arrivé. **Quoi?**
    J'ai trouvé quelque chose. **Quoi?**

NEGATION

I. In addition to the negatives mentioned in §83, we find (among others) **ne - guère** (*scarcely*), **ne - aucun** (*none*), **ne - nul** (*none*), **ne - aucunement** (*not at all*), **ne - nullement** (*not at all*):

> Il ne peut guère les voir. *He can scarcely see them.*
> Nous n'en avons aucun. *We haven't any.*
> Nul n'est arrivé. *Not one arrived.*
> Vous n'êtes aucunement à blâmer. *You are not at all to blame.*
> Ils ne veulent nullement vous voir. *They don't want to see you at all.*

II. *No* or *not*, apart from a verb, may be expressed by **non** as well as by **pas** or **point** (for emphasis sometimes by **non pas** or **non point**):

> Vous avez fait cela? Non pas! *or* Non point! *You did that? Not so!*
> Non (pas) seulement cela . . . *Not only that . . .*
> Une organisation non viable. *An organization not likely to endure.*

III. When an infinitive is negative, both parts of the negative generally precede the infinitive. This is not true however, of **ne - que** and **ne - personne:**

> Je lui ai dit de ne pas venir. *I told him not to come.*
> Il m'a ordonné de ne plus y aller. *He ordered me not to go there any more.*
> Nous étions fâchés de ne rien voir. *We were sorry not to see anything.*
> But: Il m'a promis de ne prendre que cela. *He promised me to take only that.*
> Cela nous ennuie de n'y trouver personne. *It annoys us not to find anybody there.*

NEGATION

IV. In colloquial French (not to be imitated), **ne** is sometimes omitted:

Il a pas voulu nous parler. *He wouldn't speak to us.*

V. 1. The second part of the negative may be omitted, **ne** alone being the negative, with the verbs **bouger** (*budge*), **cesser** (*cease*), **oser** (*dare*), **pouvoir** (*be able*), **savoir** (*know*):

Je lui ai dit de ne bouger. *I told him not to budge.*
Il ne cesse de parler. *He doesn't stop talking.*
Il n'ose y aller. *He daren't go there.*
Qu'a-t-il? Je ne sais. *What ails him? I don't know.*
Je ne puis le faire. *I can't do it.*

2. Ne may stand alone after **si** (*if*), **que** (*why?*), and in dependent clauses after a negative:

Il y était si je ne me trompe. *He was there if I am not mistaken.*
Que ne me l'avez-vous dit? *Why didn't you tell me so?*
Il n'y a pas de règle qu'il n'ait répétée. *There is no rule which he didn't repeat.*

VI. A pleonastic **ne** (without negative value) is used:

1. In a clause following an expression of fearing when neither clause is negative:

J'ai peur qu'il ne tombe. *I am afraid that he will fall.*
But: Je n'ai pas peur qu'il tombe. *I am not afraid that he will fall.*
J'ai peur qu'il ne vienne pas. *I am afraid he won't come.*
Je n'ai pas peur qu'il ne vienne pas. *I am not afraid that he won't come.*

2. In a clause which is the second member of an unequal comparison, the first member not being negative:

Il est plus grand que je ne le pensais. *He is taller than I thought.*
But: Il est aussi grand que je le pensais. *He is as tall as I thought.*
Il n'est pas si grand que je le pensais. *He is not so tall as I thought.*

3. After negative expressions of doubting:

Je ne doute pas qu'il n'ait fait cela. *I don't doubt he did that.*

4. In a compound tense after **depuis que, il y a, voilà**:

Il y a cinq ans qu'il n'a été ici. *It is five years since he was here.*

Il a beaucoup vieilli depuis que je ne l'ai vu. *He has grown much older since I saw him.*

VII. Note the following:

N'importe! *It doesn't matter.*
Je ne sais que faire. *I don't know what to do.*
Je n'ai que faire de cela. *I have no use for that.*
Il ne partira pas non plus. *He won't leave either.*
Ni moi non plus. *Nor I either.*

THE SUBJUNCTIVE

In addition to the uses of the subjunctive mentioned in §§60 and 64, the following may be noted:

1. In a relative clause when the antecedent is qualified by a superlative:

Voici l'histoire la plus intéressante que j'**aie** jamais lue. *This is the most interesting story that I have ever read.*

C'est la seule chose qu'il **ait** faite. *It's the only thing he did.*

2. In a relative clause of characteristic after an indefinite antecedent:

Il me faut un pardessus qui me **tienne** chaud. *I must have an overcoat which will keep me warm.*

Je cherche un livre que les enfants **puissent** lire. *I am looking for a book that the children can read.*

3. In a noun clause following upon an expression of opinion:

Il vaudra mieux qu'il ne vous **voie** pas. *It will be better if he doesn't see you.*

Il est à désirer qu'il **vienne** de bonne heure. *It is to be desired that he come early.*

Je ne trouve pas juste qu'on **fasse** cela. *I do not consider it right to do that.*

THE SUBJUNCTIVE

4. In a clause following an expression of doubt, denial or uncertainty; also after an expression which, through a negative, a question or a condition, implies doubt, denial or uncertainty:

Je sais qu'il viendra. *I know that he will come.* But: Je doute qu'il **vienne.**
J'avoue que je l'ai fait. *I confess that I did it.* But: Je nie que je l'**aie** fait.
Je suis sûr qu'il est parti. *I am sure that he has left.* But: Je ne suis pas sûr qu'il **soit** parti. Êtes-vous sûr qu'il **soit** parti? Si vous êtes sûr qu'il **soit** parti . . .
Je crois qu'il l'a fait. *I believe he did it.* But: Je ne crois pas qu'il l'**ait** fait. Croyez-vous qu'il l'**ait** fait? Si je croyais qu'il l'**ait** fait . .
Je dis qu'il est fou. *I say he is crazy.* But: Je ne dis pas qu'il **soit** fou.
Il paraît que vous avez raison. *It is evident that you are right.* But: Il semble que vous **ayez** raison. However: Il me semble que vous avez raison.

Note that a negative and an interrogative counteract each other:

Ne croyez-vous pas qu'il le fera?

5. To express indefiniteness,[1] in clauses following certain pronouns, adjectives and adverbs:

Quoi que ce **soit** . . . *Whatever it may be* . . .
Qui que ce **soit** . . . *Whoever it may be* . . .
Quel que **soit** son dessein . . . *Whatever his plan may be* . . .
Quelque grand qu'il **soit** . . . *However great he may be* ? . .
Si modestement qu'il **parle** . . . *No matter how modestly he may speak* . . .

6. In clauses introduced by certain conjunctions which in themselves require the subjunctive: **avant que**[2] (*before*), **jusqu'à ce que**[2] (*until*), **pourvu que** (*provided that, if only*), **sans que** (*without*), **pas que** (*not that*), **à moins que** (*unless*),

---

[1] Note—There is a concessive value in these expressions.
[2] With indefinite time in the future.

en attendant que[1] (*until*), **de sorte que**[2] (*so that*), **de crainte que** or **de peur que** (*for fear lest*), **que . . . ou** (*whether . . . or*), etc.

> Je le ferai avant qu'il ne **parte.** *I'll do it before he leaves.*
> Restez ici jusqu'à ce qu'il **soit** arrivé. *Stay here until he has come.*
> Pourvu qu'il **soit** à la maison! *If only he is at home!*
> Je sortirai sans qu'il le **sache.** *I'll go out without his knowing it.*
> Ce n'est pas qu'il ne **puisse** pas le faire. *It isn't that he can't do it.*
> Pas que je **sache.** *Not that I know.*
> Je partirai à moins qu'il ne **vienne.** *I'll leave unless he comes.*
> Asseyez-vous en attendant qu'il **finisse.** *Sit down until he finishes.*
> J'attends qu'on **sorte.** *I am waiting for them to come out.*
> Faites de sorte qu'il n'y **ait** personne. *Arrange so that there will be nobody.* But: J'ai fait de sorte qu'il n'y **avait** personne.
> Je le tiens de crainte (peur) qu'il ne se **sauve.** *I am holding him for fear that he might run away.* (*lest he run away*).
> Qu'il **soit** riche ou pauvre . . . *Whether he be rich or poor . . .*

7. After **que** when it repeats a conjunction that requires the subjunctive, also when it repeats a conditional **si** (which is ordinarily followed by the indicative):

> Quoique j'y aille et qu'il me **voie** . . . *Although I may go there and he may see me . . .*
> Si j'y vais et qu'il me **voie** . . . *If I go there and he sees me . . .*

8. In literary French the imperfect subjunctive not infrequently replaces the conditional of the auxiliary in a compound of the conditional in a result clause:

> Si je m'étais montré, il **eût** été surpris. *If I had appeared, he would have been surprised.*

---

[1] Likewise after any form of the verb **attendre** followed by **que** and an expression denoting time in the future.

[2] With unattained result.

THE INFINITIVE

The infinitive, although it is in very common use, is one of the most difficult constructions in French—and, perhaps, the least understood. It will generally be found disastrous to let the student who has reached the age of reason "get used to the infinitive," or trust that he will acquire a "feeling" for it. The following paragraphs will supplement the more common uses of the infinitive explained in Lessons XXXIV and XXXV.

1. A direct infinitive may be used as a subject or as a predicate nominative:

Rire vaut mieux que pleurer. *To laugh is better than to weep.*
Voir c'est **croire**. *To see is to believe.*

However, when an infinitive in the predicate may be construed as being complementary to a noun understood, the sign **de** is used:

La plus grande difficulté sera (la difficulté) **de** les **trouver**. *The greatest difficulty will be to find them.*

2. The infinitive sometimes assumes the value of a finite form, being used, without a sign, as an imperative, in an exclamation, or in a question:

Manger des fruits et des légumes; ne pas **manger** de viande. *Eat fruit and vegetables; don't eat meat.*
Moi **faire** une chose pareille! *I do such a thing!*
Que **faire**? Que **penser**? *What (was I to) do? What (was I to) think?*

3. The "historical" infinitive, with the sign **de,** is equivalent to a past tense:

Et tous **de rire.** *And all of them laughed.*

4. A direct infinitive is used in apposition:

Voilà mon intention: **vendre** tout ce que je possède et **partir.** *This is my intention: sell all I have and leave.*

5. An infinitive with the sign **à** may have adverbial value:

Elle chante **à ravir.** *She sings charmingly.*

6. An infinitive with **à** may take the place of an *if*-clause:

A vous **dire** la vérité, je n'y crois pas. *To tell you the truth (if I told you the truth), I don't believe in it.*

7. An infinitive may have passive value, although active in form. In such a case, the sign is regularly **à** except after verbs of causing, permitting and perceiving:

Cela est facile **à comprendre.** *That is easily understood.*
Une maison **à vendre.** *A house to be sold.*
C'est encore **à faire.** *It is yet to be done.*

But:

J'ai fait **faire** cet habit par votre tailleur. *I had this coat made by your tailor.*
Il s'est laissé **tromper** par son camarade. *He allowed himself to be deceived by his comrade.*
Nous avons vu **bâtir** cette maison. *We saw that house built.*

8. The sign of the infinitive sometimes has a literal prepositional value:

prendre plaisir **à** chanter *to take pleasure* **in** *singing*
s'amuser **à** lire *to amuse oneself* **by** (**in**) *reading*
s'abandonner **à** pleurer *to give oneself up* **to** *weeping*
s'abstenir **de** fumer *to abstain* **from** *smoking*
accuser **de** voler *to accuse* **of** *stealing*
capable **de** faire cela *capable* **of** *doing that*
loin **de** le penser *far* **from** *thinking so*

9. An infinitive after a comparative commonly has the sign **de**:

J'aimerais mieux vous accompagner que **de rester** ici. *I should rather go with you than stay here.*

The sign is often omitted in short sentences having the nature of proverbs:

Rire vaut mieux que **pleurer.** *To laugh is better than to weep.*

However, when an infinitive continues a preceding construction requiring **à,** it takes this sign after a comparative:

> Je prends plus de plaisir à écouter qu'**à parler.** *I take more pleasure in listening than in speaking.*

10. An infinitive connected in meaning with **assez** or **trop** has the sign **pour:**

> Je le connais assez **pour** vous présenter. *I know him well enough to introduce you.*
> Soyez assez bon **pour** me présenter. *Be so kind as to introduce me.*
> Vous marchez trop lentement **pour** y arriver dans une heure. *You are walking too slowly to get there in an hour.*

I. Some of the Verbs Followed by a Direct Infinitive:

aimer (conditional)[2]	envoyer	se rappeler
aimer autant[2]	espérer	reconnaître
aimer mieux[2]	faillir (*come near*)	regarder
aller	faire[3]	rentrer
amener (*bring*)[2]	falloir	retourner
arriver (*arrive*)[2]	s'imaginer	revenir
avoir beau	juger	savoir
compter	jurer (*swear*)[3]	sembler
courir	laisser[1, 3]	sentir
croire	manquer (*come near*)[1, 4]	sortir
daigner	mener	souhaiter
déclarer	monter	supposer
descendre (*descend*)[2]	oser	se trouver (*be*)
désirer	paraître	valoir autant
devoir	partir	valoir mieux
dire (*say*)[3]	pouvoir	venir[2, 3]
écouter	préférer	voir[2]
entendre[2]	prétendre (*claim, intend*)[2]	vouloir

[1] Or **à.**
[2] See verbs with **à.**
[3] See verbs with **de.**
[4] Or **de.**

II. Some of the Verbs Followed by an Infinitive with the Sign à:

abandonner
s'accorder (*agree*)[4]
accoutumer
aider
aimer[3]
amener (*induce*)[3]
amuser
appeler
appliquer
apprendre
apprêter
s'arrêter
arriver (*succeed*)[3]
aspirer
s'attendre (*expect*)
autoriser
avoir
chercher
commencer[2]
condamner
consacrer
consentir
consister
conspirer
continuer[2]
contribuer
décider (*induce*)[4]
se décider (*resolve*)[4]
demander[2]

dépenser
descendre (*stoop*)[3]
destiner
dévouer
disposer
donner
s'efforcer[2]
employer
encourager
s'ennuyer[2]
enseigner
s'entendre (*know how*)[3]
essayer[2]
être (*be busy with*)
exposer
forcer[2]
gagner[3]
habituer
intéresser
inviter
jouer
laisser[1, 4]
lasser[2]
manquer[1, 2]
mettre
montrer
obliger[2]
s'obstiner
s'occuper (*be busy with*)[4]

offrir[4]
s'opposer
parvenir
passer[4]
penser
perdre
se plaire
pousser
prendre garde (*take care*)[4]
prendre plaisir
se prendre (*begin*)
préparer
prétendre (*aspire*)[3]
prier (*invite*)[4]
se refuser[4]
renoncer
réussir
servir
songer
souffrir[2]
suffire
tenir (*insist*)
travailler
trembler (*tremble*)[4]
venir (*happen*)[3, 4]
voir (*see about*)[3]
vouer

---

[1] Or direct.
[2] Or **de**.
[3] See verbs with direct infinitive.
[4] See verbs with **de**.

THE INFINITIVE

III. Some of the Verbs Followed by an Infinitive with the Sign de:

s'abstenir
accorder (*grant*)[3]
accuser
achever
s'affliger
s'apercevoir
avertir
s'aviser
blâmer
cesser
charger
choisir
commencer[1]
conseiller
se contenter
continuer[1]
convaincre
convenir
craindre
décider (*decide*)[3]
dédaigner
défendre
demander[1]
se dépêcher
dire (*bid*)[2]
dispenser
se douter
s'efforcer[1]
empêcher
s'ennuyer[1]

entreprendre
essayer[1]
s'étonner
faire bien[3]
féliciter
finir
se flatter
forcer[1]
garder
gronder
se hâter
jouir
jurer (*promise*)[2]
ne pas laisser (*continue*)[2,3]
lasser[1]
manquer
se mêler
menacer
mériter
se moquer
mourir
négliger
obliger[1]
s'occuper (*be interested in*)[3]
s'offrir[3]
ordonner
oublier
pardonner
parler
se passer (*do without*)[3]

permettre
plaindre
se plaindre
prendre garde (*guard against*)[3]
prendre soin
prier (*beg*)[3]
priver
promettre
proposer
punir
refuser[3]
regretter
se réjouir
remercier
se repentir
reprocher
rire
risquer
se soucier
souffrir[1]
soupçonner
sourire
se souvenir
supplier
tâcher
tenter
trembler (*fear*)[3]
venir (*have just*)[2,3]

[1] Or à.

[2] See verbs with direct infinitive.

[3] See verbs with à.

SIMPLE TENSES OF THE THREE REGULAR CONJUGATIONS, AVOIR AND ÊTRE

Present Infinitive

donner	finir	rompre	avoir	être

Present Participle

donnant	finissant	rompant	ayant	étant

Past Participle

donné	fini	rompu	eu	été

Present Indicative

je	donne	finis	romps	ai	suis
tu	donnes	finis	romps	as	es
il	donne	finit	rompt	a	est
nous	donnons	finissons	rompons	avons	sommes
vous	donnez	finissez	rompez	avez	êtes
ils	donnent	finissent	rompent	ont	sont

Imperfect Indicative

je	donnais	finissais	rompais	avais	étais
tu	donnais	finissais	rompais	avais	étais
il	donnait	finissait	rompait	avait	était
nous	donnions	finissions	rompions	avions	étions
vous	donniez	finissiez	rompiez	aviez	étiez
ils	donnaient	finissaient	rompaient	avaient	étaient

Past Definite

je	donnai	finis	rompis	eus	fus
tu	donnas	finis	rompis	eus	fus
il	donna	finit	rompit	eut	fut
nous	donnâmes	finîmes	rompîmes	eûmes	fûmes
vous	donnâtes	finîtes	rompîtes	eûtes	fûtes
ils	donnèrent	finirent	rompirent	eurent	furent

Future

je	donnerai	finirai	romprai	aurai	serai
tu	donneras	finiras	rompras	auras	seras
il	donnera	finira	rompra	aura	sera
nous	donnerons	finirons	romprons	aurons	serons
vous	donnerez	finirez	romprez	aurez	serez
ils	donneront	finiront	rompront	auront	seront

Conditional

je	donnerais	finirais	romprais	aurais	serais
tu	donnerais	finirais	romprais	aurais	serais
il	donnerait	finirait	romprait	aurait	serait
nous	donnerions	finirions	romprions	aurions	serions
vous	donneriez	finiriez	rompriez	auriez	seriez
ils	donneraient	finiraient	rompraient	auraient	seraient

Present Subjunctive

je	donne	finisse	rompe	aie	sois
tu	donnes	finisses	rompes	aies	sois
il	donne	finisse	rompe	ait	soit
nous	donnions	finissions	rompions	ayons	soyons
vous	donniez	finissiez	rompiez	ayez	soyez
ils	donnent	finissent	rompent	aient	soient

Imperfect Subjunctive

je	donnasse	finisse	rompisse	eusse	fusse
tu	donnasses	finisses	rompisses	eusses	fusses
il	donnât	finît	rompît	eût	fût
nous	donnassions	finissions	rompissions	eussions	fussions
vous	donnassiez	finissiez	rompissiez	eussiez	fussiez
ils	donnassent	finissent	rompissent	eussent	fussent

Imperatives

donne	finis	romps	aie	sois
donnons	finissons	rompons	ayons	soyons
donnez	finissez	rompez	ayez	soyez

For synopses of compound tenses see Lesson XXXVII, §99.

IRREGULAR VERBS

Note—The principal parts of irregular verbs are here given with such other irregularities as cannot be derived from the principal parts. Under the infinitive is given the future stem. Under the present participle are given (1) irregularities in the plural of the present indicative; (2) the plural imperatives when they are not the same as the corresponding forms of the present indicative; (3) the first singular of the imperfect indicative when the imperfect does not follow the stem of the present participle; (4) the first singular of an irregular present subjunctive, in which case the same stem may be assumed to obtain in the three singulars and the third plural, the stem in the first and second persons plural being that of the present participle, unless a note states that the irregular stem is used throughout the tense. Under the past participle an irregular feminine is noted in a few cases. Under the fourth principal part are given (1) singular present indicative forms that do not follow the first singular, and (2) the singular imperative when it differs from the second singular of the present indicative other than in the omission of **s** when that form ends in **es**. Under the fifth principal part there can be no irregularities except in the use of diacritical marks.

1. aller, *to go*

aller	allant	allé	je vais	j'allai
ir-	(1) ils vont		(1) tu vas	
	(4) j'aille		il va	
			(2) va	

2. envoyer, *to send*

envoyer	envoyant [1]	envoyé	j'envoie	j'envoyai
enverr-				

[1] **oy** changes to **oi** before a mute **e**.

Thus also: **renvoyer**.

3. acquérir, *to acquire*

acquérir	acquérant	acquis	j'acquiers	j'acquis
acquerr-	(1) ils acquièrent			
	(4) j'acquière			

Thus also: **conquérir, enquérir, reconquérir, requérir**.

4. assaillir, to assail

| assaillir | assaillant | assailli | j'assaille | j'assaillis |

Thus also: **tressaillir**.

5. bouillir, to boil

| bouillir | bouillant | bouilli | je bous | je bouillis |

Thus also: **ébouillir, rebouillir**.

6. courir, to run

| courir | courant | couru | je cours | je courus |
| courr- | | | | |

Thus also: **accourir, concourir, discourir, encourir, parcourir, recourir, secourir**.

7. cueillir, to pluck, to gather

| cueillir | cueillant | cueilli | je cueille | je cueillis |
| cueiller- | | | | |

Thus also: **accueillir, recueillir, saillir** (*to project*).

8. dormir, to sleep

| dormir | dormant | dormi | je dors | je dormis |

Thus also: **endormir, redormir, rendormir**.

9. faillir, to fail

| faillir | faillant [2] | failli | je faux [1] | je faillis |
| faudr- [1] | | | | |

[1] Generally replaced by regular second conjugation forms.
[2] No imperatives.

Thus also: **défaillir** (Pres. Ind.: **je défaus**, etc.)

10. fuir, to flee

| fuir | fuyant [1] | fui | je fuis | je fuis |

[1] **uy** changes to **ui** before mute **e**.

Thus also: **enfuir**.

11. gésir, *to lie*

gésir [1]	gisant	......	......	......
	(2) lacking		(1) **il gît**	
	(4) lacking			

[1] Seldom used except in epitaphs: **Ci-gît,** *Here lies;* **Ci-gisent,** *Here lie.*

12. haïr, *to hate*

haïr	haïssant	haï	je hais	je haïs [1]

[1] Since only one orthographic sign can be used with a letter, and since the pronunciation demands the diæresis, the circumflex is omitted in the first and second persons plural of the past definite and in the third singular of the imperfect subjunctive.

13. mourir, *to die*

mourir	mourant	mort	je meurs	je mourus
mourr-	(1) **ils meurent**			
	(4) **je meure**			

14. ouvrir, *to open*

ouvrir	ouvrant	ouvert	j'ouvre	j'ouvris

Thus also: **couvrir, découvrir, entr'ouvrir, offrir, recouvrir, rouvrir, souffrir**

15. partir, *to set out*

partir	partant	parti	je pars	je partis

Thus also: **consentir   mentir   repentir   sentir**
démentir   pressentir ressentir   sortir
départir   repartir   ressortir (*to go out again*)

16. servir, *to serve*

servir	servant	servi	je sers	je servis

Thus also: **desservir.**

17. venir, *to come*

venir	venant	venu	je viens	je vins [1]
viendr-	(1) ils viennent			
	(4) je vienne			

[1] The **n** is carried throughout the past definite and the imperfect subjunctive; the **i** is circumflexed in the three usual places.

Thus also:

advenir	disconvenir	ressouvenir	abstenir	obtenir
avenir	intervenir	revenir	appartenir	retenir
circonvenir	parvenir	souvenir	contenir	soutenir
contrevenir	prévenir	subvenir	détenir	
convenir	provenir	survenir	entretenir	
devenir	redevenir	tenir	maintenir	

18. vêtir, *to clothe*

vêtir	vêtant	vêtu	je vêts	je vêtis

Thus also: **dévêtir, revêtir.**

19. absoudre, *to absolve*

absoudre	absolvant	absous	j'absous	......
		absoute		

Thus also: **dissoudre.**

20. battre, *to beat*

battre	battant	battu	je bats	je battis

Thus also: **abattre, combattre, débattre, rabattre.**

21. boire, *to drink*

boire	buvant	bu	je bois	je bus
	(1) ils boivent			
	(4) je boive			

Thus also: **emboire, imboire, reboire.**

22. clore, *to close*

clore	......	clos	je clos	......
	(1)(2)(3)lacking		(1) il clôt	
	(4) je close		(2) lacking	

Thus also: **déclore, éclore, enclore, forclore.**

23. conclure, *to conclude*

| conclure | concluant | conclu | je conclus | je conclus |

Thus also: **exclure, inclure** (Past Part.: **inclus**), **reclure** (Past Part.: **reclus**).

24. conduire, *to conduct*

| conduire | conduisant | conduit | je conduis | je conduisis |

Thus also:
construire	éconduire	luire [1]	recuire	traduire
cuire	enduire	nuire [2]	réduire	
déconstruire	induire	produire	reluire [3]	
déduire	instruire	reconduire	reproduire	
détruire	introduire	reconstruire	séduire	

[1] Past Part.: **lui**.
[2] Past Part.: **nui**.
[3] Past Part.: **relui**.

25. confire, *to preserve*

| confire | confisant | confit | je confis | je confis |

Thus also: **déconfire, circoncire** (Past Part.: **circoncis**), **suffire** (Past Part.: **suffi**).

26. connaître, *to know*

| connaître | connaissant | connu | je connais | je connus |
| | | | (1) il connaît | |

Thus also:
| apparaître | disparaître | paître[1] | reconnaître | repaître |
| comparaître | méconnaître | paraître | reparaître | |

[1] Lacks the past participle, past definite, imperfect subjunctive.

27. coudre, *to sew*

| coudre | cousant | cousu | je couds | je cousis |

Thus also: **découdre, recoudre**.

28. craindre, *to fear*

| craindre | craignant | craint | je crains | je craignis |

Thus also:
adjoindre	déjoindre	enfreindre	geindre	ratteindre
astreindre	dépeindre	enjoindre	joindre	rejoindre
atteindre	déteindre	épreindre	oindre	repeindre
ceindre	disjoindre	éteindre	peindre	restreindre
conjoindre	empreindre	étreindre	plaindre	reteindre
contraindre	enceindre	feindre	poindre	teindre

29. croire, *to believe*

| croire | croyant [1] | cru | je crois | je crus |

[1] **oy** changes to **oi** before mute **e**.

30. croître, *to grow*

| croître | croissant | crû / crue | je croîs | je crûs |

Thus also: **accroître,** [1] **décroître, recroître,** [1] **surcroître.** [1]

[1] No circumflex in past participle or 3rd sing. or 3rd plu. of past def.

31. dire, *to say, to tell*

| dire | disant | dit | je dis | je dis |
| | (1) vous dites | | | |

Thus also: contredire [1] interdire [1] médire [1] redire
dédire [1] maudire [2] prédire [1]

[1] The second plural present indicative and imperative follow the present participle.

[2] The present participle and forms derived from it double the **s**: **maudissant**.

32. écrire, *to write*

| écrire | écrivant | écrit | j'écris | j'écrivis |

Thus also: circonscrire inscrire proscrire souscrire
décrire prescrire récrire transcrire

33. être (See p. 228.)

34. faire, *to do, to make*

faire	faisant	fait	je fais	je fis
fer-	(1) vous faites			
	ils font			
	(4) je fasse [1]			

[1] This stem is used throughout the present subjunctive.

Thus also: contrefaire forfaire méfaire redéfaire satisfaire
défaire malfaire parfaire refaire surfaire

35. frire, *to fry*

| frire | .... | frit | je fris | ...... |

The second and the fifth principal parts and all forms derived from them are lacking.

36. lire, *to read*

| lire | lisant | lu | je lis | je lus |

Thus also: **élire, réélire, relire.**

37. mettre, *to put*

| mettre | mettant | mis | je mets | je mis |

Thus also: **admettre   démettre   omettre   remettre   transmettre
commettre   émettre   permettre   repromettre
compromettre entremettre   promettre   soumettre**

38. moudre, *to grind*

| moudre | moulant | moulu | je mouds | je moulus |

Thus also: **émoudre, remoudre, rémoudre.**

39. naître, *to be born*

| naître | naissant | né | je nais | je naquis |
| | | | (1) il naît | |

Thus also: **renaître.**

40. plaire, *to please*

| plaire | plaisant | plu | je plais | je plus |
| | | | (1) il plaît | |

Thus also: **complaire, déplaire, taire** (but: il tait).

41. prendre, *to take*

prendre	prenant	pris	je prends	je pris
(1) ils prennent				
(4) je prenne				

Thus also: **apprendre   déprendre   entreprendre méprendre   reprendre
comprendre désapprendre éprendre   rapprendre surprendre**

42. résoudre, *to resolve*

| résoudre | résolvant | résolu | je résous | je résolus |

43. rire, *to laugh*

| rire | riant | ri | je ris | je ris |

Thus also: **sourire.**

44. suivre, *to follow*

| suivre | suivant | suivi | je suis | je suivis |

Thus also: **ensuivre, poursuivre.**

45. traire, *to milk*

| traire | trayant [1] | trait | je trais | ...... |

[1] **ay** changes to **ai** before mute **e.**

Thus also: **abstraire   braire   extraire   retraire
           attraire   distraire rentraire   soustraire**

46. vaincre, *to conquer*

| vaincre | vainquant | vaincu | je vaincs | je vainquis |

Thus also: **convaincre.**

47. vivre, *to live*

| vivre | vivant | vécu | je vis | je vécus |

Thus also: **revivre, survivre.**

48. asseoir, *to seat*

asseoir	asseyant [2] or	assis	j'assieds [2] or	j'assis
assiér- [1]	assoyant [3]		j'assois	
asseyer-				
assoir-				

[1] Any one of these stems may be used in the future and the conditional.

[2] There are two possibilities for each of the forms derived from the second and the fourth principal parts.

[3] **oy** changes to **oi** before mute **e.**

Thus also: **messeoir, rasseoir, seoir, surseoir.**

49. avoir (See p. 228)

50. déchoir, *to decline*

déchoir	...... [1]	déchu	je déchois	je déchus
décherr-				

[1] Forms derived from the second principal part are formed on the stem **déchoy-**. oy changes to oi before mute e.
Thus also: **choir, rechoir, échoir.** [2]

[2] Used only in the third person. Has present participle: **échéant**, but forms derived from second principal part are made as above. Future and conditional may be regular. Parallel forms: Pres. Ind.: **échet**; Pres. Subj.: **échée, échéent.**

51. devoir, *to owe*

devoir	devant	dû	je dois	je dus
devr-	(1) ils doivent	due		
	(4) je doive			

Thus also: **redevoir.**

52. falloir, *to necessitate*

falloir [1]	....	fallu	....	....
faudr-	(3) il fallait		(1) il faut	il fallut
	(4) il faille			il fallût

[1] A transitive verb, but commonly rendered *to be necessary*. Used impersonally only.

53. mouvoir, *to move*

mouvoir	mouvant	mû	je meus	je mus
mouvr-	(1) ils meuvent	mue		
	(4) je meuve			

Thus also: **émouvoir** (Past Part.: **ému**), **promouvoir** (Past Part.: **promu**).

54. pleuvoir, *to rain*

pleuvoir [1]	pleuvant	plu	....	....
pleuvr-			(1) il pleut	il plut
				il plût

[1] Used impersonally only.

55. pourvoir, *to provide*

| pourvoir | pourvoyant [1] | pourvu | je pourvois | je pourvus |

[1] **oy** changes to **oi** before mute **e**.

Thus also: **dépourvoir.**

56. pouvoir, *to be able*

pouvoir	pouvant [1]	pu	je peux [3]	je pus
pourr-	(1) ils peuvent			
	(4) je puisse [2]			

[1] No imperatives.

[2] This stem is used throughout the present subjunctive.

[3] A parallel form, **je puis**, is more common, and must be used in inverted order (**puis-je**) and in **je ne puis** (without **pas**.)

57. recevoir, *to receive*

recevoir [1]	recevant	reçu	je reçois	je reçus
recevr-	(1) ils reçoivent			
	(4) je reçoive			

[1] This verb is just like **devoir** except that a cedilla must be written whenever **c** precedes **o** or **u**.

Thus also: **apercevoir, concevoir, décevoir, percevoir.**

58. savoir, *to know*

savoir	sachant [1]	su	je sais	je sus
saur-	(1) sav-		(2) sache [1]	
	(2) sach-			
	(3) sav-			
	(4) sach-			

[1] The plurals of the present indicative and the imperfect indicative have the stem **sav-**; the imperatives (singular as well as plurals) and the present subjunctive follow the present participle.

59. valoir, *to be worth*

| valoir | valant | valu | je vaux | je valus |
| vaudr- | (4) je vaille | | | |

Thus also: **équivaloir, prévaloir,** [1] **revaloir.**

[1] Present subjunctive follows present participle: **prévale**, etc.

60. voir, *to see*

voir	voyant [1]	vu	je vois	je vis
verr-				

[1] **oy** changes to **oi** before mute **e**.

Thus also: **entrevoir, prévoir,** [2] **revoir.**

[2] Future and conditional are regular: **prévoirai,** etc.

61. vouloir, *to want*

vouloir	voulant [1]	voulu	je veux	je voulus
voudr-	(1) ils veulent			
	(4) je veuille			

[1] A special imperative form, **veuillez,** is followed by an infinitive, and has the value *please* or *be so kind as to*.

ALPHABETICAL LIST OF IRREGULAR VERBS

abattre..........20
absoudre.........19
abstenir.........17
abstraire........45
accourir......... 6
accroître........30
accueillir....... 7
acquérir......... 3
adjoindre........28
admettre.........37
advenir..........17
aller............ 1
apercevoir.......57
apparaître.......26
appartenir.......17
apprendre........41
assaillir........ 4
asseoir..........48
astreindre.......28
atteindre........28
attraire.........45
avenir...........17
avoir............49

battre...........20
boire............21
bouillir......... 5
braire...........45

ceindre..........28
choir............50
circoncire.......25
circonscrire.....32
circonvenir......17
clore............22
combattre........20
commettre........37
comparaître......26
complaire........40
comprendre.......41
compromettre.....37
concevoir........57
conclure.........23
concourir........ 6
conduire.........24
confire..........25
conjoindre.......28

connaître........26
conquérir........ 3
consentir........15
construire.......24
contenir.........17
contraindre......28
contredire.......31
contrefaire......34
contrevenir......17
convaincre.......46
convenir.........17
coudre...........27
courir........... 6
couvrir..........14
craindre.........28
croire...........29
croître..........30
cueillir......... 7
cuire............24

débattre.........20
décevoir.........57
déchoir..........50

IRREGULAR VERBS

déclore..............22
déconfire...........25
déconstruire........24
découdre............27
découvrir...........14
décrire.............32
décroître...........30
dédire..............31
déduire.............24
défaillir............9
défaire.............34
déjoindre...........28
démentir............15
démettre............37
départir............15
dépeindre...........28
déplaire............40
dépourvoir..........55
déprendre...........41
désapprendre........41
desservir...........16
déteindre...........28
détenir.............17
détruire............24
devenir.............17
dévêtir.............18
devoir..............51
dire................31
disconvenir.........17
discourir............6
disjoindre..........28
disparaître.........26
dissoudre...........19
distraire...........45
dormir...............8

ébouillir............5
échoir..............50
éclore..............22
éconduire...........24
écrire..............32
élire...............36

emboire.............21
émettre.............37
émoudre.............38
émouvoir............53
empreindre..........28
enceindre...........28
enclore.............22
encourir.............6
endormir.............8
enduire.............24
enfreindre..........28
enfuir..............10
enjoindre...........28
enquérir.............3
ensuivre............44
entremettre.........37
entreprendre........41
entretenir..........17
entrevoir...........60
entr'ouvrir.........14
envoyer..............2
épreindre...........28
éprendre............41
équivaloir..........59
éteindre............28
être................33
étreindre...........28
exclure.............23
extraire............45

faillir..............9
faire...............34
falloir.............52
feindre.............28
forclore............22
forfaire............34
frire...............35
fuir................10

geindre.............28
gésir...............11

haïr................12

imboire.............21
inclure.............23
induire.............24
inscrire............32
instruire...........24
interdire...........31
intervenir..........17
introduire..........24

joindre.............28

lire................36
luire...............24

maintenir...........17
malfaire............34
maudire.............31
méconnaître.........26
médire..............31
méfaire.............34
mentir..............15
méprendre...........41
messeoir............48
mettre..............37
moudre..............38
mourir..............13
mouvoir.............53

naître..............39
nuire...............24

obtenir.............17
offrir..............14
oindre..............28
omettre.............37
ouvrir..............14

paître..............26
paraître............26
parcourir............6
parfaire............34
partir..............15
parvenir............17

peindre..........28	recuire...........24	rouvrir...........14
percevoir.........57	redéfaire..........34	saillir............ 7
permettre.........37	redevenir.........17	satisfaire.........34
plaindre..........28	redevoir..........51	savoir............58
plaire............40	redire............31	secourir.......... 6
pleuvoir..........54	redormir......... 8	séduire...........24
poindre...........28	réduire...........24	sentir............15
poursuivre.......44	réélire............36	seoir.............48
pourvoir..........55	refaire............34	servir............16
pouvoir..........56	rejoindre.........28	sortir............15
prédire.......... 31	relire..............36	souffrir..........14
prendre...........41	reluire............24	soumettre........37
prescrire..........32	remettre..........37	sourire...........43
pressentir........15	remoudre.........38	souscrire.........32
prévaloir.........59	rémoudre.........38	soustraire........45
prévenir..........17	renaître..........39	soutenir..........17
prévoir...........60	rendormir........ 8	souvenir..........17
produire..........24	rentraire..........45	subvenir..........17
promettre........37	renvoyer......... 2	suffire............25
promouvoir.......53	repaître..........26	suivre............44
proscrire 32	reparaître.........26	surcroître.........30
provenir..........17	repartir...........15	surfaire..........34
	repeindre.........28	surprendre........41
rabattre..........20	repentir...........15	surseoir..........48
rapprendre.......41	reprendre.........41	survenir..........17
rasseoir...........48	reproduire........24	survivre..........47
ratteindre........28	repromettre.......37	
reboire...........21	requérir.......... 3	taire..............40
rebouillir......... 5	résoudre..........42	teindre...........28
recevoir..........57	ressentir..........15	tenir..............17
rechoir...........50	ressortir..........15	traduire...........24
reclure...........23	ressouvenir.......17	traire..............45
reconduire...... 24	restreindre........28	transcrire.........32
reconnaître......26	reteindre..........28	transmettre.......37
reconquérir...... 3	retenir............17	tressaillir......... 4
reconstruire......24	retraire...........45	
recoudre........ 27	revaloir...........59	vaincre...........46
recourir.......... 6	revenir...........17	valoir.............59
recouvrir.........14	revêtir............18	venir..............17
récrire............32	revivre............47	vêtir..............18
recroître..........30	revoir.............60	vivre..............47
recueillir.......... 7	rire..............43	voir...............60
		vouloir...........61

GENERAL VOCABULARY

GENERAL VOCABULARY

a [a] see **avoir; il y a** *there is, there are; ago*
à [a] *at, to, in, into, on, for, by, from, with* (in descriptions)
abondance [abɔ̃dɑ̃:s] f. *abundance*
d'abord [dabɔ:r] *first* (adv.)
absence [apsɑ̃:s] f. *absence*
accompagner [akɔ̃paɲe] *to go with, accompany*
accuser [akyze] *to accuse*
acheter [aʃte] *to buy*
acteur [aktœ:r] m. *actor*
actif, active [aktif, akti:v] *active*
actrice [aktris] f. *actress*
actuel [aktɥɛl] *present* (adj.)
adieu [adjø] m. *goodbye*
admirer [admire] *to admire*
adopter [adɔpte] *to adopt*
adversaire [advɛrsɛ:r] m., f. *opponent, adversary*
aéroplane [aerɔplan] m. *airplane*
affaire [afɛ:r] f. *thing, business*
affiche [afiʃ] f. *bill, poster*
âge [ɑ:ʒ] m. *age;* **au moyen** —— *in the Middle Ages*
âgé [ɑʒe] *old*
agir [aʒi:r] *to act;* **s'**—— **de** *to be a question of, to concern*
agiter [aʒite] *to excite, agitate*
agréable [agreabl] *agreeable*
agréablement [agreabləmɑ̃] *agreeably*
ai [e] 1. s. pres. ind. of **avoir**
aie, aies, aient [ɛ] pres. subj. of **avoir**
aille [a:j] pres. subj. of **aller**
ailleurs [ajœ:r] *elsewhere*
aimable [ɛmabl] *lovable, kind*
aimer [ɛme] *to like, love*
ainsi [ɛ̃si] *thus;* **et** —— **de suite** *and so forth, etc.*
air [ɛ:r] m. *air, appearance;* **avoir l'**—— *to seem*
aise [ɛ:z] f. *ease;* **à son** —— *at one's ease, comfortably*
Alain [alɛ̃] *Alan, Allen*

---

a un, une; **two dollars a day** deux dollars par jour; **two dollars a pound** deux dollars la livre
able: to be —— pouvoir
about à peu près, autour de; **at about** (*a time*) vers
abroad à l'étranger
accompany accompagner
active actif
actor acteur *m.*
afraid effrayé; **to be** —— avoir peur
after après
afternoon après-midi *m. or f.*
afterward après, plus tard
again encore, encore une fois
age âge *m.* **What is his age?** Quel âge a-t-il? **in the Middle Ages** au moyen âge
ago il y a (*precedes time expression*)
agreeably agréablement
ail: What ails him? (*What has he?*) Qu'a-t-il? Qu'est-ce qu'il a?
air air *m.*
all tout, toute, tous, toutes; (*the whole*) tout le, toute la; **not (nothing) at all** pas (rien) du tout; **all at once** tout à coup, tout d'un coup

Alais [alɛs] [alɛ] small city near Nîmes in southern France
allemand [almɑ̃] *German*
aller [ale] *to go, to be* (well, etc.), *to be becoming;* **s'en —** *to go away;* **Comment allez-vous?** *How are you?* **allons!** *come! come now!*
allumette [alymɛt] f. *match*
Alma [alma] name of an open square and of a bridge over the Seine in Paris.
alors [alɔːr] *then* (at that time)
amateur [amatœːr] m. *lover, fancier,* "fan"
américain [amerikɛ̃] *American*
Amérique [amerik] f. *America*
ami, -e [ami] m., f. *friend*
amitié [amitje] f. *friendship, love*
amuser [amyze] *to amuse;* **s'— to enjoy oneself, have a good time***
an [ɑ̃] m. *year*
ancien, -ne [ɑ̃sjɛ̃, ɑ̃sjɛn] *old (former), ancient*
Andromaque [ɑ̃drɔmak] *Andromache* title of a tragedy by Racine (1639-1699)
anglais [ɑ̃glɛ] *English*
Angleterre [ɑ̃glətɛːr] f. *England*
animal [animal] m. *animal*
année [ane] f. *year*
anniversaire [anivɛrsɛːr] m. *anniversary* **— de naissance** *birthday*
annoncer [anɔ̃se] *to announce*
août [u] m. *August*
appareil [aparɛj] m. *outfit, set*
appartement [apartəmɑ̃] m. *apartment*
appeler [aple] *to call;* **s'— to be called, to be named.** **Il s'appelle Jean.** *His name is John.*
appétit [apeti] m. *appetite*
apporter [apɔrte] *to bring*
apprendre [aprɑ̃ːdr] *to learn*
appris [apri] past part. of **apprendre**
approcher (de) [aprɔʃe] *to approach*
après [aprɛ] *after, afterward*
après-demain [aprɛdmɛ̃] *day after tomorrow*
après-midi [aprɛmidi] m. or f. *afternoon*

---

almost presque
alone seul
along le long de
aloud *haut, à *haute voix
already déjà
also aussi
although bien que, quoique
always toujours
am suis *see* **be**
America Amérique *f.;* **South —** l'Amérique du Sud
American américain; Américain *m.*
among parmi, entre
amuse amuser
an un, une
and et
animal animal *m.*
announce annoncer
another un (une) autre; encore un (une)
answer répondre (à)
any du, de l', de la, des; de; en
anybody quelqu'un(e); **not —** (ne . . .) personne
anything quelque chose; **not —** (ne . . .) rien
apartment appartement *m.*
appear se montrer, paraître
appetite appétit *m.;* **with a good —** de bon appétit

arbre [arbr] m. *tree*
arc [ark] m. *arch*
architecture [arʃitɛktyːr] f. *architecture*
argent [arʒɑ̃] m. *money, silver*
argot [argo] m. *slang*
arrêter (s') [arɛte] *to stop*
arrivée [arive] f. *arrival;* **dès son ——** *as soon as he arrived*
arriver [arive] *to arrive; happen*
as [a] 2. s. pres. ind. of **avoir**
assassiner [asasine] *to assassinate*
asseoir [aswaːr] (p.p.: **assis**) *to seat*
assez [ase] *enough; rather*
assiette [asjɛt] f. *plate*
assis [asi] *seated, sitting*
assistant [asistɑ̃] m. *one present, witness*
assister (à) [asiste] *to witness, attend, be present*
assurance [asyrɑ̃ːs] f. *assurance*
assurer [asyre] *to assure*
attendre [atɑ̃ːdr] *to wait, wait for, await;* **s'—— à** *to expect*
attention [atɑ̃sjɔ̃] f. *care, attention*

au [o] =**à** +**le** (art.)
aucun [okœ̃]: **ne . . . ——** *no one, none*
au-dehors (de) [o d(ə)ɔːr] *outside*
au-devant [odvɑ̃]: **aller —— de** *to go to meet*
aujourd'hui [oʒurdɥi] *today*
aur- fut. and cond. of **avoir**
aussi [osi] *also, too; as;* **—— . . . que** *as . . . as*
aussitôt [osito] *at once;* **—— que** *as soon as*
Auteuil [otœːj] *suburb of Paris*
autobus [otɔbys] m. *autobus*
autocar [otɔkaːr] m. *autocar*
automne [otɔn] m. or f. *autumn*
automobile [otɔmɔbil] m. or f. *automobile*
autour (de) [otuːr] *around*
autre [oːtr] *other*
autrefois [otrəfwa] *formerly*
aux [o] =**à** +**les** (art.)
avancer [avɑ̃se] *to advance;* **l'heure avance** *time is passing, it is growing late*
avant [avɑ̃] *before* (time)

---

apple pomme *f.*
approach (s') approcher (de)
April avril *m.*
are *see* **be; here ——** voici; **there ——** voilà, il y a
arm bras *m.*
around autour (de); **go ——** faire le tour (de)
arrive arriver
as comme; **as far as** jusqu'à, aussi loin que; **as . . . as** aussi . . . que; **not so . . . as** pas si . . . que, moins . . . que; **as soon as** aussitôt que
ask, ask for demander
astonish étonner; **astonished** étonné;
to be astonished s'étonner
at à; **at the house** (*etc.*) **of** chez; **at home** à la maison; **at school** à l'école; **at once** tout de suite; **all at once** tout à coup, tout d'un coup
attend assister (à)
attention attention *f.*
August août *m.*
aunt tante *f.*
autobus autobus *m.*
automobile automobile *m. or f.;* **in an ——** en automobile
autumn automne *m. or f.;* **in ——** en automne

248   A FRENCH GRAMMAR

avant-hier [avã(t)jɛːr] *day before yesterday*
avec [avɛk] *with*
avenue [avny] f. *avenue*
Avignon [aviɲɔ̃] city of Provence
avis [avi] m. *mind, opinion*
avocat [avɔka] m. *lawyer*
avoir [avwaːr] *to have, get, receive, be, be the matter;* **Qu'a-t-il?** *What ails him?* **Qu'y a-t-il?** *What's the matter?* **Il y a** *there is (are)* **Il a dix ans.** *He is ten years old.* **avoir chaud,** etc. *to be warm,* etc.
avril [avril] m. *April*
ay- pres. part., pres. subj., imperatives of **avoir**

bain [bɛ̃] m. *bath;* **salle** (f.) **de ——(s)** *bath room*
bal [bal] m. *ball (dance)*
ballon [balɔ̃] m. *(foot)ball*

banane [banan] f. *banana*
banc [bɑ̃] m. *bench*
banque [bɑ̃ːk] f. *bank*
bas [bɑ] m. *stocking*
bas [bɑ] *low;* **en ——** *down stairs*
bateau [bato] m. *boat*
batelier [batəlje] m. *boatman*
bâton [bɑtɔ̃] m. *stick*
battre [batr] *to beat*
beau [bo] *beautiful, fine, handsome;* **faire ——** *to be fine weather*
beaucoup [boku] *much, many, very much, very many*
bel, belle [bɛl] see **beau**
besoin [bəzwɛ̃] m. *need;* **avoir —— (de)** *to need*
beurre [bœːr] m. *butter*
bibliothèque [bibliɔtɛk] f. *library*
bicyclette [bisiklɛt] f. *bicycle;* **à ——** *on a bicycle*
bien [bjɛ̃] *well, very; much, many;*

---

avenue avenue *f.*
awaken (se) réveiller
away: go away s'en aller

back de retour; **at the ——** au fond; **send ——** renvoyer
bad mauvais
bag sac *m.*
ball ballon *m.*
bank banque *f.;* **——note** billet (*m.*) de banque
bath bain *m.;* **——room** salle (*f.*) de bain(s)
be être; **—— (well, ill,** *etc.*) se porter, aller; **——(cold, warm,** *etc.*) avoir; **—— (cold, warm,** *etc.* - *impers.*) faire; *(prophetic value)*: devoir: **He is to come.** Il doit venir. **He was to come.** Il devait venir.

bear: —— a grudge en vouloir (à) [**for** = de]
beat battre
beautiful beau
because parce que; **—— of** à cause de
become devenir *p. p.:* devenu
bed lit *m.;* **——room** chambre (*f.*) à coucher; **to go to ——** se coucher; **in ——** au lit
before devant *(place)*, avant *(time)*
beg prier
begin commencer, se mettre à (+ *an infinitive*)
behind derrière
bell *(large):* cloche *f.*, *(small):* sonnette *f.*
bench banc *m.*
beside à côté de
besides du reste, au reste, d'ailleurs

GENERAL VOCABULARY

eh ——! *well!* être —— *to be comfortable;* —— à vous *yours truly;* —— entendu *of course;* —— que *although*
bientôt [bjɛ̃to] *soon*
bijou [biʒu] m. *jewel*
billet [bijɛ] m. *ticket, note;* —— en location *reserved seat*
blanc, blanche [blɑ̃, blɑ̃:ʃ] *white*
bleu [blø] *blue*
Blois [blwa] city and castle on the Loire, southwest of Paris
boire [bwaːr] *to drink*
bois [bwa] m. *wood*
Bois de Boulogne [bulɔɲ] great park just outside the gates of Paris, a favorite promenade.
boiv- see boire
bon, bonne [bɔ̃, bɔn] *good, kind;* à la bonne heure *Fine! Well and good!* de bonne heure *early*

bonbon [bɔ̃bɔ̃] m. *bonbon, candy*
bonjour [bɔ̃ʒuːr] *good day, good-bye, good morning, good afternoon*
bonne [bɔn] f. *maid*
bord [bɔːr] m. *edge, shore;* à —— *on board*
bottine [bɔtin] f. *(high) shoe, boot*
boulevard [bulvaːr] m. *boulevard*
bout [bu] m. *end*
bras [bra] m. *arm*
brave [braːv] *brave; worthy*
Bretagne [brətaɲ] f. *Brittany*
brigand [brigɑ̃] m. *brigand*
briller [brije] *to shine*
brûler [bryle] *to burn*
bu, bus, buv- see boire
bureau [byro] m. *desk, office*
but [by(t)] m. *goal, end, aim, score*

ça [sa] =cela *that*
cabine [kabin] f. *cabin*

---

best *(adj.):* le meilleur, *etc.; (adv.):* le mieux; his —— de son mieux
betake oneself se rendre
better *(adj.):* meilleur; *(adv.):* mieux
between entre
bicycle bicyclette *f.;* on a —— à bicyclette
big grand, gros
bird oiseau *m.*
birthday anniversaire *(m.)* de naissance
black noir
blackboard tableau *(m.)* noir
blow coup *m.*
blue bleu
board bord *m.;* on —— à bord; go on —— s'embarquer; black—— tableau *(m.)* noir
boat bateau *m.;* steam —— paquebot *m.*
book livre *m.*
born: to be —— naître, *p. p.:* né; he was born il est né
both tous (les) deux, toutes (les) deux
boy garçon *m.*
brave brave
bread pain *m.*
break casser
breakfast *(verb)* déjeuner
breakfast petit déjeuner *m.*
bring apporter; —— back rapporter
brother frère *m.*
busy occupé
but mais; nothing but ne . . . que
butter beurre *m.*
buy acheter
by par, à

cacher [kaʃe] *to hide*
café [kafe] m. *coffee, café;* —— **au lait** *coffee with milk*
cahier [kaje] m. *notebook*
caillou [kaju] m. *pebble*
calme [kalm] *calm*
camarade [kamarad] m. or f. *comrade, mate*
camp [kɑ̃] m. *camp, field, territory*
campagne [kɑ̃paɲ] f. *country* (not city); **à la** —— *in* (or *to*) *the country*
Canada [kanada] m. *Canada*
capitaine [kapitɛn] m. *captain*
car [kaːr] *for* (conj.), *because*
carré [kare] *square*
carte [kart] f. *map, card*
cas [kɑ] m. *case*
casser [kɑse] *to break*
cathédrale [katedral] f. *cathedral*
catholique [katɔlik] *catholic*
cause [koːz] f. *cause;* **à** —— **de** *because of*
ce [sə] (pron.) *this, that, it, he, she, they;* **ce qui, ce que,** *what*
ce [sə] (adj.) *this, that;* **ce . . .-ci** *this;* **ce . . .-là** *that*
ceci [səsi] *this* (*this thing*)
céder [sede] *to yield*
cela [səla] *that* (*that thing*)

célèbre [selɛbr] *celebrated, famous*
celle [sɛl] f. variant of **celui**
celui [səlɥi] *this, that, this one, that one, the one, he, him;* **celui-ci** *this, this one, the latter;* **celui-là** *that, that one, the former*
cent [sɑ̃] *hundred*
cerise [səriːz] f. *cherry*
ces [se] (adj.) *these, those;* **ces . . .-ci** *these;* **ces . . .-là** *those*
cesser [sɛse] *to cease, stop*
cet, cette [sɛt] see **ce** (adj.)
ceux [sø] m. pl. of **celui**
chacun [ʃakœ̃] *each one*
chaise [ʃɛːz] f. *chair*
Chambord [ʃɑ̃bɔːr] *castle near Blois*
chambre [ʃɑ̃ːbr] f. (*private*) *room* —— **à coucher** *bedroom*
chameau [ʃamo] m. *camel*
champ [ʃɑ̃] m. *field*
Champs-Élysées [ʃɑ̃z‿elize] *fine avenue in Paris*
changer [ʃɑ̃ʒe] *to change*
chanter [ʃɑ̃te] *to sing*
chapeau [ʃapo] m. *hat*
chapelle [ʃapɛl] f. *chapel*
chaque [ʃak] *each*
Charles [ʃarl] *Charles*
charmant [ʃarmɑ̃] *charming*
chat [ʃa] m. *cat*

---

cabin cabine *f.*
cake gâteau *m.*
call appeler; **to be called** s'appeler
calm calme
can *see* pouvoir
Canada Canada *m.*
candy bonbon *m.*
care attention *f.*, soin *m.;* **Take ——!** Faites attention!
carriage voiture *f.;* **in a ——** en voiture
carry porter
castle château *m.*
cat chat *m.*
cathedral cathédrale *f.*
chair chaise *f.*
chalk craie *f.*
change changer
change monnaie *f.;* **small ——** (petite) monnaie

GENERAL VOCABULARY 251

château [ʃɑto] m. *castle*
chaud [ʃo] *warm, hot;* **avoir —** *to be warm;* **faire —** *to be warm* (impersonal)
chauffeur [ʃofœːr] m. *chauffeur*
chemin [ʃəmɛ̃] m. *road;* **— de fer** *railroad*
chemise [ʃəmiːz] f. *shirt*
cher, chère [ʃɛːr] *dear, expensive*
Cherbourg [ʃɛrbuːr] city on the northwest coast of France
chercher [ʃɛrʃe] *to seek, look for, (go and) get*
cheval [ʃəval] m. *horse;* **à —** *on horseback, astride*
cheveu [ʃəvø] m. *hair*
chez [ʃe] (prep.) *at the house of, to the house of, at (to, in) the shop (office, etc.) of*
chien [ʃjɛ̃] m. *dog*
chimère [ʃimɛːr] f. *chimera*
Chine [ʃin] f. *China*
chinois [ʃinwa] *Chinese*
Chinon [ʃinɔ̃] city and castle
chocolat [ʃɔkɔla] m. *chocolate*
choisir [ʃwaziːr] *to choose*
chose [ʃoːz] f. *thing;* **quelque —** (neuter) *something*
chou [ʃu] m. *cabbage*
cinq [sɛ̃ːk] [sɛ̃] *five*

cinquante [sɛ̃kɑ̃ːt] *fifty*
cinquième [sɛ̃kjɛm] *fifth*
circulation [sirkylasjɔ̃] f. *traffic, communication*
cité [site] f. (old word for) *city* **Ile de la —** island in the Seine, the original city of Paris
clair [klɛːr] *clear, bright;* m. *light*
classe [klɑːs] f. *class, classroom*
cloche [klɔʃ] f. *(large) bell*
Cluny [klyni] museum containing an interesting collection of objects of historical interest; built on the site of Roman baths, some ruins of which remain
cœur [kœːr] m. *heart*
coin [kwɛ̃] m. *corner*
collège [kɔlɛːʒ] m. *college; preparatory school;* **— de France** graduate school in the Latin Quarter in Paris
combien? [kɔ̃bjɛ̃] *how much? how many?* **— de temps?** *how long?*
commander [kɔmɑ̃de] *to order, command*
comme [kɔm] *as, like, such as; how!*
commencer [kɔmɑ̃se] *to begin, start*
comment? [kɔmɑ̃] *how?*
commerce [kɔmɛrs] m. *trade*
compagnon [kɔ̃paɲɔ̃] m. *companion*

Charles Charles
charming charmant
cheap (à) bon marché
cheese fromage *m.*
cherry cerise *f.*
child enfant *m. or f.*
chocolate chocolat *m.*
choose choisir
church église *f.*
city ville *f.*

class classe *f.*
classmate camarade (*m. or f.*) de classe
classroom (salle de) classe *f.*
clean propre
climb grimper
close fermer
clothes vêtements *m. pl.*
coat pardessus *m.*
coffee café *m.*

complet [kɔ̃plɛ] *complete, full*
comprendre [kɔ̃prɑ̃ːdr] *to understand*
compter [kɔ̃te] *to count; to intend*
comte [kɔ̃ːt] m. *count (noble)*
concierge [kɔ̃sjɛrʒ] m. or f. *porter*
conducteur [kɔ̃dyktœːr] m. *conductor*
confiserie [kɔ̃fizri] f. *confectionery*
confiture [kɔ̃fityːr] f. *jam, preserves*
confortable [kɔ̃fɔrtabl] *comfortable*
connaiss- see **connaître**
connaître [kɔnɛːtr] *to know, be acquainted with*
connu, connus, etc. see **connaître**
consentir [kɔ̃sɑ̃tiːr] *to consent*
construction [kɔ̃stryksjɔ̃] f. *construction*
conte [kɔ̃ːt] m. *tale, short story*
content [kɔ̃tɑ̃] *glad, happy, pleased, contented*
continuer [kɔ̃tinɥe] *to continue*
contre [kɔ̃ːtr] *against*
convive [kɔ̃viːv] m. or f. *guest, table companion*
copie [kɔpi] f. *copy*
corde [kɔrd] f. *rope, cord*
cordial [kɔrdjal] *cordial*
corps [kɔːr] m. *body*
côte [koːt] f. *coast*
côté [kote] m. *side;* de ce —— *on this side;* de l'autre —— *on the other side;* à —— de *beside*
coucher [kuʃe] *to put to bed;* se —— *to go to bed, lie down;* **chambre à** —— *bedroom*
coup [ku] m. *stroke, blow, draught, "drop";* —— de pied *kick;* tout à ——, tout d'un —— *suddenly, all at once*
cour [kuːr] f. *court, yard*
courant [kurɑ̃] m. *current;* **tenir au** —— *to keep informed*
courir [kuriːr] *to run*
course [kurs] f. *errand, race, course*
court [kuːr] *short*
couru [kury] p.p. of **courir**
cousin, -e [kuzɛ̃] [kuzin] m., f. *cousin*
couteau [kuto] m. *knife*
coûter [kute] *to cost*
craie [krɛ] f. *chalk*
cravate [kravat] f. *necktie*
crayon [krɛjɔ̃] m. *pencil*
créer [kree] *to create*
cri [kri] m. *cry*
croire [krwaːr] *to believe*
croix [krwa] f. *cross*
cuiller [kyjɛːr] f. *spoon*
cuisine [kɥizin] f. *kitchen, cooking*

---

cold froid; **to be** —— avoir froid; (*impersonally*) faire froid
collar faux-col *m.*
come venir, *p. p.:* venu; —— **back** revenir; —— **in** entrer; —— **up** monter; —— **down** descendre
companion compagnon *m.*, compagne *f.;* **travelling** —— compagnon de voyage
continue continuer
cook cuisinier *m.*, cuisinière *f.*
corner coin *m.*
cost coûter
could *see* pouvoir
count compter
count comte *m.*
country (*not city*) campagne *f.;* (*district*) pays *m.;* **in the** —— à la campagne
course: of —— bien entendu
cousin cousin, -e *m. f.*
cow vache *f.*

GENERAL VOCABULARY

cuisinier [kɥizinje] m. *cook*
cuisinière [kɥizinjɛːr] f. *cook*
culotte [kylɔt] f. *breeches*

d'abord [dabɔːr] *first* (adv.)
dame [dam] f. *lady*
dangereux [dɑ̃·ʒrø] *dangerous*
dans [dɑ̃] *in, into*
danser [dɑ̃se] *to dance*
Daudet [dodɛ] French writer (1840-1897)
de [də] *of, from, in, with, to, by, for; than; some, any*
débarquer [debarke] *to land*
debout [dəbu]: **être** —— *to be standing*
décembre [desɑ̃ːbr] m. *December*
décider [deside] *to decide; persuade, induce;* **se** —— *to decide*
déclarer [deklare] *to declare*
dedans [dədɑ̃] *within, in it, in them*
défendre [defɑ̃ːdr] *to forbid*
déjà [deʒa] *already*
déjeuner [deʒøne] *to eat lunch or breakfast*
déjeuner [deʒøne] m. *luncheon;* **petit** —— *breakfast*
demain [dəmɛ̃] *tomorrow*
demander [dəmɑ̃de] *to ask, ask for;* **se** —— *to wonder*

demeurer [dəmœre] *to live (dwell); remain*
demi [dəmi] *half*
dent [dɑ̃] f. *tooth*
départ [depaːr] m. *departure*
(se) dépêcher [depɛʃe] *to hurry*
depuis [dəpɥi] *since* (prep.); —— **que** *since* (conj.); —— **quand?** —— **combien de temps?** *since when? how long?*
dernier, dernière [dɛrnje] [dɛrnjɛːr] *last*
derrière [dɛrjɛːr] *behind*
des [de] =**de** +**les** (art.)
dès [dɛ] *as early as, even at*
descendre [desɑ̃ːdr] *to descend, go down, get out* (of a vehicle); *to take* (or *bring*) *down; to put up* (at a hotel); **Tout le monde descend!** *All change!*
désirer [dezire] *to want, desire*
desquels [dekɛl] =**de** +**lesquels**
deux [dø] *two;* **tous les** —— *both*
devant [dəvɑ̃] *before* (place), *in front of*
devenir [dəvniːr] (p.p.: **devenu**) *to become*
devoir [dəvwaːr] *to owe.* See Vocabulary of Lesson XXXV.

---

cross traverser
cry pleurer, crier, s'écrier; —— **out** s'écrier
cup tasse *f.*
curtain rideau *m.*

dance danser
daughter fille *f.*
day jour. *m.*, journée *f.;* —— **before yesterday** avant-hier; —— **after tomorrow** après demain; **every**

(**each**) —— tous les jours, chaque jour; **next** —— lendemain *m.;* **second** —— **following** surlendemain *m.*
deal: a great —— beaucoup
dear, (dearly) cher
December décembre *m.*
deck pont *m.*
depart partir
departure départ *m.*
desire désirer

devr- see **devoir**
différent [diferɑ̃] *different*
difficile [difisil] *difficult, hard*
difficulté [difikylte] f. *difficulty*
dimanche [dimɑ̃:ʃ] m. *Sunday*
dîner [dine] *to dine*
dîner [dine] m. *dinner*
dire [di:r] *to say, tell*
dis-, dit- see **dire**
disposition [dispozisjɔ̃] f. *arrangement*
distinguer [distɛ̃ge] *to distinguish*
dix [dis] [di] *ten*
dix-huit [dizɥit] [dizɥi] *eighteen*
dix-neuf [diznœf] [diznœ] *nineteen*
dix-sept [dissɛt] [dissɛ] *seventeen*
dois, doiv- see **devoir**
dollar [dɔla:r] m. *dollar*
dommage [dɔma:ʒ] m. *injury, pity;* **C'est —!** *It's a pity!* **Quel —!** *What a pity!*
donc [dɔ̃(:k)] *so, then, therefore*
donner [dɔne] *to give;* **— la main (à)** *to shake hands (with);* **— sur** *to open upon, look out upon*
dont [dɔ̃] *whose, of whom, of which*
dormir [dɔrmi:r] *to sleep*
douane [dwan] f. *custom-house*
douanier [dwanje] m. *custom-house official*

doute [dut] m. *doubt*
doux [du] *gentle, mild*
douzaine [duzɛn] f. *dozen*
douze [du:z] *twelve*
drapeau [drapo] m. *flag*
droite [drwat] f. *right;* **à —** *on the right*
drôle [dro:l] *funny, strange*
du [dy] =**de** +**le** (art.)
dû, dus, etc. see **devoir**
duc [dyk] m. *duke*
duchesse [dyʃɛs] f. *duchess*
duquel [dykɛl] =**de** +**lequel**
dur [dy:r] *hard*

eau [o] f. *water*
école [ekɔl] f. *school;* **à l'—** *in (at, to) school*
écouter [ekute] *to listen, listen to*
(s')écrier [ekrie] *to shout, cry out*
écrire [ekri:r] (p.p.: **écrit**) *to write*
écriteau [ekrito] m. *sign*
écriv- see **écrire**
égal [egal] *equal*
église [egli:z] f. *church;* **à l'—** *at (to, in) church*
eh [e]: **eh bien!** *well!*
Eiffel [ɛfɛl] Eiffel Tower, 1000 feet high, built for the exposition of 1889, now used as a radio station

---

desk bureau *m.*, pupitre *m.*
die mourir, *p. p.:* mort
difficult difficile
difficulty difficulté *f.*
dine dîner
dining-room salle (*f.*) à manger
dinner dîner *m.*
dirty sale, malpropre
do faire
doctor médecin *m.*

dog chien *m.*
don't: don't you? n'est-ce pas?
door porte *f.*
down: go (come) — descendre; **— stairs** en bas
downtown en ville
dozen douzaine *f.*
drawing-room salon *m.*
dress s'habiller
dress robe *f.*

GENERAL VOCABULARY

élève [elɛːv] m. or f. *pupil*
s'élever [elve] *to rise (up)*
elle [ɛl] *she, her, it*
elles [ɛl] *they, them*
s'embarquer [ɑ̃barke] *to set sail, go on board*
empêcher [ɑ̃pɛʃe] *to prevent*
emplette [ɑ̃plɛt] f. *purchase;* **faire des emplettes** *to go shopping*
employé, -e [ɑ̃plwaje] m., f. *employé*
employer [ɑ̃plwaje] *to employ, use*
en [ɑ̃] *some, any; of it, of them*
en [ɑ̃] *in, into, to, on, as, like;* (with present participle): *while;* —— **bas** *downstairs;* —— **haut** *upstairs*
encore [ɑ̃kɔːr] *yet, still, again; more;* ——**un (deux,** etc.) *one (two,* etc.) *more;* —— + a partitive *some more*
encre [ɑ̃ːkr] f. *ink*
endroit [ɑ̃drwa] m. *place, location*
enfant [ɑ̃fɑ̃] m. or f. *child*
enfin [ɑ̃fɛ̃] *finally, at last*
ennuyer [ɑ̃nɥije] *to bore, weary;* **s'**—— *to be bored*
ensemble [ɑ̃sɑ̃ːbl] *together*
ensuite [ɑ̃sɥit] *then, next*
entendre [ɑ̃tɑ̃ːdr] *to hear;* **bien entendu** *of course*
entr'acte [ɑ̃trakt] m. *intermission*
entre [ɑ̃ːtr] *between, among*

entrée [ɑ̃tre] f. *entrance, entry*
entrer [ɑ̃tre] *to enter*
enverr- fut. and cond. of **envoyer**
envie [ɑ̃vi] f. *wish, desire, longing*
environs [ɑ̃virɔ̃] m. pl. *vicinity*
envoyer [ɑ̃vwaje] *to send*
épais [epɛ] *thick*
épaule [epoːl] f. *shoulder*
équipe [ekip] f. *team*
es [ɛ] 2 s. pres. ind. of **être**
escalier [ɛskalje] m. *stairway*
espérer [ɛspere] *to hope*
essayer [ɛsɛje] *to try*
est [ɛ] 3 s. pres. ind. of **être; est-ce que?** [ɛskə] (Literally: *Is it that?*) an expression used to make a declarative sentence interrogative; **n'est-ce pas?** [nɛspa] *Is it not so?*
est [ɛst] m. *east*
et [e] *and*
ét- see **être**
étage [etaːʒ] m. *story* (of a house) **au premier** —— *on the second floor*
États-Unis [etaz‿yni] m. pl. *United States*
été [ete] p.p. of **être**
été [ete] m. *summer*
étendre [etɑ̃ːdr] *to extend, spread*
êtes [ɛt] 2. pl. pres. ind. of **être**
étoile [etwal] f. *star*

---

drink boire
dry sécher
dry sec, sèche
during pendant
duty devoir *m.;* **to be one's** —— devoir

each chaque *(adj.),* chacun *(pron.);* ——**other** nous, vous, se, l'un(e) l'autre, l'un(e) à l'autre, les un(e)s les autres, les un(e)s aux autres
early de bonne heure, tôt
easy facile
eat manger
eight *huit
eighteen dix-huit
eighty quatre-vingts
either *(after a negative)* non plus; ——**... or** ou ... ou
eleven *onze

étonner [etɔne] *to astonish;* s'—— *to be astonished*
étranger [etrɑ̃ʒe] *foreign;* m. *foreigner;* à l'—— *abroad*
être [ɛːtr] *to be*
étudiant, -e [etydjɑ̃] [etydjɑ̃ːt] m., f. *student*
étudier [etydje] *to study*
eu [y] p.p. of avoir
Europe [œrɔp] f. *Europe*
eus [y] etc. past def. of avoir
eux [ø] *they, them*
exactement [ɛgzaktəmɑ̃] *exactly*
examiner [ɛgzamine] *to examine*
excursion [ɛkskyrsjɔ̃] f. *excursion*
exemple [ɛgzɑ̃ːpl] m. *example;* par —— *for example*
expliquer [ɛksplike] *to explain*

façade [fasad] f. *façade, front*
face [fas] f. *face;* en —— (de) *opposite*
fâché [faʃe] *angry, sorry*

facile [fasil] *easy*
façon [fasɔ̃] f. *manner*
faible [fɛːbl] *weak*
faille [faːj] pres. subj. of **falloir**
faim [fɛ̃] f. *hunger;* avoir —— *to be hungry*
faire [fɛːr] *to do, make, take* (a step, a journey, etc.), *to have* (done), *cause, matter, be* (in impersonal expressions of the weather); —— venir *to call, send for, have (cause to) come;* —— attention *to pay attention, take care;* —— une malle *to pack a trunk;* —— la queue *to stand in line;* —— visite (à) *to visit*
fais- [fəz-] see **faire**
fait [fɛ], faites [fɛt] see **faire;** tout à fait *quite, entirely, altogether*
falloir [falwaːr] *to be necessary, take* (time), *require, demand* (an impersonal verb); il ne faut pas *you* (one) *must not*

---

employ employer
end fin *f.*
England Angleterre *f.*
English anglais; —— **language** anglais *m.* ——**man** Anglais *m.*
enough assez
enter entrer
Europe Europe *f.*
even même (*adv.*)
evening soir *m.*, soirée *f.*; **in the** —— le soir
ever jamais
every tout, chaque; —— **day** tous les jours
everybody tout le monde *m. s.*
everything tout, (*all things*) toutes les choses *f. pl.*
everywhere partout

exactly exactement, précisément; —— **eight o'clock** huit heures précises
example exemple *m.*; **for** —— par exemple
excite agiter
expect attendre, s'attendre à
expensive cher
explain expliquer
eye œil *m., pl.:* yeux

face figure *f.*
fail manquer
fall tomber
family famille *f.*
famous célèbre
far loin; **as . . . as** jusqu'à
fast vite

famille [fami:j] f. *family*
fass- pres. subj. of **faire**
fatal [fatal] *fatal, disastrous*
fatigué [fatige] *tired*
faubourg [fobu:r] m. *suburb*
faudr- fut. and cond. of **falloir**
faut [fo] pres. ind. of **falloir**
faux, fausse [fo] [fo:s] *false*
faux-col [fokɔl] m. *collar*
femme [fam] f. *woman, wife*
fenêtre [fənɛ:tr] f. *window*
fer- fut. and cond. of **faire**
fermer [fɛrme] *to close, shut*
fête [fɛ:t] f. *holiday*
feuille [fœ:j] f. *leaf, sheet* (of paper)
février [fevrie] m. *February*
fier [fjɛ:r] *proud*
figure [figy:r] f. *face, figure*
fil [fil] m. *thread, wire;* **sans —** *wireless*
filet [filɛ] m. *net*
fille [fi:j] f. *daughter;* **jeune —** *girl, young woman;* **petite—** *little girl*
filleul [fijœl] m. *godson*
fils [fis] m. *son*
fin [fɛ̃] f. *end*
finir [fini:r] *to finish;* **— par** + infinitive *(to do) finally*
fis [fi] etc. past def. of **faire**
flatter [flate] *to flatter*
fleur [flœ:r] f. *flower*
fleuve [flœ:v] m. *(large) river*
fois [fwa] f. *time (occasion)*
fond [fɔ̃] m. *bottom, back, farther end*
fonder [fɔ̃de] *to found*
font [fɔ̃] 3. pl. pres. ind. of **faire**
fontaine [fɔ̃tɛn] f. *fountain*
football [futbal] m. *football*
formalité [fɔrmalite] f. *formality*
fort [fɔ:r] *strong*
fou, fol, folle [fu, fɔl] *mad, crazy*
Foulard [fula:r] proper name
fourchette [furʃɛt] f. *fork*
franc [frɑ̃] m. *franc* (normally about

---

father père *m.*
fear avoir peur (de)
fear peur *f.*
February février *m.*
few peu; **a —** quelques, quelques-uns
field champ *m.*; **in the fields** aux champs, dans les champs
fifteen quinze
fifth cinquième
fifty cinquante
find trouver
fine beau; **—!** À la bonne heure!
finish finir
first premier *(adj.);* d'abord *(adv.)*
— (ground) floor rez-de-chaussée *m.*
five cinq
flag drapeau *m.*
flatter flatter
floor plancher *m.*, étage *m.*; **ground —, first —** rez-de-chaussée *m.* **second —** premier étage *m.*
flower fleur *f.*
follow suivre
foot pied *m.*; **on —** à pied; **on one's feet** debout
football football *m.*
for pour; **(since)** depuis; **(during)** pendant
foreign étranger
forget oublier
fork fourchette *f.*
former ancien; **the —** celui-là, *etc.*
formerly autrefois
forty quarante

twenty cents)
français [frãsɛ] *French;* **le ——** *m.*
French (language)
Français [frãsɛ] *m. Frenchman,*
Frenchmen, French people
François [frãswa] *Francis*
frapper [frape] *to knock, strike*
frère [frɛːr] *m. brother*
froid [frwa] *cold;* **avoir ——** *to be*
cold; **faire ——** *to be cold* (impersonal)
fromage [frɔmaːʒ] *m. cheese*
fruit [frɥi] *m. fruit*
fus [fy] etc. past def. of **être**

gai [ge] *gay, cheerful*
galerie [galri] f. *gallery*
gant [gã] *m. glove*
garçon [garsɔ̃] *m. boy, waiter, steward,*
bachelor
garder [garde] *to keep, guard*
gare [gaːr] *f. (railway) station*
gargouille [gargu:j] *f. gargoyle*
gâteau [gato] *m. cake*
gauche [goːʃ] *f. left* **à ——** *on the left*
géant [ʒeã] *m. giant*
geler [ʒəle] *to freeze*
général [ʒeneral] *m. general*
genou [ʒənu] *m. knee*
gens [ʒã] *m.* or *f.* pl. *people (indi-*

four quatre
fourteen quatorze
fourth quatrième, (un) quart
franc franc *m.*
France (la) France *f.*
free libre
French français; **—— language** français *m.;* **—— lesson** leçon (*f.*) de français; **—— man, —— people** Français *m.*
Friday vendredi *m.*
friend ami *m.,* amie *f.*
from de, à; **—— it** en
front façade *f.;* **in ——of** devant
fruit fruit *m.*
full plein

game jeu *m.,* match *m.*
garden jardin *m.*
gentleman monsieur *m.; pl.:* messieurs
get avoir; (**go and**) **——** chercher; **—— in** (*a vehicle*) monter; **—— out** (*of a vehicle*) descendre; **—— up** se lever; **—— tired** se lasser.

girl jeune fille *f.;* **little ——** petite fille *f.*
give donner
glad heureux, content
glass verre *m.*
glove gant *m.*
go aller, se rendre, partir, marcher; **—— and get** aller chercher; **—— around** faire le tour (de); **—— away** s'en aller, partir; **—— back** retourner; **—— down** descendre; **—— home** rentrer (à la maison); **—— in** entrer; **—— on board** s'embarquer; **—— out** sortir; **—— to bed** (aller) se coucher; **—— up** monter; **—— with** accompagner
goal but *m.*
good bon; **——-bye!** au revoir! adieu!
graceful gracieux
grand grand
granddaughter petite-fille *f.*
grandfather grand-père *m.*
grandmother grand'mère *f.*
grandson petit-fils *m.*
grass herbe *f.*

viduals); **jeunes** —— *young men*
gentil, -le [ʒɑ̃ti] [ʒɑ̃tiːj] *nice*
glace [glas] *f. ice; mirror*
gracieux, gracieuse [grasjø] [grasjøːz] *graceful, gracious*
grand [grɑ̃] *large, tall, great*
grandir [grɑ̃diːr] *to grow large*
grand'mère [grɑ̃mɛːr] *f. grandmother*
grand-père [grɑ̃pɛːr] *m. grandfather*
grêler [grɛle] *to hail*
grimper [grɛ̃pe] *to climb*
gros, -se [gro] [groːs] *big, bulky*
ground [graund] *m. grounds, field*
guère [gɛːr]: **ne ... ——** *scarcely*
guerre [gɛːr] *f. war*

guichet [giʃɛ] *m. ticket window*
Guise [giːz] noble French family of the XVIth and XVIIth centuries

(s')habiller [abije] *to dress*
habiter [abite] *to live (in), dwell, inhabit*
***haut** [o] *high; aloud;* **en ——** *upstairs*
hélas! [elɑːs] *alas!*
Henri [ɑ̃ri] *Henry*
herbe [ɛrb] *f. grass*
heure [œːr] *f. hour, time, o'clock*
à la bonne ——! *Fine! Well and*

---

great grand
greatly beaucoup
green vert
ground terre *f.;* **—— floor** rez-de-chaussée *m.*
grow: **—— tired** se lasser, s'ennuyer
grudge: bear a —— en vouloir (à) [**for** = de]
gull mouette *f.*

half moitié *f.,* demi; **—— past six** six heures et demie
hall salle *f.,* galerie *f.,* corridor *m.*
hand main *f.*
handsome beau
happen arriver
happy heureux, content
hard difficile; dur; ferme
has *see* avoir; **hasn't he?** n'est-ce pas?
hat chapeau *m.*
have avoir; **—— just** venir (*pres.*) + de + *infinitive;* **had just** venir (*imperf.*) + de + *infinitive;* (**cause**) faire; (**obliged to**) falloir,

devoir; **haven't they?** n'est-ce pas?
he il, lui, ce
head tête *f.;* **——ache** mal (*m.*) à la tête; **to have a ——ache** avoir mal à la tête
health santé *f.*
hear entendre
her (*pron.*): la, lui, elle, celle; (*adj.*): son, sa, ses
here ici; **—— is (are)** voici
hers le sien, *etc.;* à elle
herself se, elle-même
high *haut; **—— shoe** bottine *f.*
him le, lui; celui
himself se, lui, lui-même
his (*pron.*): le sien, *etc.,* à lui; (*adj.*): son, sa, ses; **in —— hand** à la main
history histoire *f.*
hold tenir
home: at —— à la maison, chez moi, *etc.;* **at the —— of** chez; **to go ——** rentrer (à la maison)
honor honneur *f.;* **in —— of** en l'honneur de
hope espérer

good! de bonne —— *early*
heureux, heureuse [œrø] [œrø:z] *happy, glad, fortunate*
*****hibou** [ibu] m. *owl*
hier [jɛːr] [ijɛːr] *yesterday*
histoire [istwaːr] f. *story, history*
historique [istɔrik] *historical*
hiver [ivɛːr] m. *winter*
homme [ɔm] m. *man*
honneur [ɔnœːr] m. *honor*
hospitalier [ɔspitalje] *hospitable*
hôte, hôtesse [oːt] [otɛs] m., f. *host, hostess*
hôtel [ɔtɛl] m. *hotel*
*****huit** [ɥit] [ɥi] *eight;* —— **jours** *a week*

ici [isi] *here*
idée [ide] f. *idea*
ignorer [iɲɔre] *not to know, to be ignorant of*

---

horse cheval *m.*; **on horseback** à cheval
host hôte *m.*
hot chaud; **it is** —— il fait chaud; **I am** —— j'ai chaud
hotel hôtel *m.*
hour heure *f.*
house maison *f.*; **at (to) the** —— **of** chez
how? comment? ——! comment! comme . . . ! que . . . ! —— **much?** —— **many?** combien? —— **long?** depuis quand? depuis (pendant) combien de temps? —— **old is he?** quel âge a-t-il?
hundred cent
hungry: to be —— avoir faim *f.*
hurry (se) dépêcher
husband mari *m.*

il [il] *he, it*
île [iːl] f. *island*
ils [il] *they*
(s')imaginer [imaʒine] *to imagine*
imposer [ɛ̃poze] *to impose*
impression [ɛ̃prɛsjɔ̃] f. *impression*
Indes [ɛ̃ːd] f. pl. *India*
ingénieur [ɛ̃ʒenjœːr] m. *engineer*
intention [ɛ̃tɑ̃sjɔ̃] f. *intention;* **avoir l'**—— **(de)** *to intend*
intéressant [ɛ̃terɛsɑ̃] *interesting*
intéresser [ɛ̃terɛse] *to interest*
intérieur [ɛ̃terjœːr] m. *interior*
inviter [ɛ̃vite] *to invite*
ir- fut. and cond. of **aller**

jamais [ʒamɛ] *ever, never;* **ne . . .**—— *never*
janvier [ʒɑ̃vje] m. *January*
jardin [ʒardɛ̃] m. *garden*

I je, moi
ice glace *f.*; —— **cream** glace *f.*, crème (*f.*) à la glace
if si
ill malade
immediately tout de suite, immédiatement
impossible impossible
in dans, à, en, de; —— **front of** devant; —— **it (them)** y; —— **my (his, her, your) hand** à la main
inform mettre au courant (de); **to keep informed** tenir au courant (de)
ink encre *f.*
insist (upon) tenir à
instead au lieu (de)
intend avoir l'intention (de), compter
interest intéresser; **to be interested**

je [ʒə] *I*
Jean [ʒɑ̃] *John*
Jeanne d'Arc [ʒan dark] *Joan of Arc*
jersey [ʒɛrsɛ] m. *jersey*
jetée [ʒəte] f. *pier, mole*
jeter [ʒəte] *to throw (away) cast*
jeu [ʒø] m. *play, game*
jeudi [ʒødi] m. *Thursday*
jeune [ʒœn] *young*
joie [ʒwa] f. *joy, delight*
joli [ʒɔli] *pretty*
jouer [ʒwe] *to play*
joueur [ʒwœːr] m. *player*
joujou [ʒuʒu] m. *plaything, toy*
jour [ʒuːr] m. *day;* **tous les jours** *every day;* **huit jours** *a week;* **quinze jours** *two weeks*
journal [ʒurnal] m. *newspaper*
journée [ʒurne] f. *day*
juillet [ʒyjɛ] m. *July*

juin [ʒɥɛ̃] m. *June*
jusqu'à [ʒyska] *to, up to, until, as far as*
justice [ʒystis] f. *justice, law;* **Palais de ——** *Palace of Justice, (court house, law courts)*

kilomètre [kilɔmɛtr] m. *kilometer*
kodak [kɔdak] m. *kodak*

l' see **la** and **le**
la [la] *the; her, it*
là [la] *there*
là-bas [labɑ] *down there, yonder*
laisser [lɛse] *permit, let, leave;* **—— tranquille** *to leave alone*
lait [lɛ] m. *milk;* **café au ——** *coffee with milk*
langue [lɑ̃ːg] f. *language*
laquelle [lakɛl] see **lequel**

---

s'intéresser
interest intérêt *m.*
interesting intéressant
into dans, en, à; **—— it (them)** y
invite inviter
is see être & devoir; **here ——** voici; **there is** voilà, il y a; **isn't he? is it not so?** n'est-ce pas?
it il, elle, ce, le, la, lui; **in (into) ——** y; **of ——** en
its son, sa, ses

jam confiture *f.*
January janvier *m.*
jersey jersey *m.*
John Jean
journey voyage *m.*
July juillet *m.*
jump sauter
June juin *m.*

just: —— the same tout de même; **to have ——** ... venir de ...

keep garder, tenir; **—— informed** tenir au courant; **kept on ... ing** (*expressed by imperfect tense*)
kick coup (*m.*) de pied
kind espèce *f.*, sorte *f.*
king roi *m.*
kitchen cuisine *f.*
knee genou *m.*
knife couteau *m.*
knock frapper
know savoir, connaître; **—— how** savoir
kodak kodak *m.*

lady dame *f.*
land débarquer
land terre *f.*, pays *m.*

large [larʒ] *broad, wide*
lasser [lase] *to weary, tire;* **se —** *to grow weary*
latin [latɛ̃] *Latin*
laver [lave] *to wash*
le [lə] *the; him, it*
leçon [ləsɔ̃] f. *lesson*
légume [legym] m. *vegetable*
lendemain [lɑ̃dmɛ̃] m. *next day*
lentement [lɑ̃·tmɑ̃] *slowly*
lequel [ləkɛl] *which, who, whom; which one?*
les [le] *the; them*
lesquels, lesquelles [lekɛl] see **lequel**
lettre [lɛtr] f. *letter*
leur [lœːr] (pers. pron.) *to or for them*
leur(s) [lœːr] (poss. adj. or poss. pron.) *their, theirs*
lever [ləve] *to raise;* **se —** *to rise, get up;* **être levé** *to be up*
liberté [libɛrte] f. *liberty*
libre [libr] *free, unengaged*
lieu [ljø] m. *place, stead;* **au — de** *instead of*

linge [lɛ̃ːʒ] m. *linen, laundry*
lire [liːr] *to read*
lis- see **lire**
lit [li] m. *bed*
littérature [literatyːr] f. *literature*
livre [liːvr] m. *book*
livre [liːvr] f. *pound*
location [lɔkɑsjɔ̃] f.: **billet en — reserved seat**
loin [lwɛ̃] *far*
Loire [lwaːr] f. *river in France*
Londres [lɔ̃ːdr] *London*
long, longue [lɔ̃] [lɔ̃ːg] *long;* **le long de** *along*
longtemps [lɔ̃tɑ̃] (adv.) (a) *long (time)*
louer [lwe] *to rent; praise*
Louvre [luːvr] m. *formerly palace of French kings, now a museum*
lu [ly] p.p. of **lire**
lui [lɥi] *to (or for) him, or her, or it; he, him*
lumière [lymjɛːr] f. *light*
lundi [lœ̃di] m. *Monday*
lune [lyn] f. *moon*

---

language langue *f.*
large grand
last dernier, passé; **— night** hier soir, cette nuit; **at — enfin**
late tard, en retard
Latin latin
(the) latter celui-ci, *etc.*
lead mener, conduire
learn apprendre, *p. p.:* appris
leave quitter (*trans.*), partir (*intrans.*), laisser
left gauche; **on (to) the —** à gauche
less moins
lesson leçon *f.*
let laisser

letter lettre *f.*
library bibliothèque *f.*
lie: — down se coucher
light lumière *f.*
like aimer, vouloir
like (*prep.:*) comme; **nothing — it** rien de tel
line queue *f.;* **stand in —** faire la queue
linen (clothes) linge *m.*
listen écouter; **— to** écouter
little petit; **(not much):** peu; **a —** un peu
live vivre; **(dwell):** demeurer, habiter

M. =monsieur
ma [ma] *my*
machine [maʃin] f. *machine, engine*
madame [madam] f. *madam, Mrs., mistress*
mademoiselle [madmwazɛl] f. *Miss*
magasin [magazɛ̃] m. *store, shop*
magnifique [maɲifik] *magnificent*
mai [mɛ] m. *May*
main [mɛ̃] f. *hand;* **à la —** *in my (his, her, your) hand;* **donner la — (à)** *to shake hands (with)*
maintenant [mɛ̃tnɑ̃] *now*
mais [mɛ] *but; why!* **— oui (non)!** *Why yes (no)!*
maison [mɛzɔ̃] f. *house;* **à la — (at)** *home*
Maisons-Alfort [mɛzɔ̃ alfɔːr] suburb of Paris
maître [mɛːtr] m. *master, teacher*
mal [mal] m. *evil, illness;* (adv.): *badly;* **— à la tête** *headache;* **— de mer** *sea-sickness*
malade [malad] *sick*
malgré [malgre] *in spite of*

malheur [malœːr] m. *misfortune*
malheureusement [malœrøzmɑ̃] *unhappily, unfortunately*
malheureux [malœrø] *unhappy, unfortunate*
malle [mal] f. *trunk;* **faire une —** *to pack a trunk*
manger [mɑ̃ʒe] *to eat;* **salle à —** *dining-room*
manquer [mɑ̃ke] *to miss, fail, lack*
marchand [marʃɑ̃] m. *merchant*
marché [marʃe] m. *market, bargain;* **(à) bon —** *cheap, cheaply*
marcher [marʃe] *to walk, march, go, move, travel*
mardi [mardi] m. *Tuesday*
mari [mari] m. *husband*
Marie [mari] *Mary*
mars [mars] m. *March*
Marthe [mart] *Martha*
match [matʃ] m. *game;* **— nul** *tie game*
matin [matɛ̃] m. *morning;* **le —** *in the morning*
matinal [matinal] (adj.) *up early*

---

lively vif
London Londres
long long; longtemps; **how —?** depuis quand? depuis (pendant) combien de temps? **a — time** longtemps; **longer** plus longtemps; **no (not any) longer** ne . . . plus
longing envie *f.*; **have a —** avoir envie (de)
look regarder; **— at** regarder; **— for** chercher; **— out upon** donner sur
lose perdre
lover amateur *m.*
low bas; **— shoe** soulier *m.*

lunch (*verb*) déjeuner
luncheon déjeuner *m.*

---

madam madame *f.* (Mme)
maid bonne *f.*
make faire
man homme *m.*; **young men** jeunes gens
many (*or* **very many**) beaucoup, bien; **how —?** combien? **so —** tant; **too —** trop
map carte *f.*
march marcher
March mars *m.*
market marché *m.*

matinée [matine] f. *morning; afternoon performance*
mauvais [movɛ] *bad;* **faire —** *to be bad weather*
me [mə] *me, to (for) me, myself*
médecin [mɛtsɛ̃] m. *doctor, physician*
meilleur [mɛjœːr] (adj.) *better;* **le — *best***
même [mɛːm] *same; very; self;* (adv.): *even;* **tout de —** *just the same*
mener [məne] *to lead*
mer [mɛːr] f. *sea;* **en pleine —** *on the open sea*
merci [mɛrsi] *thank you*
mercredi [mɛrkrədi] m. *Wednesday*
mère [mɛːr] f. *mother*
méridional [meridjɔnal] *southern*
merveilleux [mɛrvɛjø] *marvelous*
mes [me] *my*
messe [mɛs] f. *mass* (church service)
messieurs [mesjø] m. pl. *gentlemen*
mètre [mɛtr] m. *meter*
Métro [metro] =**Métropolitain** [metrɔpɔlitɛ̃] m. name of Paris underground railway

mettre [mɛtr] *to put, put on;* **se — à** + infinitive *to begin*
Mexique [mɛksik] m. *Mexico*
midi [midi] m. *noon; South* (of France)
mien, -ne [mjɛ̃] [mjɛn] *mine* (poss. pron.)
mieux [mjø] (adv.) *better;* **le — *best;*** **(faire) de son —** *(to do) one's best*
mil [mil] *thousand* (used in dates)
milieu [miljø] m. *middle*
mille [mil] *thousand*
milliard [miljaːr] m. *billion*
million [miljɔ̃] m. *million*
minuit [minɥi] m. *midnight*
minute [minyt] f. *minute*
mis [mi] see **mettre**
Mlle = **mademoiselle**
MM. = **messieurs**
Mme = **madame**
moderne [mɔdɛrn] *modern*
moi [mwa] *I, me*
moins [mwɛ̃] *less;* **le — *least;* — ... que** *less ... than; not so ... as*

Martha Marthe
Mary Marie
mass messe *f. (church service)*
master maître *m.*
match allumette *f.*
matter: What's the **—?** Qu'y a-t-il? Qu'est-ce qu'il y a? **What's the — with him (her)?** Qu'a-t-il (elle)? Qu'est-ce qu'il (elle) a?
May mai *m.*
me me, moi
meal repas *m.*
mean vouloir dire, signifier
meat viande *f.*
meet rencontrer, se rencontrer; **go (come) to —** aller (venir) à la rencontre de, aller (venir) au-devant de
merchant marchand *m.*
middle milieu *m.;* **in the — Ages** au moyen âge
midnight minuit *m.*
milk lait *m.*
mine le mien, etc., à moi
misfortune malheur *m.*
miss manquer
miss mademoiselle *f.* (Mlle)
mistake, be mistaken se tromper
moment moment *m.*
Monday lundi *m.*

mois [mwa] m. *month*
moitié [mwatje] f. *half*
moment [mɔmɑ̃] m. *moment*
mon [mɔ̃] *my*
monde [mɔ̃:d] m. *world; people;* tout le —— *everybody;* beaucoup de —— *many people;* du —— *(some) people*
monnaie [mɔnɛ] f. *coin, change*
monsieur [məsjø] m. *gentleman, Mr., sir*
Mont-Saint-Michel [mɔ̃ sɛ̃miʃɛl] m. island off the coast of Normandy
monter [mɔ̃te] *to mount, get in* (a vehicle); *to take up, to bring up*
montre [mɔ̃:tr] f. *watch*
montrer [mɔ̃tre] *to show;* se —— *to appear*
monument [mɔnymɑ̃] m. *monument, public building*
morceau [mɔrso] m. *piece*
mort [mɔ:r] p.p. of **mourir**
mort [mɔ:r] f. *death*
mot [mo] m. *word*
mou, mol, molle [mu] [mɔl] *soft*
mouchoir [muʃwa:r] m. *handkerchief*

mouette [mwɛt] f. *gull*
mourir [muri:r] *to die*
moyen [mwajɛ̃] m. *means;* au —— âge *in the Middle Ages*
mule [myl] f. *mule*
mûrir [myri:r] *to ripen*
musée [myze] m. *museum*
musique [myzik] f. *music*

naissance [nɛsɑ̃:s] f. *birth;* anniversaire (m.) de —— *birthday anniversary*
naître [nɛ:tr] *to be born;* p.p. né
nation [nasjɔ̃] f. *nation*
naturellement [natyrɛlmɑ̃] *naturally*
ne [nə]: ne ... pas *not;* ne ... jamais *never;* ne ... plus *no more, no longer;* ne ... point *not* (emphatic); ne ... personne *nobody;* ne ... que *only, nothing but;* ne ... rien *nothing;* ne ... ni ... ni, ne ... ni ... ne *neither ... nor*
né [ne] p.p. of **naître**
nécessaire [nesɛsɛ:r] *necessary*
neiger [nɛʒe] *to snow*

---

money argent *m.*
month mois *m.*
more plus; two (three) —— encore deux (trois); some (any) —— encore du (des, *etc.*); no (not any) —— ne ... plus
morning matin *m.,* matinée *f.;* in the —— le matin; six o'clock in the —— six heures du matin; good —— bonjour; the whole —— toute la matinée
most le (la, les) plus; la plupart *f.*
mother mère *f.*
mount monter
Mr. monsieur *m.* (M.)

Mrs. madame *f.* (Mme)
much (*or* very much) beaucoup, bien; how ——? combien? so —— tant; too —— trop
museum musée *m.*
music musique *f.*
must *see* falloir & devoir
my mon, ma, mes; in —— hand à la main
myself me, moi-même

name nom *m.;* to be named s'appeler; His —— is John. Il s'appelle Jean.
napkin serviette *f.*

neuf [nœf] [nœ] *nine*
neuvième [nœvjɛm] *ninth*
nez [ne] m. *nose*
ni [ni] *neither;* see **ne**
Nîmes [ni(ː)m] city of Provence in southern France
noir [nwaːr] *black;* **tableau** —— *blackboard*
nom [nɔ̃] m. *name*
nombre [nɔ̃ːbr] m. *number*
non [nɔ̃] *no, not;* —— **plus** (after a negative) *either*
nord [nɔːr] m. *north*
Normandie [nɔrmɑ̃di] f. old province in northern France
nos [no] *our*
notre [nɔtr] *our*
nôtre [noːtr] *ours*
Notre-Dame [nɔtrə dam] (*Our Lady*) Paris cathedral
nous [nu] *we, us, to (for) us, ourselves, each other, to (for) each other*
nouveau, nouvel, nouvelle [nuvo] [nuvɛl] *new*
nouvelles [nuvɛl] f. pl. *news;* **une nouvelle** *a piece of news*
novembre [nɔvɑ̃ːbr] m. *November*
nuage [nɥaːʒ] m. *cloud*
nuit [nɥi] f. *night, darkness*
nul [nyl] *no, none, not any, null;* **match**—— *tie game*
numéro [nymero] m. *number*

objet [ɔbʒɛ] m. *object*

---

naturally naturellement
near (to) près (de), auprès (de)
necessary nécessaire; **to be** —— falloir; **it is** —— il faut
need besoin *m.;* **to** ——, **to have** —— (**of**) avoir besoin (de)
neither ni l'un(e) ni l'autre; —— . . . **nor** (ne . . .) ni . . . ni, ne . . . ni . . . ne
never (ne . . .) jamais
new nouveau
news nouvelles *f. pl.;* **a piece of** —— une nouvelle
newspaper journal *m.*
New York New-York
next prochain, voisin, suivant; —— **day** lendemain *m.;* **the** —— **time** la prochaine fois
next (*adv.*) ensuite
nice gentil
night nuit *f.;* **last** —— hier soir, cette nuit
nine neuf
nineteen dix-neuf
ninety quatre-vingt-dix; ——**-three** quatre-vingt-treize
no non; (**not any**) pas de; **Why no!** Mais non! **no more** (ne . . .) plus
nobody (ne . . .) personne; —— **but** ne . . . que
noon midi *m.*
nor ni; **neither . . .** —— (ne . . .) ni . . . ni, ne . . . ni . . . ne
Normandy Normandie *f.*
not (ne . . .) pas, (ne . . .) point; —— **at all** (ne . . .) pas du tout
note billet *m.*
notebook cahier *m.*
nothing (ne . . .) rien; —— **at all** (ne . . .) rien du tout; —— **but** ne . . . que
notice remarquer
novel roman *m.*
November novembre *m.*
now maintenant, à présent, en ce moment

occupé [ɔkype] *occupied, busy*
octobre [ɔktɔbr] m. *October*
Odéon [ɔdeɔ̃] m. theater in Paris
œil [œːj] m. *eye*
officier [ɔfisje] m. *official*
oiseau [wazo] m. *bird*
olivier [ɔlivje] m. *olive tree*
ombre [ɔ̃ːbr] f. *shade, shadow*
on [ɔ̃] *one, somebody, people, we, you, they*
oncle [ɔ̃ːkl] m. *uncle*
ont [ɔ̃] 3. pl. pres. ind. of **avoir**
*****onze** [ɔ̃ːz] *eleven*
opposition [ɔpozisjɔ̃] f. *opposition, resistance*
or [ɔːr] m. *gold*
orage [ɔraːʒ] m. *storm*

ôter [ote] *to remove, take off*
ou [u] *or*
où [u] *where; in (to, at, on) which*
oublier [ublie] *to forget*
ouest [wɛst] m. *west*
*****oui** [wi] *yes*
ouvert [uvɛːr] *open, opened*
ouvrage [uvraːʒ] m. *work*
ouvrir [uvriːr] *to open;* p.p. **ouvert**

pain [pɛ̃] m. *bread*
paire [pɛːr] f. *pair*
paix [pɛ] f. *peace*
palais [palɛ] m. *palace*
pape [pap] m. *pope*
papier [papje] m. *paper*
paquebot [pakbo] m. *steam-boat*

---

number numéro *m.*, nombre *m.*

o'clock heure(s) *f.*
October octobre *m.*
of de, à; —— **course** bien entendu; —— **it (them)** en
office bureau *m.;* **at (to, in) the** —— **of** chez
officer officier *m.*
often souvent
old vieux (vieil, vieille), âgé; (**former, ancient**): ancien; **How old is he?** Quel âge (*m.*) a-t-il? **He is ten years old.** Il a dix ans. Il est âgé de dix ans.
on sur, à, de; —— **this (the other) side** de ce (l'autre) côté
once une fois; **at** —— tout de suite **all at** —— tout à coup, tout d'un coup
one on; **the** —— celui(-ci), celui(-là); **that** —— celui-là; **this** —— celui-ci
one un, une

oneself se, soi-même
only seul (*adj.*), seulement (*adv.*); ne ... que
open ouvrir; —— **on** donner sur
open (*adj.*) ouvert; **on the** —— **sea** en pleine mer
opposite en face (de), de l'autre côté
or ou; **either ... or** ou ... ou
order commander
order: in —— **to** pour; **in** —— **that** pour que, afin que
other autre; **each** —— *see* each
ought *see* devoir & falloir
our notre, nos
ours le nôtre, *etc.*, à nous
ourselves nous, nous-mêmes
out sorti; **get** —— (*of a vehicle*) descendre; **go** —— sortir
over: —— **there** là-bas
overcoat pardessus *m.*
owe devoir
own propre (*before the noun*)

par [paːr] *by, through, during, on, over, "per"*
paraître [parɛːtr] *to appear*
parc [park] m. *park*
parce que [pars kə] *because*
pardessus [pardəsy] m. *overcoat*
pardon [pardɔ̃] m. *pardon; I beg your pardon*
parent, -e [parɑ̃] [parɑ̃ːt] m., f. *relative*
Paris [pari] m. *Paris*
parisien [parizjɛ̃] *Parisian*
parler [parle] *to speak, talk*
parmi [parmi] *among*
particulier [partikylje] *private; peculiar*
partie [parti] f. *part*
partir [partiːr] *to leave, depart, set out, start;* **Nous voilà partis!** *We're off!*
partout [partu] *everywhere;* **un peu ——** *almost everywhere*
pas [pɑ]: **ne ... ——** *not;* **—— du tout** *not at all*
passeport [paspɔːr] m. *passport*
passer [pɑse] *to pass; spend* (time)
pauvre [poːvr] *poor*
paver [pave] *to pave*
payer [pɛje] *to pay, pay for*

pays [pɛi] m. *country* (political division or district)
paysage [pɛizaːʒ] m. *landscape*
peine [pɛn] f. *pain, trouble*
peinture [pɛ̃tyːr] f. *painting*
pendant [pɑ̃dɑ̃] *during, for* (a time); **—— que** *while*
pénétrer [penetre] *to penetrate, enter*
penser [pɑ̃se] *to think;* **—— à** *to have in mind;* **—— de** *to have an opinion of*
pension [pɑ̃sjɔ̃] f. *boarding-house*
perdre [pɛrdr] *to lose, waste*
père [pɛːr] m. *father*
permettre [pɛrmɛtr] *to permit;* p.p. **permis**
personne [pɛrsɔn] f. *person;* (**ne ...**) **——** (neuter) *nobody*
petit [pəti] *little, small*
petite-fille [pətit fiːj] f. *granddaughter*
petit-fils [pətifis] m. *grandson*
peu [pø] *little, not much, few, not many;* **un ——** *a little; somewhat*
peuple [pœpl] m. (a) *people, race; lower classes*
peur [pœːr] f. *fear;* **avoir ——** *to be afraid*
peut, peuv-, peux see **pouvoir**
peut-être [pøt‿ɛːtr] *perhaps*
Philippe [filip] *Philip*

---

pack (*a trunk, bag, etc.*) faire
pair paire f.
paper papier m.; **news——** journal m.
Paris Paris m.
Parisian parisien
park parc m.
part partie f.
pass passer
passport passeport m.
past passé; **a quarter —— eight** huit heures et quart; **half —— eight** huit heures et demie
pay payer; **—— for** payer
peace paix f.
pen plume f.
pencil crayon m.
people on, (du) monde m., personnes f. pl. peuple m., gens m. or f. pl.
permit permettre, laisser
person personne f.
Philip Philippe
piano piano m.

phrase [frɑːz] f. *sentence*
piano [pjano] m. *piano*
Picardie [pikardi] f. *Picardy* (old province of France; capital: Amiens)
pièce [pjɛs] f. *room; play; coin*
pied [pje] m. *foot;* à —— *on foot*
pierre [pjɛːr] f. *stone*
pittoresque [pitɔrɛsk] *picturesque*
place [plas] f. *place, seat, space, public square*
plaire [plɛːr] *to please*
plaisir [plɛziːr] m. *pleasure*
plaît [plɛ] 3. s. pres. ind. of **plaire** *s'il vous* —— *please, if you please*
plein, -e [plɛ̃] [plɛn] *full;* **en pleine mer** *on the open sea*
pleurer [plœre] *to weep, cry*
pleut [plø] pres. ind. of **pleuvoir**
pleuvoir [plœvwaːr] *to rain*
pluie [plɥi] f. *rain*
plume [plym] f. *pen*
plupart [plypaːr] f. *most, the majority*
plus [ply] *more;* **le** —— *most;* (ne ...) —— *no more, no longer;* **non** —— (after a negative) *either*
plusieurs [plyzjœːr] *several*
poche [pɔʃ] f. *pocket*
point [pwɛ̃] m. *point;* (**ne . .**) ——

not (emphatic)
pomme [pɔm] f. *apple;* —— **de terre** *potato*
pont [pɔ̃] m. *bridge; deck*
porte [pɔrt] f. *door; gate*
porter [pɔrte] *to carry; wear;* **se** —— *to be* (well, ill, etc.)
poser [poze] *to put, ask* (a question)
possible [pɔsibl] *possible*
postal [pɔstal] *postal*
poteau [pɔto] m. *post*
pou [pu] m. *louse*
pour [puːr] *for, to, in order to*
pourquoi [purkwa] *why*
pourr- fut. and cond. of **pouvoir**
pouvoir [puvwaːr] *to be able*
précieux [presjø] *precious*
précis [presi] *precise;* **deux heures précises** *exactly two o'clock*
préférer [prefere] *to prefer*
premier, première [prəmje] [prəmjɛːr] *first* (adj.)
prendre [prɑ̃ːdr] *to take;* p.p. **pris**
préparer [prepare] *to prepare*
près (de) [prɛ] *near*
à présent [prezɑ̃] *at present, now*
présenter [prezɑ̃te] *to present, introduce*
président [prezidɑ̃] m. *president*

---

picture tableau *m.*, image *f.*
piece morceau *m.*
pity pitié *f.*; **it's a** —— c'est dommage; **what a** ——! quel dommage!
place endroit *m.*, lieu *m.*, place *f.*
plate assiette *f.*
play jouer; —— (*a game*) jouer à; —— (*an instrument*) jouer de
play pièce *f.*
pleasant agréable
please plaire; (**if you**) —— s'il vous

plaît
pleasure plaisir *m.*; **take** —— (**in**) prendre plaisir (à)
poor pauvre
porter concierge *m. or f.*
possible possible
post card carte (*f.*) postale
potato pomme (*f.*) de terre
pound livre *f.*
prefer aimer mieux, préférer
prepare préparer

presque [prɛsk] *almost*
prêt [prɛ] *ready*
prier [prie] *to pray, beg, request*
printemps [prɛ̃tɑ̃] m. *spring;* **au —** *in spring*
pris [pri] see **prendre**
prix [pri] m. *price, prize*
prochain [prɔʃɛ̃] *next*
procurer [prɔkyre] *to procure*
professeur [prɔfɛsœːr] m. *professor, teacher*
profiter [prɔfite] *to profit*
promenade [prɔmnad] f. *walk, ride* **faire une —** *to take a walk,* etc.
se promener [prɔmne] *to take a walk,* etc.
promesse [prɔmɛs] f. *promise*
promettre [prɔmɛtr] *to promise*
propre [prɔpr] *clean; own*
propriété [prɔpriete] f. *property, estate*
Provence [prɔvɑ̃ːs] f. old province in the south of France
province [prɔvɛ̃ːs] f. *province*
pu, pus, etc. see **pouvoir**
puis, puiss- see **pouvoir**
puis [pɥi] *then (afterward)*
puisque [pɥiskə] *since* (causal)
pupitre [pypitr] m. *desk*

quai [ke] m. *quai, wharf, platform* (of a railway station)
quand [kɑ̃] *when;* **depuis —?** *since when? how long?*
quarante [karɑ̃ːt] *forty*
quart [kaːr] m. *quarter (one-fourth)*
quartier [kartje] m. *quarter, district*
quatorze [katɔrz] *fourteen*
quatre [katr] *four*
quatre-vingt-dix [katrə vɛ̃ dis] *ninety*
quatre-vingts [katrə vɛ̃] *eighty*
quatrième [katriɛm] *fourth*
que [kə] *whom, which, that; what* (pron.)
que [kə] (conj.) *that, than;* **aussi . . . —** *as . . . as;* **pas si . . . —** *not so . . . as;* **plus (moins) . . . —** *more (less) . . . than;* **ne . . . —** *only, nothing but*
que! [kə] *how!*
quel, -le [kɛl] *which, what* (adj.) **— homme!** *what a man!*
quelque [kɛlk(ə)] *some* (limited), *a small quantity;* **quelques** *a few;* **— chose** *something*
quelquefois [kɛlkəfwa] *sometimes*
quelques-uns [kɛlkəz‿œ̃] *some*
quelqu'un [kɛlkœ̃] *somebody*
question [kɛstjɔ̃] f. *question*

---

present (adj.) actuel, présent; **one — assistant** m.; **those —** les assistants m. pl.; **to be — (at)** assister (à)
preserves confiture f.
pretty joli
private particulier
procure (se) procurer
promise promettre
pupil élève m. or f.
purchase emplette f.

put mettre, p. p.: mis; **— on** mettre; **— up (at)** (a hotel) descendre (dans)
quarter (un) quart; quartier m.
question question f.; **be a — of** s'agir de
quick, quickly vite
quite tout, tout à fait, bien

railroad chemin (m.) de fer

queue [kø] f. *queue, tail, line;* **faire la —** *to stand in line*
qui [ki] (rel.) *who, whom, which, that*
qui? [ki] *who, whom*
quinze [kɛ:z] *fifteen;* **— jours** *two weeks*
quitter [kite] *to leave*
quoi [kwa] *what, which;* **sur —** *whereupon;* **de —** *wherewith*
quoique [kwak ə)] *although*

raconter [rakɔ̃te] *to tell, relate*
radioconcert [radjɔkɔ̃sɛ:r] m. *wireless concert*
raison [rɛzɔ̃] f. *reason; right;* **avoir —** *to be right*
rampe [rɑ̃:p] f. *flight of stairs*
rappeler [raple] *to call back;* **se —** *to remember*
rapporter [rapɔrte] *to bring back*
rayon [rɛ‿ɔ̃] m. *shelf; ray, beam*
récemment [resamɑ̃] *recently*
receveur [rəsvœ:r] m. *conductor, ticket collector*
recevoir [rəsvwa:r] *to receive, accept*
recevr-, reçois reçoiv-, reçu see **recevoir**
récompenser [rekɔ̃pɑ̃se] *to repay*
réfléchir [refleʃi:r] *to reflect*
refuser [rəfyze] *to refuse*

raise lever
rapidly vite
rather assez; plutôt
read lire, *p. p.:* lu
ready prêt
receive recevoir
red rouge
refuse refuser
relative parent *m.*, parente *f.*
remain rester
remember se rappeler

regarder [rəgarde] *to regard, look, look at, watch*
règle [rɛ‿gl] f. *rule*
reine [rɛ:n] f. *queen*
remarquer [rəmarke] *to notice*
remercier [rəmɛrsje] *to thank*
rencontre [rɑ̃kɔ̃:tr] f. *meeting;* **aller (venir) à la — de** *to go (come) to meet*
rencontrer [rɑ̃kɔ̃tre] *to meet*
rendre [rɑ̃:dr] *to return, give back* **— visite** *to pay a call;* **se —** *to go (betake oneself)*
rentrer [rɑ̃tre] *to re-enter, return (home)*
renvoyer [rɑ̃vwaje] *to send back (or away)*
repartir [rəparti:r] *to set out again*
repas [rəpɑ] m. *meal*
répéter [repete] *to repeat*
répondre [repɔ̃:dr] *to answer, respond*
réponse [repɔ̃:s] f. *reply, answer*
(se) reposer [rəpoze] *to rest*
restaurant [rɛstɔrɑ̃] m. *restaurant*
reste [rɛst] m. *rest remainder, remains, remnant;* **du —, au —** *besides, moreover, however*
rester [rɛste] *to remain, stay*
retard [rəta:r] m. *delay;* **en —** *late*

rent louer
repeat répéter
reply réponse *f.*
reserved réservé; **— seats** billets (*m.*) en location (*f.*)
rest (se) reposer
restaurant restaurant *m.*
return: (come back) revenir; **(go back)** retourner; **(bring back)** rapporter; **(give back)** rendre; **— (home)** rentrer

retenir [rətniːr] *to detain*
retour [rətuːr] m. *return;* **de** —— *back*
retourner [rəturne] *to return (go back);* **se** —— *to turn around*
(se) réveiller [revɛje] *to awaken*
revenir [rəvniːr] *to return (come back);* p.p. **revenu**
revoir [rəvwaːr] *to see again;* **au** —— *good-bye*
rez-de-chaussée [red̥ʃose] m. *ground floor*
rideau [rido] m. *curtain*
rien [rjɛ̃] *nothing;* **ne ...** —— *nothing*
robe [rɔb] f. *dress*
roi [rwa] m. *king*
romain [rɔmɛ̃] *Roman*
roman [rɔmɑ̃] m. *novel*
rompre [rɔ̃ːpr] *to break*
Rouen [rwɑ̃] *city in Normandy*
rouge [ruːʒ] *red*

rouler [rule] *to roll*
route [rut] f. *road, way;* **en** —— *on the way, Let's go!*
royal [rwajal] *royal*
ruban [rybɑ̃] m. *ribbon*
rue [ry] f. *street*
ruine [rɥin] f. *ruin*
rusé [ryze] *sly*

s' = **se** or **si**
sa [sa] *his, her, its, one's*
sac [sak] m. *sack, (hand) bag, valise*
sach- see **savoir**
saint [sɛ̃] *holy, sacred;* m. *saint*
Saint-Cloud [sɛ̃ klu] *suburb of Paris*
Saint-Malo [sɛ̃ malo] *French seaport*
sais [se] [sɛ] 1. or 2. s. pres. ind. of **savoir**
saison [sɛzɔ̃] f. *season*
sale [sal] *dirty*

---

right (*adj.*): droit; (*noun*): droit *m.*, droite *f.*, raison *f.;* **on the** —— à droite; **to be** —— avoir raison
ring sonner
rise se lever
road chemin *m.*, route *f.;* **on the** —— (**to**) en route (pour)
Roman romain
room pièce *f.*, salle *f.*, chambre *f.;* (**place, space**): place *f.;* **bath**—— salle de bain(s); **bed**—— chambre à coucher; **dining** —— salle à manger; **drawing**—— salon *m.*
rule règle *f.*
run courir, *p. p.:* couru

sail, set —— s'embarquer
saint saint,-e *m. f.*
same même; **just the** —— tout de même

satisfied content
Saturday samedi *m.*
say dire, *p. p.:* dit
school école *f.;* **at (in, to)** —— à l'école
sea mer *f.;* **on the open** —— en pleine mer; ——**sickness** mal (*m.*) de mer; **to be** ——**sick** avoir le mal de mer
seat place *f.;* **reserved** —— billet (*m.*) en location
seated assis
second deuxième, second; **on the** —— **floor** au premier (étage)
see voir; rendre (*or* faire) visite (à)
seek chercher
sell vendre
send envoyer; —— **for** envoyer chercher, faire venir; —— **back** renvoyer
sentence phrase *f.*

salle [sal] f. *room, hall;* —— **à manger** *dining-room;* —— **de bains** *bathroom*
salon [salɔ̃] m. *drawing-room*
salutation [salytasjɔ̃] f. *greeting*
samedi [samdi] m. *Saturday*
sans [sɑ̃] *without*
santé [sɑ̃te] f. *health*
saur- fut. and cond. of **savoir**
sauter [sote] *to jump*
savoir [savwaːr] *to know (have knowledge), know how*
scène [sɛn] f. *scene, stage*
sculpture [skyltyːr] f. *sculpture, carving*
se [sə] *himself, herself, itself, oneself, themselves, to (for) himself,* etc., *each other, to (for) each other*
sec, sèche [sɛk] [sɛʃ] *dry*
sécher [seʃe] *to dry*

second [səgɔ̃] *second*
seize [sɛːz] *sixteen*
semaine [səmɛn] f. *week*
sembler [sɑ̃ble] *to seem*
sentiment [sɑ̃timɑ̃] m. *sentiment, regard*
sept [sɛt] [sɛ] *seven*
septembre [sɛptɑ̃ːbr] m. *September*
ser- fut. and cond. of **être**
service [sɛrvis] m. *service*
serviette [sɛrvjɛt] f. *napkin, towel*
servir [sɛrviːr] *to serve*
ses [se] *his, her, its, one's*
seul [sœl] *alone*
seulement [sœlmɑ̃] *only* (adv.)
si [si] (conj.) *if, whether*
si [si] (adv.) *so;* **pas si . . . que** *not so . . . as*
Sicile [sisil] f. *Sicily*
siècle [sjɛkl] m. *century, cycle*

September septembre *m.*
set appareil *m.*
set out partir
set sail s'embarquer
seven sept
seventeen dix-sept
seventy soixante-dix; ——**-five** soixante-quinze
several plusieurs
shade ombre *f.*
shake: —— **hands** donner la main à, se donner la main
shall *see the future*
she elle, ce
sheet *(of paper)* feuille *f.*
shelf rayon *m.*
shirt chemise *f.*
shoe: **(low)** —— soulier *m.;* **(high)** —— bottine *f.*
shop magasin *m.;* **at (to, in) the** ——

of chez; ——**keeper** marchand *m.*
short court
shortly peu
should *see the conditional, also* devoir *and* falloir
shout crier, s'écrier
show montrer
sick malade; **to be sea**—— avoir le mal de mer
side côté *m.;* **on this** —— de ce côté
sidewalk trottoir *m.*
sign signer
sign signe *m.;* **make a** —— faire signe
since *(prep.):* depuis; *(temporal conj.):* depuis que; *(causal conj.):* puisque
sing chanter
sir monsieur *m.*
sister sœur *f.*

sien, -ne [sjɛ̃] [sjɛn] *his, hers, its*
signal [siɲal] m. *signal*
signe [siɲ] m. *sign, signal*
signer [siɲe] *to sign*
silence [silɑ̃:s] m. *silence;* **passer sous** —— *to pass over in silence*
simple [sɛ̃:pl] *simple, mere*
singulier [sɛ̃gylje] *strange, funny, singular*
six [sis] [si] *six*
sœur [sœ:r] f. *sister*
soif [swaf] f. *thirst;* **avoir** —— *to be thirsty*
soir [swa:r] m. *evening;* **le** —— *in the evening*
soirée [sware] f. *evening*
sois, soit, soient [swa] see **être**
soixante [swasɑ̃:t] *sixty*
soixante-dix [swasɑ̃·t dis] *seventy*

soleil [sɔlɛ:j] m. *sun*
sombre [sɔ̃:br] *dark, somber*
somme [sɔm] f. *sum*
sommeil [sɔmɛ:j] m. *sleep;* **avoir** —— *to be sleepy*
sommes [sɔm] 1. pl. pres. ind. of **être**
son [sɔ̃] *his, her, its, one's*
sonner [sɔne] *to sound, ring, strike (of a clock)*
sonnette [sɔnɛt] f. *(small) bell*
sont [sɔ̃] 3. pl. pres. ind. of **être**
Sorbonne [sɔrbɔn] f. *part of the University of Paris (college of arts?)*
sorte [sɔrt] f. *sort, kind;* **de la** —— *thus, in this (or that) way*
sortir [sɔrti:r] *to go out*
sou [su] m. *sou (one cent)*
soulier [sulje] m. *(low) shoe, oxford*

---

sit (to be sitting) être assis; —— **down (to seat oneself)** s'asseoir, *p. p.:* assis
six six
sixteen seize
sixty soixante
slang argot *m.*
sleep dormir
sleep sommeil *m.;* **to be sleepy** avoir sommeil
small petit
so si, tellement; —— **much** (*or* **many**) tant; **not** —— ... **as** pas si ... que, moins ... que; —— **that (in order that)** pour que, afin que
some du, de la, de l', des, de; en; quelque(s), quelques-uns
somebody quelqu'un, on
something quelque chose
sometimes quelquefois
son fils *m.*

soon bientôt, tôt; **as** —— **as** aussitôt que; **too** —— trop tôt, trop vite
sorry fâché; **to be sorry** être fâché (de), regretter (de)
sort espèce *f.*, sorte *f.*
south sud *m.*, midi *m.;* —— **America** l'Amérique (*f.*) du Sud
speak parler
spend dépenser; —— (*time*) passer
spoon cuiller *f.*
sport sport *m.*
spring printemps *m.;* **in** —— au printemps
square place *f.*
square carré
stadium stade *m.*
stage scène *f.*
stairs, stairway escalier *m.;* **down** —— en bas; **go down** —— descendre; **up** —— en *haut; **go up** —— monter
stand être debout; —— **in line** faire

sous [su] *under*
souterrain [sutɛrɛ̃] *underground*
souvenir [suvniːr] m. *memory*
souvent [suvɑ̃] *often*
soy- see **être**
spirale [spiral] f. *spiral*
sport [spɔːr] m. *sport, athletics*
sportif [spɔrtif] *sporting, athletic*
stade [stad] m. *stadium*
statue [staty] f. *statue*
su, sus, etc. see **savoir**
sucre [sykr] m. *sugar*
sud [syd] m. *south*
suis [sɥi] 1. s. pres. ind. of **être**
Suisse [sɥis] f. *Switzerland*
suisse [sɥis] *Swiss*
suite [sɥit]: **tout de** —— *immediately, at once;* **et ainsi de** —— *and so forth, etc.*

suivre [sɥiːvr] *to follow*
sur [syːr] *on, upon, over*
Suresnes [syrɛːn] suburb of Paris
surlendemain [syrlɑ̃dmɛ̃] m. *(the) second day following*
surprendre [syrprɑ̃ːdr] *to surprise*
surtout [syrtu] *above all, especially*
système [sistɛːm] m. *system*

ta [ta] *thy*
tabac [taba] m. *tobacco*
table [tabl] f. *table*
tableau [tablo] m. *picture;* —— **noir** *blackboard*
tandis que [tɑ̃di(s) k(ə)] *while*
tant [tɑ̃] *so much, so many*
tante [tɑ̃ːt] f. *aunt*
Tarascon [taraskɔ̃] city of Provence
tard [taːr] *late*

---

la queue; **remain standing** rester debout
start commencer; partir
station gare *f.*
statue statue *f.*
stay rester, demeurer
steamer paquebot *m.*
steward garçon *m.*
stick bâton *m.*
still encore, toujours; **(quiet)**: tranquille
stone pierre *f.*
stop (s')arrêter, cesser
store magasin *m.*
storm orage *m.*
story histoire *f.*; **short** —— conte *m.*
street rue *f.*; **... Street** rue de . . . ;
—— **car** tramway *m.*
strike frapper, sonner *(of a clock)*
strong fort
student étudiant,-e *m. f.*

study étudier
such tel; —— **a** un tel
suddenly tout à coup, tout d'un coup
sugar sucre *m.*
sum somme *f.*
summer été *m.;* **in** —— en été
sun soleil *m.*
Sunday dimanche *m.*
surprise étonner, surprendre;
surprised étonné, surpris; **to be** —— s'étonner
Swiss suisse

table table *f.*
take prendre, mener, conduire; ——
a walk se promener (à pied), aller se promener, faire une promenade;
—— **care** faire attention; ——
pleasure (in) prendre plaisir (à)
talk parler; **(chat)** causer
tall grand

tasse [tɑːs] f. *cup*
taxi(mètre) [taksi(mɛtr)] m. *taxicab*
te [tə] *thee, to (for) thee, thyself*
tel [tɛl] *such;* **rien de —** *nothing like it*
téléphonie [telefɔni] f. *telephone*
temps [tã] m. *time; weather;* **de — en —** *from time to time*
tenir [təniːr] *to hold, keep;* **— à** *to insist upon, to want to, be anxious to* **— au courant** *to keep informed*
terrain [tɛrɛ̃] m. *field, ground*
terrasse [tɛras] f. *terrace*
terre [tɛːr] f. *earth;* **pomme de terre** *potato*
tes [te] *thy*

tête [tɛːt] f. *head*
thé [te] m. *tea*
théâtre [teɑːtr] m. *theater;* **— Français** leading theater in Paris
tien- see **tenir**
tien, -ne [tjɛ̃] [tjɛn] *thine*
tiers [tjɛːr] m. *(one-)third*
tins, etc. [tɛ̃] see **tenir**
toi [twa] *thou, thee*
toilette [twalɛt] f. *toilet*
tomber [tɔ̃be] *to fall*
ton [tɔ̃] *thy*
tort [tɔːr] m. *wrong, error;* **avoir —** *to be wrong*
tôt [to] *early, (too) soon*
touchant [tuʃã] *touching*

---

taxi(cab) taxi(mètre) *m.*
tea thé *m.*
teacher maître (d'école) *m.*, maîtresse (d'école) *f.*, professeur *m.*
team équipe *f.*
telephone téléphone *m.*, téléphonie *f.*
tell dire, *p. p.:* dit; **(relate)** raconter
ten dix
than que, de
thank remercier; **— you** merci, *or* je vous remercie
that *(rel. pron.):* qui, que, lequel
that *(demons. pron.):* ce, cela, ça, celui, celui-là; **— one** celui, celui-là
that *(adj.):* ce, cet, cette, ce . . . -là, *etc.*
that *(conj.):* que; **so —** pour que, afin que
the le, la, l', les
theater théâtre *m.*
thee te, toi

their leur
theirs le leur
them les, leur, eux, elles; **of —** en
themselves se, eux-mêmes, elles-mêmes
then puis; ensuite; alors; donc
there là, y; **— is (are)** voilà, il y a; **over —** là-bas
these *(pron.)* ceux(-ci), *etc.*, ce
these *(adj.)* ces, ces . . .-ci
they ils, elles, eux, on, ce
thing chose *f.*; **(belongings)** affaires *f. pl.*
think penser; **— of** penser à **(to have in mind)**, penser de **(to have an opinion of)**
third troisième; (un) tiers
thirsty: to be — avoir soif *(f.)*
thirteen treize
thirty trente
this *(pron.):* ce, ceci, celui(-ci); **— one** celui-ci
this *(adj.):* ce, cet, cette, ce . . .-ci, *etc.*

toujours [tuʒuːr] *always, still*
tour [tuːr] m. *tour, turn, trick;* **faire le —— (de)** *to go around*
tour [tuːr] f. *tower*
Touraine [turɛn] f. *old province in central France*
tourner [turne] *to turn, go around*
Tours [tuːr] *city on the Loire in Touraine*
tout [tu] (adj.) *each, all;* (pron.) *everything;* (adv.) *entirely, quite, very;* **—— le . . .** *the whole;* **—— le monde** *everybody;* **tous les deux** *both;* **pas du ——** *not at all;* **—— à coup, —— d'un coup** *all at once;* **—— à fait** *quite, entirely, altogether;* **—— de même** *just the same;* **—— de suite** *at once, immediately*
train [trɛ̃] m. *train*
tram, tramway [tram] [tramwe] m. *street car*
tranquille [trãkil] *quiet, tranquil;* **laisser ——** *to leave alone;* **Soyez ——!** *Don't worry!*
travail [travaːj] m. *work*
travailler [travaje] *to work*
traverser [travɛrse] *to cross*
treize [trɛːz] *thirteen*
trente [trãːt] *thirty*
très [trɛ] *very*
trésor [trezɔːr] m. *treasure, treasury*
tricolore [trikɔlɔːr] *tricolored;* **dra-**

---

those (*pron.*): ceux(-là), *etc.;* ce
those (*adj.*): ces, ces . . . -là
thou tu, toi
thousand mille, mil
three trois
through par
throw jeter
Thursday jeudi *m.*
thus ainsi
thy ton, ta, tes
thyself te, toi-même
ticket billet *m.;* **—— window** guichet *m.*
time temps *m.;* (**occasion**) fois *f.;* (**hour**) heure *f.;* **a long ——** longtemps; **next ——** la prochaine fois; **to have a good ——** s'amuser; **from —— to ——** de temps en temps
tired fatigué; **get (grow) ——** se lasser, s'ennuyer
to à, en, chez, pour, de, jusqu'à; **—— the house of** chez; (**in order**) **——** pour
tobacco tabac *m.*
today aujourd'hui
together ensemble
tomorrow demain; **day after ——** après-demain
too aussi; trop; **—— much (many)** trop
tower tour *f.*
traffic circulation *f.*
train train *m.*
tram tram(way) *m.*
travel voyager, marcher
travels voyages *m. pl.;* **travelling companion** compagnon (*m.*) de voyage
tree arbre *m.*
tricolor drapeau (*m.*) tricolore
trunk malle *f.*
Tuesday mardi *m.*
turn tourner; **—— around** se retourner
twelve douze; **—— o'clock** midi *m.* minuit *m.*
twenty vingt
two deux

peau (*m.*) —— *French flag*
triomphe [triɔ̃ːf] *m. triumph*
trois [trwɑ] *three*
troisième [trwɑzjɛm] *third*
tromper [trɔ̃pe] *to deceive;* **se** —— *to be mistaken*
trop [tro] [trɔ] *too, too much, too many;* **pas** —— *not so very*
trottoir [trɔtwaːr] *m. sidewalk*
trouver [truve] *to find;* **se** —— *to be*
tu [ty] *thou*

un [œ̃] *a, an, one*
une [yn] *a, an, one*
université [ynivɛrsite] *f. university*

va [va] 3. s. pres. ind. *or* imper. of **aller**
vacances [vakɑ̃ːs] *f. pl. vacation*
vache [vaʃ] *f. cow*
vague [vag] *f. wave*
vaincre [vɛ̃ːkr] *to conquer*
vais [ve] [vɛ] 1. s. pres. ind. of **aller**
valoir [valwaːr] *to be worth;* —— **mieux** *to be better, to be worth more*

vas [va] 2. s. pres. ind. of **aller**
vaut [vo] 3. s. pres. ind. of **valoir**
vendre [vɑ̃ːdr] *to sell*
vendredi [vɑ̃drədi] *m. Friday*
venir [vəniːr] *to come;* **faire** —— *to call, send for;* —— **à** + infinitive *to happen;* —— **de** + infinitive *to have just* (*done*)
vent [vɑ̃] *m. wind*
venu [vəny] p.p. of **venir**
verr- fut. and cond. of **voir**
verre [vɛːr] *m. glass*
vers [vɛːr] *towards, at about* (time)
Versailles [vɛrsɑːj] *city about twelve miles southwest of Paris, famous for its magnificent royal palace and gardens*
vert [vɛːr] *green*
vêtement [vɛtmɑ̃] *m. garment*
veuill-, veul-, veut, veux see **vouloir**
viande [vjɑ̃ːd] *f. meat*
victoire [viktwaːr] *f. victory*
vide [vid] *empty*
vie [vi] *f. life*
vien- see **venir**

---

ugly vilain
uncle oncle *m.*
under sous
understand comprendre
unfortunately malheureusement
United States États-Unis *m. pl.*
university université *f.;* —— **Street** rue (*f.*) de l'Université
until jusqu'à
up: to be —— être levé; **to get** —— se lever; **to go** —— monter; —— **stairs** en *haut
us nous
use employer, faire usage de, se servir de; **used to** + *infinitive expressed by the imperfect tense*

vacation vacances *f. pl.*
vegetable légume *m.*
very très, bien; même
vicinity environs *m. pl.;* **in the** —— aux environs
visit visiter, faire (*or* rendre) visite à
visit visite *f.*
voice voix *f.*

wait, wait for attendre
waken réveiller
walk marcher, aller à pied; **go for a** —— (**take a** ——) se promener (à pied), faire une promenade, aller se promener
walk promenade *f.*

vieux, vieil, vieille [vjø] [vjɛːj] *old*
vif [vif] *lively, quick, keen*
vilain [vilɛ̃] *ugly*
village [vilaːʒ] m. *village*
ville [vil] f. *city, town;* **en —** *about town, downtown*
vin [vɛ̃] m. *wine*
vingt [vɛ̃] *twenty*
vins, etc. [vɛ̃] *past def. of* **venir**
vis, etc. [vi] *past def. of* **voir**
visite [vizit] f. *visit, inspection; visitor;* **faire (rendre) —** *to visit*
visiter [vizite] *to visit, inspect*
vite [vit] *quick, quickly*
vitrail [vitraːj] pl.: **vitraux** [vitro] m. *stained glass window*
vivre [viːvr] *to live*
voici [vwasi] *here is, here are;* **nous — ** *here we are*
voilà [vwala] *there is, there are;* **nous —** *here we are;* **Nous — partis!** *We're off!*
voir [vwaːr] *to see*
voisin [vwazɛ̃] *near, contiguous;* m. *neighbor*

voiture [vwatyːr] f. *carriage;* **en —** *in a carriage; All aboard!*
voix [vwa] f. *voice*
voler [vɔle] *to steal, rob; fly*
vont [vɔ̃] 3. pl. pres. ind. of **aller**
vos [vo] *your*
votre [vɔtr] *your*
vôtre [voːtr] *yours*
voudr- fut. and cond. of **vouloir**
vouloir [vulwaːr] *to want, wish;* **— bien** *to be willing;* **— dire** *to mean;* **en — à quelqu'un de quelque chose** *to bear someone a grudge for something*
vous [vu] *you, to (for) you, yourself, yourselves, each other, to (for) each other*
voy- see **voir**
voyage [vwajaːʒ] m. *journey*
voyager [vwajaʒe] *to travel*
vrai [vrɛ] *true*
vu [vy] p.p. of **voir**
vue [vy] f. *view, sight*
wagon [vagɔ̃] [wagɔ̃] m. *(railway) coach;* **—lit** m. *sleeping car*

---

want désirer, vouloir
warm chaud; **to be —** avoir chaud, *(impersonally)*: faire chaud
was *see* être & devoir; **wasn't he? wasn't it?** n'est-ce pas?
wash laver
waste perdre
watch regarder
watch montre *f.*
water eau *f.*
wave vague *f.*
way chemin *m.*, route *f.;* **(means)**; moyen *m.;* **on the — (to)** en route (pour)
we nous, on
wear porter

weary lasser
weather temps *m.*
Wednesday mercredi *m.*
week semaine *f.*, huit jours; **last —** la semaine dernière (*or* passée)
well bien; **—!** eh bien! **very —** très bien; à la bonne heure! **— and good!** à la bonne heure! **be — se** porter bien
wharf quai *m.*
what? (*pron.*): que? qu'est-ce qui? quoi?
what (= that which) ce qui, ce que, *etc.*
what (*adj.*): quel; **— a . . . !** quel . . . !

y [i] *there, to it, to them, in it,* etc.
il y a *there is, there are;* **il y avait** *there was (were);* **il y a** + expression of time *ago;* **il y a longtemps que**
vous étudiez trop *you have long been studying too much*
yeux [jø] m. pl. *eyes*

---

when quand
where où
whether si
which (*rel. pron.*): qui, que, ce qui, ce que, lequel, quoi; **from** —— dont, duquel, d'où; **of** —— dont, duquel; **in (to, at, on)** —— où
which (*adj.*): quel; —— **one?** lequel?
while pendant que, en (+ *pres. part.*)
white blanc
who qui, lequel, quel
whole: the —— ... tout le ..., toute la ...; **a** —— ... tout(e) un(e) ...
whom qui, que, lequel; **of** —— dont, duquel, de qui
whose dont, de qui, duquel
whose? de qui? à qui?
why pourquoi; —— **yes (no)!** Mais oui (non)!
wide large
wife femme *f.*
will vouloir; *see the future*
willing: to be —— vouloir bien
wind vent *m.*
window fenêtre *f.;* **ticket** —— guichet *m.*
windy: to be —— faire du vent
wine vin *m.*
winter hiver *m.;* **in** —— en hiver
wireless sans fil (*m.*); —— **telephone set** appareil (*m.*) de téléphonie (*f.*) sans fil
wish désirer, vouloir

with avec, de, chez, (*in descriptions*): à
without sans
woman femme *f.;* **young** —— jeune femme, jeune fille *f.*
wonder se demander
won't: won't they? n'est-ce pas?
word mot *m.*, parole *f.*
work travailler
work travail *m.*, ouvrage *m.*
world monde *m.*
worry: Don't worry! Soyez tranquille!
worthy brave, digne
would *see* vouloir, *also the conditional;* **wouldn't you?** n'est-ce pas?
write écrire, *p. p.:* écrit
wrong tort *m.;* **to be** —— avoir tort
wrong faux, inexact

yard cour *f.*
year an *m.*, année *f.;* **last** —— l'année passée (*or* dernière); **in the** —— en l'an
yes *oui, si; **why** ——! mais oui!
yesterday hier; **day before** —— avant-hier
yet encore; déjà
yonder là-bas
you vous, (tu, te, toi,) on
young jeune; **young men** jeunes gens
your votre, vos; **in** —— **hand** à la main
yours le vôtre, à vous
yourself vous, vous-même